history of

20th century
literature

Executive Editor Julian Brown
Senior Editor Trevor Davies
Creative Director Keith Martin
Senior Designer Peter Burt
Designer Leslie Needham
Picture Research Liz Fowler
Senior Production Controller Sarah Scanlon and Louise Hall

First Published in Great Britain in 2001 by Hamlyn
an imprint of Octopus Publishing Group Limited
2-4 Heron Quays, Docklands, London E14 4JP

Copyright © 2001 Octopus Publishing Group Limited

ISBN 0 60059807 1

A catalogue record for this book is available from the
British Library

Produced by Toppan
Printed in China

Facing page: Ernest Hemingway (1899–1961)
This page: Virginia Woolf (1882–1941)
           William Faulkner (1897–1962)

hamlyn

history of

20th century literature

simon beesley
sheena joughin

contents

Introduction 6

Chapter 1

NEW CENTURY, OLD FACES 8
America in Europe 9
The craft of the novel 10
New directions in drama 12
Eminent Victorians 14
American naturalists 16
The novel in Europe 18

Chapter 2

EARLY 20TH-CENTURY POETRY 20
W.B. Yeats 21
Philosopher poets 22
Profound simplicities 24
Russian poets 26

Chapter 3

MODERNISM AND THE
    AVANT-GARDE 28
Symbolism, imagism
    and after 29
Eliot and Pound 30
Modern –isms in Europe 32
American moderns 34

Chapter 4

THE NEW NOVEL 36
Virginia Woolf 37
Marcel Proust 38
Franz Kafka 40
James Joyce 42
D.H. Lawrence 44

Chapter 5

THE FIRST WORLD WAR AND
    ITS AFTERMATH 46
The war poets 47
The lost generation 48
Moveable feasts 50
The jazz age 52
Expatriates 54

Chapter 6

BETWEEN THE WARS 56
Forster and Lewis 57
English disaffections 58
American fiction 60
American modernism 62
The novel in France 64
The novel in Germany 66
Other European voices 68
Experiments in the theatre 70

Chapter 7

WOMEN ON WOMEN 72
Colette 73
Pioneers 74
The second sex 76
Surfacing 78

Chapter 8

DEPRESSION AND AFTER 80
British poets of the 1930s 81
Political novels 82
The proletarian novel 84
Dramatic realism 86

Chapter 9

NEW MOVEMENTS IN THE
    50s AND 60s 88
Existentialism 89
The French 'New Novel' 90
The Beats 92
In opposition 94
Cult fiction 96

Chapter 10

POST-WAR FICTION	98
Fact-based fiction	99
Jewish-American writing	100
Into the 1960s	102
The short story in America	104
African-American writing	106
Englishmen abroad	108
Post-war Britain	110
Feminine perspectives	112
The novel in Europe	114
Latin American fiction	116
The international experience	118

Chapter 11

POST-WAR THEATRE	120
Samuel Beckett	121
The theatre of the absurd	122
The British renaissance	124
American drama	126
New directions	128
Onto the screen	130

Chapter 12

GENRE FICTION	132
Science fiction and fantasy	133
Science fiction: contemporary masters	134
Spy fiction	136
The detective story	138
Private eyes	140
Horror fiction	142
Bestsellers: adventure and faction	144
Bestsellers: saga and romance	146

Chapter 13

POETRY SINCE THE WAR	148
Stevens and Moore	149
American candour	150
The British Isles	152
Modern masters	154

Chapter 14

POST-MODERN FICTION	156
Literary latin	157
Magic Realism	158
Metafictions	160
Post-modern Americans	162

Chapter 15

THE WORLD IN PRINT	164
The novel in Japan	165
European novelists	166
Latin-American fiction	168
Post-colonial literature	170
Literature in Australia and Canada	172

Chapter 16

MODERN WRITERS	174
Generation X	175
Recent American fiction	176
Afro-American women writers	178
Women writers in America	180
Recent fiction in Britain	182
International fiction now	184

Nobel Prize for Literature winners	186
20th-Century timeline	187

Index	188

introduction

The history of literature in the 20th century is to a large extent the history of its leading writers. Poetry, drama and fiction (unlike some other art forms) cannot generally be discussed in terms of short-term movements. Of course, writers are influenced by new ideas, new literary techniques and each other, but the greater the writer the more individual their voice. There have certainly been more writers in the 20th century than any other; literature is no longer mostly written – and read – by educated white Europeans. One of many tremendous changes during this period has been the fact of mass literacy and increased leisure time, which, along with technological developments, has meant that more books have been printed (and subsequently translated) than ever before.

Modernism, however, which began at the close of the 19th century, is the one movement which has affected all aspects of our culture in the 20th century. A somewhat vague term, modernism refers to a revolution in the arts, whereby traditional methods of representing reality – which in literature means telling a story, relating an event, reflecting on an emotion – were seen to be limited and limiting. 'Make it New', said Ezra Pound, and writers attempted to do that, with varying degrees of success, for 40 years or more. While every generation experiences itself as 'new' to a certain extent, people living through the first 50 years of the 20th century, really did live in a world which fast became unprecedentedly 'modern'. The revolutionary ideas of Freud, Darwin, Nietzsche and other thinkers had redefined man's relationship to history and to himself. Two World Wars changed the physical, political, economic and social shape of Europe in ways we are still coming to terms with. The arrival of the aeroplane, the car, the telephone and television changed forever the way people experienced each other. In literature, these tumultuous circumstances resulted in a new focus on personal

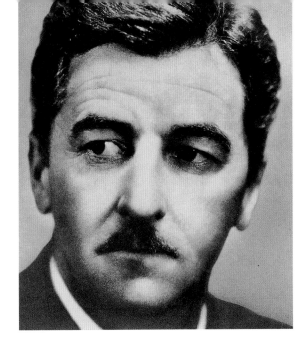

consciousness, the unconscious, memory, perception. The omnipotent narrator and linear narrative no longer dominated fiction. Poetry no longer had to scan or to rhyme. Plays no longer needed scenery, plot or realistic dialogue. Like paintings, books no longer had to be 'about' anything except themselves. The extremes of experimentation which modernism inspired slowly gave way to more accessible literature again, but without people like Ezra Pound, James Joyce, Rilke, Proust and Pirandello, the shape of contemporary literature would be very different.

The technology that wrought such change in the earlier part of the century brought with it new sources of entertainment, which challenged literature, especially in the last 30 years. Cinema, radio, and, most importantly, TV are now at least as popular diversions as books are. Poetry, particularly, has a reduced readership. Drama is often on television, but the avant-garde or contentious is rarely filmed, and watching a play on a small screen at home is hardly a 'theatrical' experience. Fiction, on the other hand, is booming – despite talk of the 'decline of the novel'. Whether this is because the difference between 'literature' and popular fiction has widened, or whether the abundance of screenplays based on 19th-century novels has sent people back to the bookshops (in search of more of the same or to find something to distract them from costume drama) is not for this introduction to say. Certainly there is no dearth of new fiction to read. Rather there is so much being currently printed that it is hard, at this stage, to know what will last and what will not. We can be sure though, that with so many emerging and disparate voices, some at least will last long into the 21st century; maybe even as long as there are people to read them.

1 New century, old faces

American-born Henry James settled in London at the age of 34. His ideas on the interplay between character and action had an enormous impact on the 20th-century novel.

Some of the most significant changes in literature occurred at least ten years before the turn of the century. Henry James was working on a new conception of the novel. Knut Hamsun had written a manifesto calling writers to attend the 'secret stirrings in the remote parts of the mind'. And Henrik Ibsen's turn towards a more realistic, less artificial drama had already taken place. Most readers at the close of the 19th century would have been unaware of these developments. Many of the works we now consider turning points in literature were ignored in their own time.

America in Europe

HENRY JAMES (1843–1916)

Henry James was born in New York, the son of a distinguished writer on theology and philosophy, and the younger brother of William James, a psychologist and philosopher, who received as much acclaim in his own field as Henry did in literature. Feeling that American culture was too raw for his own imaginative purposes, James moved to Europe in 1875 and settled in London two years later. The contrast between the civilizations of the New World and the Old provided the subject for many of his works. Where America is innocent and exuberant, Europe is seen with fascination as worldly and wise, but also corrupt and devious. As often as not, however, the villains in James's novels are Americans who have been tarnished by their residence in Europe.

The book that made James's reputation was a short one, *Daisy Miller* (1879). A high-spirited American girl travels to Rome with her wealthy mother. The local community of expatriate Americans is offended by Daisy's freedom from convention and ostracizes her. In *The Portrait of a Lady* (1881), the masterpiece of his middle period, James treats this same theme in greater depth and with considerable subtlety. Isabel Archer, the American heroine, inherits a fortune in England and falls under the influence of two corrupt Americans living in Italy. By the end of the book she has lost her innocence and the reader has come to see her as a victim of her own naivety and of her refusal to understand that Europe is not what it seems.

For James, characters were not people with stories that had to be told, as they had been for 19th-century novelists; instead, they were part of the story itself. As he said: 'What is action but the development of character? What is character but the development of action?' He achieved a great virtuosity in presenting events from the point of view of a single character as opposed to presenting them through an omniscient narrator. The true nature of the malicious American dilettante who marries Isabel Archer for her money is revealed to us slowly as the book proceeds and only through her. We never know more about him than she does. This technique is common now, but James was breaking new ground in creating what has come to be called the 'psychological novel'. *What Maisie Knew* (1897) is a perfect example of both the reader and the central character (a child of divorced parents) sharing the same confusion about what is happening.

In his later years James's novels became increasingly abstract as he pursued his interest in the complexities of human relations. His long sentences became even longer and more ambiguous during this period. His last three books – *The Wings of the Dove* (1902), *The Ambassadors* (1903) and *The Golden Bowl* (1904) – are considered to be among his greatest works, but many people find them daunting.

James's friend the novelist Edith Wharton once asked him: 'What was your idea in suspending the four principal characters in *The Golden Bowl* in the void? ... Why have you stripped them of all the human fringes we necessarily trail after us through life?' It is a tribute to the integrity of his vision that his reply was: 'My dear – I didn't know I had!'

> 'It is art that makes life, makes interest, makes importance, for our consideration and application of these things, and I know of no substitute whatever for the force and beauty of the process.'

HENRY JAMES *From a letter to H.G. Wells (1906)*

The craft of the novel

In the 19th century novels had mostly been concerned to tell a story without troubling the reader too much with the characters' inner states or the manner in which the story was told. In the early 20th century novelists turned their attention to more complex and hidden aspects of human behaviour. This resulted in new narrative techniques and new ways of engaging the reader.

Conrad's boyhood in Poland was steeped in English literature (his father translated Shakespeare). After many years at sea, he published his first novel in English at the age of 38.

JOSEPH CONRAD (1857–1924)

Joseph Conrad is unusual in that he is a major novelist writing in a language that was not his mother tongue. 'English for me was neither a matter of choice nor adoption,' he wrote. 'It was I who was adopted by the genius of the language.' Born in the Ukraine, he was the son of a Polish poet and political exile, and his real name was Józef Teodor Konrad Korzeniowski. A seaman for 20 years (16 of which were spent in the British merchant navy, where he became a master mariner), he moved to Britain in 1896, and began writing in English, his third language, after Polish and French.

The sea provides the background for much of Conrad's fiction, and in his own time his reputation was mainly as a writer of sophisticated adventure stories and 'romances' set in exotic locations. Modern criticism, however, recognizes a far more complex and pessimistic strain in Conrad, and his greatest novels – *Nostromo* (1904), *The Secret Agent* (1907), *Under Western Eyes* (1911) and *Victory* (1915) – are now seen as classics of English literature. He is 'the novelist of man in extreme situations' and has a remarkable ability to evoke each character's particular vision of reality. In a rich and highly coloured prose, he explores ideas of corruptibility, vulnerability, solitude and human evil. Civilization, he seems to suggest, is a flimsy veil for innate barbarism. Conrad's most celebrated short work, 'Heart of Darkness' (1902), was the inspiration for the film *Apocalpyse Now*. In this story the white man, Mr Kurtz, is a corrupted idealist who sets up his own kingdom in the Congo and is drawn into savagery; his dying words are: 'The horror! The horror!'

RUDYARD KIPLING (1865–1936)

Kipling's father was a museum curator in Lahore, India, and when Rudyard was six his parents left him with a family in England, where he and his sister spent five unhappy years. He recalled the miseries of this time in the short story 'Baa, Baa, Black Sheep' (1888), although he never blamed his parents afterwards, insisting they were the 'best of parents'. Kipling's denial was highly characteristic of both the man and the writer. He was an odder, more contradictory figure than most popular accounts of him allow. On the face of it, he was the great celebrator of the British Empire, the 'Poet of Empire', whose attitudes towards imperialism and colonialism have dated rather badly. But Kipling was also an astonishingly gifted writer, capable of empathizing with values very different from those of the British Raj. 'His talent I think quite diabolically great,' was Henry James's comment.

Kipling started writing fiction as a journalist in India. His first collections of short stories, of which *Plain Tales from the Hills* (1888) is probably the best, brought him instant celebrity. A succession of verses, based on ballads and hymns, together with his children's tales – *The Jungle Book* (1894) and *Just So Stories* (1902) – made him immensely popular with ordinary readers at the very time critical opinion began to cool. From a large and varied output, the novel *Kim* (1901) is regarded as his finest work. A vivid and panoramic picture of India, the book shows great imaginative sympathy for British and Indian characters alike. Kim ('Little Friend of all the World') is a young Irish orphan who moves with equal ease between the two cultures.

The reaction against his jingoism and what is perceived as vulgarity has tended to distract attention from the brilliance of Kipling's writing. His fascination with language and mastery of technique recall that of later writers such as James Joyce, while his handling of dialogue has rarely been equalled. In particular, Kipling perfected the art of paring down a story to maximize its emotional force. 'I have had tales by me for three or five years which shortened themselves almost yearly.' Some of his later short stories, such as 'Mrs Bathhurst' (1904) and 'Dayspring Mishandled' (1928), are small masterpieces of compression. He was awarded the Nobel prize for Literature in 1907.

EDITH WHARTON (1862–1937)

Like her friend Henry James, Edith Wharton was concerned with the ways in which individuals are thwarted by their social milieu. Brought up in a wealthy family to take her place in New York high society, she came to find that society intolerably narrow and uncultivated. Her novel *The Age of Innocence* (1920) is a witty, ironic and touching study of a love frustrated by the pressures of convention – and by the kind of people 'who dreaded scandal more than disease, who placed decency above courage'. An earlier novel, *The House of Mirth* (1905), tells the more sombre story of Lily Bart, whose efforts to take her rightful place in society are undone by her own honesty and gullibility. By the end of the book Lily is penniless and kills herself with an overdose, but her downfall is presented dispassionately: as the way things are rather than as a tragedy. Edith Wharton insisted that the task of the novelist was to find out what the characters 'being what they are, would make of the situation', but her novels invariably show people as victims of their situation, with little choice over the outcome of their lives. The book in which she departed from the setting of polite society, *Ethan Frome* (1911), is a grim tale of revenge and human helplessness on a poor New England farm.

> In the days beyond compare and before the Judgements, a genius called Graydon foresaw that the advance of education and the standard of living would submerge all mind-marks in one mudrush of standardized reading matter.

RUDYARD KIPLING, *'Dayspring Mishandled'* (1928)

New directions in drama

At the beginning of the century dramatists were deeply indebted to Henrik Ibsen (1828–1906), the Norwegian playwright who more than anyone else was responsible for modern dramatic realism. Ibsen freed playwrights from the dead-weight of a 19th-century theatrical tradition that relied on artifice, histrionic acting and contrived set pieces. Even Chekhov could not dispense with such 'tricks of the trade' as a pistol shot ringing out off-stage until his last plays – and he would not have done so without Ibsen.

ANTON CHEKHOV (1860–1904)

It is sometimes said that the greatest writers are unclassifiable. Of no one is this more true than the Russian dramatist and short-story writer Anton Chekhov. He insisted that his plays were comedies, yet their mood is overwhelmingly poignant and tragic. His stories avoid any obvious rhetorical or poetic effects and are characterized by a tremendous naturalness and realism, but they are also strangely atmospheric and haunting: 'Reading them one gets the impression of holding life itself, like a fluttering bird, in one's cupped hand.' Chekhov has been variously described as a realist, a pessimist, a satirist, an impressionist, a master of psychological observation and the 'master prose stylist' of the Russian language. He is all these things, but in a way not easily reduced to the terms of critical categories.

Chekhov (also spelled Chekov and Tchekhov) was the son of a grocer and the grandson of a serf. He studied medicine and divided his time between writing and working as doctor. As he wrote to a friend: 'Medicine is my lawful wife, and literature is my mistress. When I get fed up with one, I spend the night with the other.' He started by contributing humorous pieces to newspapers and magazines, but as he began to receive acclaim the stories took an increasingly dark tone. Chekhov is the supreme master at charting the vain hopes and futile aspirations of ordinary people: peasants, impoverished landed gentry, middle-class professionals in provincial towns, soldiers and a wide range of other figures from pre-Revolutionary Russia. What contributes to the special distinction of the stories – many regard him as the greatest short-story writer of the century – is his sympathy with his characters and his refusal ever to pass judgement on them.

In his four most popular plays – *The Seagull* (1896), *Uncle Vanya* (1897), *The Three Sisters* (1901) and *The Cherry Orchard* (1904) – Chekhov aspired to complete realism: 'A play should be written in which people arrive, go away, have dinner, talk about the weather and play cards. Life must be exactly as it is – not on stilts.' He succeeds brilliantly in his aim. *The Three Sisters*, for example, concerns three sisters in a provincial town, yearning to move to Moscow but never actually going there. Like many Chekhovian characters, they are forced to abandon their dreams and accept their situation. The play is short on plot and dramatic incident, but Chekhov's mastery is such that he manages to make it a powerfully moving tragedy of everyday life.

> The Lord God has given us vast forests, immense fields, wide horizons; surely we ought to be giants, living in such a country as this.

ANTON CHEKHOV, *The Cherry Orchard* (1904)

Left: Physician, dramatist and short-story writer of genius, Anton Chekhov (left) with his fellow countryman Leo Tolstoy, the giant of 19th-century Russian fiction.

Right: George Bernard Shaw – as famous for his witty and paradoxical sayings as for his drama, now best-known for *Pygmalion* which was the basis for the musical *My Fair Lady*.

AUGUST STRINDBERG (1849–1912)

The Swedish dramatist and novelist August Strindberg was one of the most prolific of writers, with more than 50 plays, as well as novels, short stories, poems and an autobiography, to his credit. His early works – conventional historical dramas and tales of rural life – are rarely performed now, but with *The Father* (1887), *Miss Julie* (1888) and *The Creditors* (1888) he began a radical new phase in his drama. These bold and intense works were written in a spirit of revolt against the prevailing social conventions and values. Using the techniques of dramatic naturalism – unaffected dialogue, stark scenery, the use of stage props as symbols – Strindberg mercilessly exposes human frailties. His concern is with extreme states of mind, particularly as expressed in the war between the sexes (which women always win). The later works – *The Dance of Death* (1901), *A Dream Play* (1902) and *Ghost Sonata* (1907) – are tortured psychic dramas, which push the analysis of the sex war further than before.

GEORGE BERNARD SHAW (1856–1950)

Few writers could be as different from Strindberg as the Anglo-Irish playwright George Bernard Shaw. He had little interest in human emotion and psychology; his characters rarely come alive; and his plays are generally lacking in dramatic force. Shaw's aim was to use drama as a vehicle for putting forward ideas. A passionate advocate of socialism, women's rights, equality of income and reform in general, he believed strongly in the power of reason and intelligence to bring about change. In plays such as *Man and Superman* (1903),

Major Barbara (1905) and *Heartbreak House* (1919) Shaw expounds his ideas with great wit and clarity and through brilliant paradox. The didactic purpose of these plays, however, now tends to be lost on contemporary audiences, and the works that remain popular (and still figure in the international repertoire) are the more light-weight 'comedies with a moral', such as *Arms and the Man* (1898) and *Pygmalion* (1912). He was awarded the Nobel prize in 1925.

J.M. SYNGE (1871–1909)

The Irish dramatist John Millington Synge was educated at Trinity College, Dublin, and then spent some years in Paris, where he met W.B. Yeats (see page 20) in 1896. Acting on Yeats's advice, Synge went to the Aran Islands, off the west coast of Ireland, to write of Irish peasant life. His first play, *In the Shadow of the Glen* (1903), first performed at the Abbey Theatre, Dublin – where all but the last of his works were staged – is a grim one-act comedy, in which a peasant feigns his own death in order to test his wife's fidelity.

Reported death is also at the centre of Synge's most famous play, *The Playboy of the Western World* (1907), which caused a sensation on its first performance, not least for the startling poetry of its language, which was drawn from rural speech. Christy arrives in a peasant community with the story of how he killed his father. This is a lie, but the point of the play is to illustrate that stories are more potent than truth. Christy becomes the 'playboy' he decided to be and is free to go on 'romancing through a romping lifetime ... to the dawning of the Judgement Day'.

Eminent Victorians

'He has a ponderously warm manner of saying nothing in infinite sentences,' Thomas Hardy said of Henry James. This reaction was generally typical of his contemporaries, who were indifferent to, or even mystified by, the very works now regarded as modern classics. The majority of English writers born in the second half of the 19th century clung to the values and outlook of the Victorian age and saw no need to introduce radical change to the art of the novel.

Thomas Hardy, the great 19th-century novelist whose poetic gift came to fruition late in life after the death of his much-missed wife.

THOMAS HARDY (1840–1912)

Hardy wrote the last of his novels, *Jude the Obscure*, in 1895, and like his other novels it belongs firmly in the fictional tradition of the 19th century. Henry James, incidentally, took as unsympathetic a view of Hardy's fiction as Hardy did of his. In a review of *Far from the Madding Crowd* he wrote: 'Mr Hardy has gone astray very cleverly, and his superficial novel is a really curious imitation of something better.'

The significance of Hardy in the 20th century rests with his poetry. He wrote poetry all his life, and some of the novels contain passages in which he turned his early poems into prose. But it was not until after the death of his wife Emma in 1912 that, at the age of 74, he wrote his greatest poems. These are, in effect, elegies for his marriage, and as his mind filled with memories of their first few happy years, he also recalled his later indifferent and sometimes hostile behaviour towards Emma. The poems were in part triggered by remorse and guilt. 'They lament not the death of Emma but the squandering of love.' Hardy sought to write in a language close to ordinary speech, avoiding what he called the 'jewelled line'. His reputation as a poet has risen steadily since his death. If not a great poet, he undoubtedly wrote a number of major poems.

SAMUEL BUTLER (1835–1902)

In spite of his iconoclasm, Samuel Butler is very much a Victorian figure. The novel for which he is best known, *The Way of All Flesh* (1903), was, in fact, written in the 1880s and published posthumously. This is a savage and powerful attack on Victorian institutions, particularly the Church and the family. A work of great satirical force, it probably had more influence on the early 20th-

> Woman much missed, how you call to me, call to me,
> Saying that now you are not as you were
> When you had changed from the one that was all to me,
> But as at first, when our day was fair.
>
> THOMAS HARDY, 'The Voice' (1914)

century revolt against Victorianism than any other single book. Ernest Pontifex, the product of three generations of tyrannical fathers, is intended for the Church. After various misadventures, including a period in prison, he escapes from his family's despotism and succeeds in making a living through literature. The novel is semi-autobiographical in retracing Butler's own path. He himself avoided being ordained as a clergyman by moving to New Zealand, where he achieved success as a sheep-farmer. After five years, he returned to England and took up painting.

ARNOLD BENNETT (1867–1931)

Late in his life, Enoch Arnold Bennett became the epitome of the stodgy, old-fashioned writer for the new young novelists of England. Even Henry James accused his books of 'dripping with detail' and of having 'no scheme, no conception of character, no subject'. Bennett was deeply indebted to French 19th-century realism, particularly Honoré de Balzac and Gustave Flaubert, but his books are by no means simply derivative. The son of a self-educated Staffordshire solicitor, he wrote about life in the Pottery towns he had known in his youth. *Anna of the Five Towns* (1902) was the first of a number of novels to describe the rich but humdrum life he grew up with. This sequence continued with the Clayhanger trilogy (1910–16), which charts the quiet goings-on in a provincial town with documentary detail. *Old Wives' Tales* – his finest achievement – leaves the confines of this world to trace the lives of two sisters over a 40-year period. One stays at home, while the other elopes to Paris with a commercial traveller. The book's real theme is time and the inevitable change it brings to women, first seen in the flower of their youth.

As well as being a novelist, Bennett was a successful journalist and critic, whose stream of potboilers, reviews, self-help books – *Literary Taste: How to Form It* and *How to Live on 24 Hours a Day*, for example – were immensely popular with middle-brow readers. But it is for the craft and warmth with which he observes everyday life that he is enjoyed today.

ENGLISH HUMORISTS

Saki, the pseudonym of Hector Hugh (H.H.) Munro (1870–1916), is known chiefly for comic short stories, which have a strong flavour of the macabre and grotesque. Two of his best collections of short stories, *Reginald in Russia* (1910) and *The Chronicles of Clovis* (1911), feature the sardonic and mischievous young men, Reginald and Clovis, who specialize in puncturing the pretensions of their fellow guests at country house parties. In a typical Saki story, a gruesome or sinister incident is related in a farcical manner. Some of his most memorable stories involve animals that take revenge on their owners.

Sir Max Beerbohm (1872–1956) wrote a handful of short stories – of which 'Enoch Soames' is a comic and

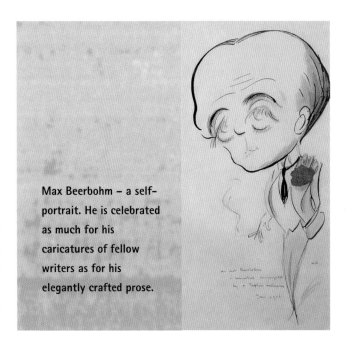

Max Beerbohm – a self-portrait. He is celebrated as much for his caricatures of fellow writers as for his elegantly crafted prose.

satirical masterpiece – and one novel, *Zuleika Dobson* (1911). The latter is a light-hearted satire – written in impeccable and elegant prose – about a great beauty who visits Oxford University and breaks the hearts of all who meet her. His greatest talent, however, was as caricaturist, in both words and pictures. In *A Christmas Garland* (1912) he wrote a series of parodies in the style of Henry James, Rudyard Kipling, H.G. Wells and other writers of the time. Beerbohm's parodies are some of the most brilliant in the language; in fact, only the contemporary American humorous writer Peter de Vries comes close to them. No one has ever caught the intricacies (some would say convolutions) of Henry James's later style more accurately and with such flair.

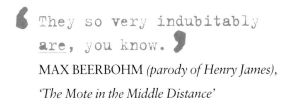

‘ They so very indubitably are, you know. ’
MAX BEERBOHM *(parody of Henry James)*,
'The Mote in the Middle Distance'

American naturalists

These writers were concerned to write about life as it is lived by ordinary people. They themselves came mainly from humble backgrounds and had experienced at first hand the hardships they described. Sympathy for working people and a disenchantment with the values of a country dedicated to material success lie at the heart of their work.

THEODORE DREISER (1871–1945)

Theodore Dreiser grew up in poverty in a small town in Indiana. He became a journalist and ended up as editor of the popular woman's magazine *Delineator*. His own experience of the realities of working life left him implacably opposed to American capitalism, and towards the end of his life he joined the Communist Party. Dreiser's novels deal with the harsher aspects of American prosperity, seen as governed by a Darwinian process by which only the most ruthless and predatory are able to survive.

His first book, *Sister Carrie* (1900), is an account of a working girl's rise to the 'tinsel and shine' of worldly success and her ultimate failure. At the time it caused some controversy for its depiction of her sexuality and ambition. His best novel, *An American Tragedy* (1925), similarly traces the rise and fall of a boy from a poor evangelist family in his struggle to enter the world of wealth and privilege; on the brink of good fortune, he drowns his pregnant girlfriend (partly by accident) and is executed for the crime. Dreiser has often been dismissed for his clumsy style, but his passionate indictment of his native land gives the novels a force which is often lacking in more conventional literary works. As the critic H.L. Mencken put it: 'Dreiser can feel, and, feeling, he can move. The others are very skilful with words.'

SHERWOOD ANDERSON (1876–1941)

Anderson's critique of American materialism is more subtle than Dreiser's, and it is expressed with much greater literary craft. Nevertheless, it remains just as damning. When he was 36 years old Anderson suffered a nervous breakdown, walked out of his job as manager of a paint factory and moved to Chicago to pursue a literary career. Although he wrote seven novels, his reputation rests mainly on his acknowledged masterpiece, *Winesburg, Ohio* (1919), a collection of short stories about people in a small town. The book is a markedly unsentimental and realistic picture of contemporary America, revealed through the lives of the town's citizens. All of them are shown to be to some degree frustrated, lost and misunderstood. It is written in a style that has been described as 'the most idiomatic, unliterary prose' in American fiction since Mark Twain and that has had a considerable influence on later writers, particularly William Faulkner and Ernest Hemingway, who attempted to disavow his debt to Anderson with a parody of his style in *The Torrents of Spring* (1926).

JACK LONDON (1876–1916)

In less than 20 years, Jack (John Griffith) London produced 50 books of fiction and non-fiction, becoming the bestselling American author of his time. His reputation declined in later years, although he continued to be enormously popular abroad, particularly in Russia. Jack London's own life is a saga of overcoming hardship and poverty: virtually self-educated, he rode freight trains the length of America as a hobo, sailed to Japan, took part in the Klondike gold rush, hunted in Alaska and generally lived the life of adventure he was to re-enact in much of his fiction. The Jack London hero is usually an idealized, rather macho figure, struggling

with adversity and triumphing over it through sheer vigour and determination. Some of the views London expressed in his fiction – an odd mixture of militant socialism and ideas of the Nietzschean superman – now seem quaintly absurd, if not repellent. Yet his books remain highly readable for their pace and energy. London had an unusual gift for storytelling, which he combined with a special sympathy for the animal world and outdoor existence. In *The Call of the Wild* (1903) he could be said to be exploring his own wildness with the story of a dog who joins a wolf pack. *Martin Eden* (1909) is perhaps his best work, an autobiographical novel whose hero finally commits suicide – as London himself was to do seven years later.

STEPHEN CRANE (1871–1900)

Strictly speaking, Stephen Crane is a 19th-century novelist. The single work by which he is now remembered, *The Red Badge of Courage* (1895), is a brilliantly imag-ined study of the reactions of an inexperienced soldier to battle in the American Civil War. In its mixture of naturalism and psychological realism, the novel has, however, more in common with the fiction of the 20th century. It combines highly naturalistic dialogue – 'We've helt 'em back; derned if we haven't' – with impressionistic and poetic language – 'The bugles called to each other like brazen gamecocks'. Crane died at the early age of 29, after a hectic life as a war reporter in Mexico, Cuba and Greece, and a bohemian life with Cora Taylor, a rebellious Bostonian whom he met when she was managing a brothel in Florida.

The novel in Europe

Of those European writers whose lives and works spanned the 19th and 20th centuries, some of the most original were more or less ignored in the English-speaking world until 50 or 60 years later. Hermann Hesse's novels, for example, received full recognition only when they became cult books for the alternative culture of the 1960s and 1970s, while Knut Hamsun's classic novel *Hunger* was not translated into English until 1967.

Non-English speaking authors have become widely available in the past 30 years, but the innovative work of these early masters is undiminished.

KNUT HAMSUN (1859–1952)

Born into a peasant family, the Norwegian writer Knut Hamsun, whose real name was Knut Pedersen, spent his childhood in the remote Lofoten islands and had no formal education. He started to write when he was 19 years old and working as a shoemaker's apprentice. He is now seen as one of the founding fathers of the modern novel. Isaac Bashevis Singer went so far as to say that the 'whole modern school of fiction stems from Knut Hamsun'. As early as 1890, he spoke of a new kind of writing that was sensitive to the 'secret stirrings that go unnoticed in the remote parts of the mind'. It would capture 'the strange workings of the nerves, the whisper of the blood, the entreaty of the bone, all the unconscious life of the mind'. In his novel *Sult* (*Hunger*, 1890) he had used a vivid lyrical prose to record the fragmentary and hallucinatory consciousness of a solitary wanderer, suffering from semi-starvation. (Hamsun himself had spent ten years working as a casual labourer in America and Norway.) The novel concentrates on the narrator's sensations and perceptions almost to the exclusion of everything else, and as a reaction against the excesses of naturalism it had an electrifying effect on European writers.

Even though it was written eight years before the century began, Hamsun's *Mysterier* (*Mysteries*, 1892) has been described as 'one of the half-dozen greatest novels of the 20th century' and one that contains the seeds of much of the experimentation in fiction that was to occur later in the century. A new translation in 1971 made it an instant bestseller in the United States. The mysteries of the title are those experienced by a young man who spends a summer in a small resort, trying to make sense of his relationship with himself and other people. Like many of Hamsun's characters, he is an isolated and asocial individual, whose alienation in the end destroys him.

Hamsun's view of the world, which was influenced by the German philosopher Friedrich Nietzsche, was fiercely individualistic and contemptuous of the modern view of progress. In later works, such as *Markens Grode* (*The Growth of the Soil*, 1917), his antipathy to contemporary Western culture softens somewhat, although this novel, too, with its back-to-nature philosophy, is marked by a strong, sometimes savage, irony. He won the Nobel prize in 1920, but his reputation was damaged by his outspoken support for the Nazis during the German occupation of Norway.

HERMANN HESSE (1877–1962)

Among the pioneers of 20th-century fiction, the German-born novelist Hermann Hesse was the least interested in technical or formal innovation. He was happy to rely on traditional forms of storytelling, and his great originality comes from the themes he pursued over a writing career lasting 40 years. In a lifelong quest for self-understanding and self-liberation, he explored through his novels the conflicts between sensuality and spirituality, between bourgeois existence and the life of the artist. These concerns, informed by his deep interests in Eastern mysticism and Jungian psychoanalysis, were what later made him a cult figure for many young people in western Europe and the United States.

The early novels *Peter Camenzind* (1904) and *Rosshalde* (1914) focus on the problems attending artistic success in a civilization essentially hostile to spiritual and aesthetic values. He wrote his first major work, *Demian* (1919), after a personal crisis had led him into psychoanalysis with a follower of Karl Jung. The novel, which is an examination of the growth of self-awareness in a troubled adolescent, had an immediate impact in Germany and made Hesse famous. *Siddhartha* (1922), a more directly mystical novel in which the Hindu hero strives to resolve the clash between the flesh and the spirit, was inspired by a trip to India.

Hesse's most successful novels are *Steppenwolf* (1927) and *Das Glasperlenspiel* (*The Glass Bead Game*, 1943). The first, which has elements of fantasy and Magic Realism, is the story of someone who feels himself to be half-man, half-wolf. Harry Heller (a self-portrait of Hesse) is 48 years old and has decided to commit suicide at the age of 50. He finds a solution to the division in his nature when he stumbles across the sign: 'MAGIC THEATRE. ENTRANCE NOT FOR EVERYBODY: FOR MADMEN ONLY.' In *The Glass Bead Game* Hesse again explores the dualism of the spiritual and the active life through the figure of a supremely talented intellectual. The game, which incorporates all spiritual, artistic and scientific knowledge in the year 2400, is played by scholars in the utopian province of Castilia, far from normal human existence. Joseph Knecht, Master of the Glass Bead Game, personifies the perfection of a life dedicated to contemplation and the intellect. In an ambiguous ending, Knecht tries

Above left: In novels such as *Steppenwolf* and the *Glass Bead Game*, Hermann Hesse anticipated many of the concerns of the later half of the 20th century, making him a posthumous success as a cult author.

Above: Edvard Munch's *The Dance of Life*. Munch's dark vision of human existence mirrored Hesse and Hamsun's view of life as a struggle between rationality, the unconscious and the demands of the flesh.

to introduce the same perfection to the outside world, only to sacrifice himself by leaping into a river. Hesse was awarded the Nobel prize in 1946.

2 Early 20th-century poetry

W.B. Yeats as a young man, determined to confront the new century while celebrating the old. His failure to achieve complete happiness in either produced profoundly beautiful poetry in both.

The poets who slid into the 20th century from the 19th did so with varying degrees of unease. For some, the metropolis, the factory, political upheaval and cultural fragmentation were stimulants – a call to overthrow conventional form and sensibility. For others, however, modernity meant the end of 'the great song' of eternal truths. ('Talk to me of originality and I will turn to you with rage,' cried Yeats.) The most enduring work of this period engages passionately with the tensions between tradition and innovation and hears 'The rattles of the pebbles on the shore/Under the receding wave,' while observing what the turning tide reveals.

W.B. Yeats (1865-1939)

WILLIAM BUTLER YEATS is widely regarded as the 20th century's greatest poet writing in the English language. Born in Dublin, he was the eldest son of a lawyer turned painter, John Butler Yeats (1839–1922). The family moved to London, where Yeats was educated at the Godolphin School in Hammersmith. He later studied at the School of Art in Dublin, where a fellow student, George Russell (1867–1935), shared his interest in mysticism and the supernatural. Yeats attended his first seance in 1886. Encouraged by his father, he began to write poetry in his late teens.

Influenced by both the Pre-Raphaelites and William Blake, Yeats's initial aim was to re-create a specifically Irish literature. He drew on fairy stories, folktales, Gaelic legends and contemporary spiritualism, to which he was exposed by his mentor, Lady Augusta Gregory. They worked together on her investigation into the Irish peasantry, *Visions and Beliefs in the West of Ireland* (1922), and together they created the movement known as the Irish Literary Renaissance, which culminated in the establishment of the Abbey Theatre, Dublin, which opened in 1904. By now Yeats was interested in lacing formal language with colloquialisms and the language of dreams – the conflict between ethereal immaterial notions and the concrete nature of Irish nationalism is the subject of his best early poetry.

The most crucial event for Yeats's poetry occurred in 1889, when he fell in love with the fiery and beautiful Republican, Maud Gonne (1866–1953). His obsession with her was to haunt his work forever. Another crucial meeting was with Ezra Pound (see page 31) in 1909. Pound's influence was to make Yeats's work tauter and more authoritative, and to make Yeats himself more determined to strip away the masks of his previous poetry and to find a resolute 'I'. 'Now that my ladder's gone,' he wrote, 'I must lie down where all the ladders start,/In the foul rag and bone shop of the heart.' His own heart was gesturally won from Maud (to whom he proposed perpetually – and to her daughter, too, as a last resort) by Georgie Hyde Lees. Marriage made his life 'serene and full of order' and provided the starting point for a new conjunction of the romantic and realist strains in his poetry, when his wife started to produce reams of 'automatic writing' to help her husband. This led to a bizarre collection, *A Vision* (1926), dealing with types of human personality, with the 'gyres' (spirals) of history and with the supernatural. His greatest books, *The Tower* (1928) and *The Winding Stair* (1929), include elements of the symbolic notions foreshadowed in *A Vision*.

Yeats's poetry has grand surfaces, a textural richness, a precision and a passion, which in his final years became lustfully romantic – he underwent an operation to 'rejuvenate' his sexuality in 1934. His plays, first performed at the Abbey Theatre, are secondary to his poems, but have a special fascination, ranging from the Romantic, to bleak expressionism and grotesque farce. He was awarded the Nobel prize in 1923.

> I pray – for fashion's word is out
> And prayer comes round again –
> That I may seem, though I die old,
> A foolish, passionate man

W. B. YEATS *'A Prayer for Old Age'* (1928)

Philosopher poets

Frost, Rilke and Valéry are singular figures in the history of 20th-century poetry, whose only common ground is an uncompromising idea of the poet's vocation and the role of poetry. Whereas many poets of the early 20th century were preoccupied with form and language, these men saw poetry as the highest expression of thought and consciousness. They belong to a long – and necessary – tradition in which poets are a race apart. They are, in Shelley's words, 'the unacknowledged legislators of the world'.

ROBERT FROST (1874–1963)

Robert Lee Frost was born in San Francisco, but when his father died of tuberculosis in 1885 his family moved to New England, where he lived most of his life until he was 39 years old. He was successful at school but found academic life restrictive. He tried his hand at mill work, shoe-making, journalism and farming before taking his wife and large family to London in 1912. He had the manuscript of his first book, *A Boy's Will*, with him. This, like most of his work to date, had been rejected by American publishers, but Britain was more receptive to experimental work, and it was published, with the help of Edward Thomas, in 1913. Amy Lowell reviewed his second book, *North of Boston* (1913), in America, where it was enthusiastically read, and by the time he returned there in 1915 he was a bestselling author. He bought a farm in New Hampshire, where he continued to write his distinctive, quiet poetry about ordinary people in everyday situations.

For Frost the poem constituted a 'momentary stay against confusion', and his work is concerned with domestic, rural activities – mending fences, sharpening saws, swinging birches and the like – which trigger wider reflection. One of his best known poems, 'Mending Wall', for example, is 'about' the barriers between

'Home is the place where, when you have to go there,
They have to take you in'
'I should have called it
Something you somehow haven't to deserve.'
ROBERT FROST, *The Death of the Hired Man*, *North of Boston* (1913)

Above: Rainer Maria Rilke in an uneasy pose. He was a restless, wandering poet – 'the Santa Claus of unhappiness' – at home only in his relentless search for poetic truth.

Far left: Robert Frost reads at the Inauguration Ceremony of J.F. Kennedy in 1961. Frost's quiet insights into the significance of the everyday made him a potent figure in the American national consciousness.

coast in the castle of a princess when he wrote his most famous work, *Duineser Elegien* (*Duino Elegies*, 1923), which he completed in an astonishing three weeks. His most significant mistress was Lou Andreas-Salome, to whom Nietzsche had proposed and whose correspondence with Freud is famous. They met in 1897 and travelled together to Russia, the most important of his many 'elective homelands'. Here he began his first serious work, *Das Stunden-Buch* (*The Book of Hours*, 1905), in which his self-celebratory, devotional and musical voice was already developing.

Each poem represents the struggle of the act of writing. Rilke defined his writing method as 'making objects out of fear', objects achieved through a process he called 'reversion', whereby poems were received, by him, from some universal dictating consciousness. His themes are love, death, the terrors of childhood, the idolization of women and, most importantly, the question of 'God', which he saw as a necessary 'tendency of the heart' rather than as an identifiable supreme being. 'This life suspended over an abyss is, in fact, impossible,' he wrote, but it was that impossibility that drove him to create. He died of undiagnosed leukaemia, from which he had been suffering for many years.

PAUL VALÉRY (1871–1945)

Valéry's poetry has been described as 'perhaps the most sheerly beautiful of the century', but there is relatively little of it. He wrote for three years, from 1888, but stopped when an unrequited love affair prompted him to renounce all emotional preoccupations and dedicate himself to the 'idol of the intellect'. He wanted desperately to be thought of as a thinker, rather than as a poet, and between 1894 and 1945 recorded his thoughts each day in the famous Cahiers (notebooks), while living the uneventful life of a civil servant.

In 1912 the novelist André Gide pressed him to revise his early works for publication, and Valéry began writing again, beginning the five-year labour of *La Jeune parque* (*The Young Fate*, 1917). This long poem about the youngest of the three Fates of classical mythology, which symbolized the three stages of life, brought him immediate fame. His reputation was consolidated with the luminous *L'Album de vers anciens* (1920) and *Charmes* (*Enchantments*, 1922), which contains his famous meditation on death, 'La Cimetière marin' ('The Graveyard by the Sea'), and what may be his best known line: 'Le vent se lève! ... il faut tenter de vivre!' ('The wind is rising! ... We must try to live!').

people and ends with the acceptance that 'Good fences make good neighbours'. One critic has noted that 'there is loneliness in every poem'; there is also dark humour and a pessimistic but enduring affection. His most famous poems are to be found in *Mountain Interval* (1916). Other books include *New Hampshire* (1923), *Collected Poems* (1930) and the darkly affirmative last volume, *In the Clearing* (1962).

RAINER MARIA RILKE (1875–1926)

Apart from working in Paris as secretary to the sculptor Auguste Rodin for a short time, Rilke did nothing but write. He wrote in Prague – where he was born and where his education (a 'primer of horror') took place – in Russia, Spain, France, Austria, Switzerland and Italy. He was funded in his life's work by a variety of patrons (mainly rich and cultured older women who fell in love with him), and he was, typically, living on the Adriatic

Profound simplicities

Many poets of this era strove to express a profound sense of detachment and of the disquieting strangeness of being alive – an experience so complex that the simplest of language was necessary to explore it. What Graham Greene called a 'sense of banishment' pervades their work. There is a desperate insistence that 'all is otherness', which led to deeply introverted expressions of objective alienation.

FERNANDO PESSOA (1888–1935)

'A solemn investigator of futile things,' the deeply melancholic Pessoa was born in Lisbon in 1888. His father died and his mother remarried, and in 1896 the family moved to Durban, South Africa, where Pessoa received an English education. In 1905 he returned to Portugal and hardly stirred from Lisbon for the next 30 years, until his death of sclerosis of the liver.

He had a number of jobs, including translating for commercial firms, from which he earned enough to allow him to devote himself to poetry. He never married, his love life was inhibited and sad, and the few friends he had committed suicide or went mad. His 'uneventful' life was in contrast to his busy genius, which led him to write poetry under four different names (heteronyms, he called them) – four separate poetic identities – the first of which presented himself on 8 March 1914 and wrote 30 poems in one go. This was Alberto Caeiro. 'My master had appeared in me,' Pessoa said and quickly found Ricardo Reis and Alvaro de Campos to write poems for him as well. 'Into each of them I have put a deep conception of life,' he wrote. They were as 'alert to the mysterious importance of existing' as Pessoa was when he wrote under his own name. Little of his work was published during his lifetime, although he prepared a book of 150 poems, *Mensagem (Song-Book)*, the year before he died. After his death a trunk with the manuscripts of nearly 300 poems was discovered, and these were slowly published. 'An extraordinary, complex man who wrote simply,' Pessoa's poems are beautiful if harrowing journeys through the state of un-belonging in the world.

```
I know, I alone
How much it hurts, this heart
With no faith nor law
Nor melody of thought.


Only I, only I
And none of this can I say
Because feeling is like the sky -
Seen, nothing in it to see.
```

FERNANDO PESSOA, 'I Know, I Alone' (1932)

CONSTANTINE CAVAFY (1863–1933)

Constantine Cavafy, the pseudonym of Konstantinos Pétrou Kaváfis, was born in Alexandria into a Greek merchant family. Like Pessoa, he had an English education, after the death of his father in 1870. His family moved to Liverpool, but Cavafy returned to Alexandria when he was 14 years old. He lived there the rest of his life except for three years in Constantinople, where he wrote many poems and started the life of homosexual encounters that were to become the subject of much of his work. He earned his living as a civil servant, printing

Above: **Constantine Cavafy's beloved Alexandria,** *circa* **1900. The intimate possibilities of city life are at the heart of his intensely sexual poetry.**

Right: **Pablo Neruda, a man of profound communist principle, for whom 'the closest thing to poetry', was 'a loaf of bread or a ceramic dish, or a piece of wood lovingly carved'.**

his poems privately, and took little interest in the fame he slowly began to acquire.

Cavafy valued above all a human tolerance that 'forgives, justifies and includes everything, because it understands'. 'I only speak,' he wrote, 'but I don't think my words useless. Someone else will act. And my words – coward that I am – will assist his energy.' In a quiet way, Cavafy addressed timeless and fundamental issues of love, sexual longing, nostalgia and the purpose of art. One critic remarked that 'he hardly ever seems to raise his voice above a whisper'. His poetry is simply written, often conversational and full of minutely observed dramas which, through his vision, are transformed into universal statements.

PABLO NERUDA (1904–73)

'To write simply has been my most difficult task,' Neruda wrote. He achieved it, however, and endowed apparently straightforward lines like 'I am sad. But I am always sad' with a unique potency. The son of a railway worker, he was born Ricard Eliecer Neftalí Reyes in Parral, Chile, and adopted the pseudonym Pablo Neruda in 1920, having decided to write poetry. His first collection, *Veinte poemas de amor y una canción desesperada* (*Twenty Love Poems and a Song of Despair*, 1924), brought him overnight fame, but he continued his work in the diplomatic service, working as Chilean consul and, later, ambassador, in Burma, Ceylon, Singapore, Barcelona and Madrid. He was dismissed when he became a communist in 1936, and he was even forced to go into hiding at one point, crossing the Andes on a horse. He is a poet of the multitude who achieves universality by writing about his most intimate desires. 'We have to disappear into the midst of those we don't know,' he explained, 'so that they will suddenly pick up something of ours from the streets, from the sand, from the leaves that have fallen for a thousand years.' He was awarded the Nobel prize for literature in 1971.

Russian poets

The beginning of the 20th century saw the genesis of a new spirit in Russian poetry. The Poets' Guild was formed in 1911, giving rise to the movement known as Acmeism, whose aims were similar to those of the imagist group in London. The Bolshevik Revolution of 1917 halted the greatest achievements of Russian modernism, but its energy was sustained, despite the violent repression of what Osip Mandelstam called 'this tyrant century'.

ANNA AKHMATOVA (1889–1966)

Born Anna Andreevna Gorenko, Akhmatova first became famous in pre-Revolutionary St Petersburg for the 'vertiginous brevity' of her love poems. She had started writing poetry as an adolescent, following a serious illness, when she adopted her Tartar grandmother's name as her nom-de-plume in 1906. She studied law and Latin in Kiev, and agreed to marry Nikolai Gumilyev – whom she had met when she was 14 – in 1910. They visited Switzerland and Paris, where she was painted by Modigliani. On her return to St Petersburg she met Mikhail Kuzmin who started the magazine *Apollon*, which carried a manifesto entitled 'Concerning Beautiful Clarity' in its first issue. By 1917 Akhmatova had published three collections – 'Evening', 'Rosary' and 'White Flock' – which were remarkable for their frank lyricism. 'She brought to the Russian lyric the wealth of the 19th-century Russian novel', noted Osip Mandelstam.

The Revolution completely changed her life and her work. Gumilyev, from whom she was separated, was arrested for counter-revolutionary sentiments and executed in 1921. Her son, Lev Gumilev, was arrested in 1934, and she spent 17 months trying to secure his release from a Leningrad prison. She was described by Stalin's cultural minister as being 'half nun, half whore', and her work was banned between 1923 and 1940. She was expelled from the Union of Writers, but none of this broke her spirit and she continued to write out of her unshakeable conviction that poetry needs to tell harsh truths. Her private sufferings began to seem representative of the suffering around her, and her genius was to speak of complex social generalities from the perspective of particular and private pain.

OSIP MANDELSTAM (1891–1938)

The son of a Jewish leather merchant, Mandelstam was born in Warsaw but brought up in St Petersburg. He travelled in Europe between 1907 and 1910, spending time in Italy and at the Sorbonne in Paris. He returned to Russia to study romance and German philosophy at St Petersburg University. He met Anna Akhmatova, and became famous in literary circles after the publication of his first collection, *Stone* (1913), which had the

Long closed the roads to the past,
'And what is the past to me now?
What is to be found there? Bloodstained flagstones,
Or a bricked-up door,
Or an echo that still refuses
To keep quiet, though I ask it to ...
The same thing happened to the echo
As with what I carry in my heart'
ANNA AKHMATOVA, *'Echo'*

brevity and clarity of language that the Acmeist group demanded. A second collection, *Tristia* (1922), confirmed his reputation and widened his range, but during the 1920s he was increasingly criticized for being 'out of step' with the new Soviet age. His insistence that the poet has the right to tell the truth about what he sees and feels led to his arrest in 1934: he had written a poem explicitly denouncing Stalin. During his three-year internal exile he wrote 'The Verona Notes', but was arrested again in May 1938 and never seen again. His wife, Nadezhda, wrote two volumes of autobiography – *Hope Against Hope* (1970) and *Hope Abandoned* (1974) – which not only describe Osip's tragic life but are also powerful and harrowing descriptions of life under 20th-century totalitarian rule.

BORIS PASTERNAK (1890–1960)

Pasternak, who was born in Moscow, studied music until he was 18 years old, when he started writing poetry, which showed the influence of Rilke, Alexander Blok and Andrei Bely. In 1912 Pasternak went to Marburg in Germany to study philosophy, but on his return to Russia he became involved with the Futurist poets and published his first collection, *A Twin In The Clouds* in 1914.

Pasternak's work is difficult, but it is meant to be. He was instrumental in the evolution of a technique known as 'making strange', whereby everyday objects, people and events are 'defamiliarized' – made bizarre and new – by being described by the poet in 'strange' ways. 'Things splintered into sensations and created anew ... turned out to be different things, never seen before,' he explained. Associative links are missed out, so the readers have to supply their own and decode the idea or feeling of the poem as they read. In the 1930s Pasternak began what he called his 'long, silent duel with Stalin'. His poetry was banned in 1933, and he earned his living as a translator. His last years were spent working on the novel *Doctor Zhivago* (1957), a testament to the experience of the Russian intelligentsia before and after the Revolution. He was awarded the Nobel prize – which he refused – in 1958.

Right and below: **Russian Revolutionary posters like these embody the enthusiasm and optimism felt by many writers and intellectuals at the time. Yet their avant-garde literary experiments soon fell foul of the increasingly repressive Soviet regime, and the revolution devoured its own children.**

3 Modernism and the avant-garde

The closing years of the 19th century had seen the beginnings of what was effectively a revolution in artistic representation. Traditional forms were no longer adequate to convey the complex experience of the modern world. Art and literature of this period was concerned particularly with technique and with the need to show its audience that it was, indeed, a craft and need not be confined to the traditional forms that had been used so far.

Right: The opening of the First International Dada Fair, on the 5th July 1925 in Dr. Burchard's bookshop, Berlin. George Grosz is standing at the far right. The collagist Hannah Hoch is seated front left.

Far right: Experimentation in Europe blurred boundaries between different art forms. Here, the painter Raoul Dufy illustrates a poem by Apollinaire – 'Carp, how long you live!... has death forgotten you, melancholy fish'.

Symbolism, imagism and after

The word symbolism derives from the Greek *symballein*, 'to throw together'. A symbolist movement began in the 1880s in France, using as a basis for artistic expression the idea that a poem or a painting need not explain overtly what it is about but rather could 'throw up' a meaning from what it describes. Instead of dwelling on the nature of loneliness, for example, a poem might reveal that state through describing a lonely bird, as Charles Baudelaire's 'L'Albatross' does.

In England this idea of abstraction was developed by, among others, T.E. Hulme. Hulme had studied in Paris and wanted to break with the sentimental self-indulgence of the Romantic tradition. The resulting imagist movement began in London around 1908. The imagists' thesis was that a poem does not communicate logically but by bringing together things that are not normally associated with each other. Two aspects of the same thing might be juxtaposed to reveal another, quite different reality. The poems were hard, precise 'images', which aimed to change the way ordinary things are perceived and to trigger unacknowledged emotion through that physical revelation. 'Make it New', Ezra Pound famously advised. One 'instant of time', perfectly captured, he wrote, would be more powerful than dozens of lines of traditional poetry.

The imagists were much influenced by the Japanese noh plays and by their poetic forms, particularly the haiku, of which Pound's 'In a Station of the Metro' (1916) is probably the most famous:

> The apparition of those faces in the crowd;
> Petals on a wet, black bough.

These two lines are the end product of what began as a 32-line poem.

La Carpe.

Dans vos viviers, dans vos étangs,
Carpes, que vous vivez longtemps !
Est-ce que la mort vous oublie,
Poissons de la mélancolie.

T.E. HULME (1883–1917)

Thomas Ernest Hulme was born in Staffordshire and began his adult life studying mathematics at Cambridge. He was sent down in 1902 and went to Canada where 'the flat spaces and wide horizons of the virgin priaree' made him realize 'the necessity of verse'. He went to Paris and studied with the philosopher Henri Bergson before returning to Britain, where he founded the Poets Club in London in 1908. It was here that Ezra Pound, Amy Lowell and Hilda Dolittle (H.D.) met. Oriental verse forms were discussed, and the notion of *vers libre* – a poetry with no formal rhythm or rhyme sequence – was approved as a way forward. Hulme was insistent that poetry should consist of 'absolutely accurate representation and no verbiage'. The poet's personality should not 'interfere' with his work, and language itself must be used differently, so that a new 20th-century reality could emerge through art. Hulme was killed in action in Flanders in 1917, but his ideas changed the way poetry was written, irreversibly.

Eliot and Pound

It is rare in any biography of any important figure in the history of modernism not to find that there was a significant meeting with Ezra Pound, whose own work, particularly *The Cantos*, informed the taste of an entire generation. Without Pound's contribution, Eliot's seminal poem *The Waste Land* might never have been published.

good and made Eliot the most respected avant-garde writer of his day.

Critics often dwell on the difficulty of Eliot's work – its erudite references and mythical structures – but his poetry is concerned with human themes: isolation, the difficulty (impossibility, even) of communication, the fragmentation of the physical world in the aftermath of the First World War, the spiritual sterility of the present and an intense and inherent longing for stability. His writing often includes snatches of ordinary conversation, intermingled with fragments of old songs, lines from Shakespeare or the Greek myths and dramatic

T.S. ELIOT (1888–1965)

Thomas Stearns Eliot, the seventh child of Henry Eliot, was born and raised in a strict Unitarian family in St Louis, Missouri. In 1906 he went to Harvard, where he studied Greek, Latin, Renaissance literature and French and German philosophy. He also edited the student magazine and began writing poetry. By the time he was 21 years old, he had completed 'Portrait of a Lady' and 'The Love Song of J. Alfred Prufrock', two of his most famous works. He moved to London in 1914 and met the imagists, who influenced his thinking – particularly Ezra Pound, who would one day cut *The Waste Land* (which is dedicated to him), from 800 lines to 433.

Eliot spent a year teaching at the Highgate School, before beginning his brief career as a clerk at Lloyds Bank. At the time, he was also editing and writing drama, poetry and literary criticism. In 1919 he published *Poems*, which contained 'Gerontion', a meditative interior monologue in blank verse – 'Thoughts of a dry brain in a dry season' – which was immediately recognized as a breakthrough in English poetry. *The Waste Land* was published in 1922, and its appearance changed English poetry for

'What shall I do now? What shall I do?'
'I shall rush out as I am, and walk the street
'With my hair down, so. What shall we do tomorrow?
'What shall we ever do?'
                    The hot water at ten.
And if it rains, a closed car at four.
And we shall play a game of chess,
Pressing lidless eyes and waiting for a knock upon the door.

T.S. ELIOT, *The Waste Land* (1922)

Above: A portrait of Ezra Pound by Wyndham Lewis, whose vorticist movement Pound invented. Much of his work involved supporting other writers, but his poetry sequence *The Cantos* is seminal to the modernist era.

Left: A caricature of American-born T.S. Eliot, whose intense poem of contemporary sterility, 'The Waste Land' established him, in 1922, as the key figure in English-language modernism.

EZRA POUND (1885–1972)

When Pound died in Venice after 60 years of publishing activity, he had produced 70 books of his own, contributions to about 70 others and more than 1500 articles. He had been a leader of the imagist movement in Britain, but he quickly moved on to form the vorticist group with Wyndham Lewis and others. He had been responsible, too, for the initial publishing of Eliot and James Joyce. As editor of various literary reviews in London, he became a dominant figure in Anglo-American verse and was the first person to recognize many major talents, including Robert Frost, D.H. Lawrence and Henri Gaudier-Brzeska.

Pound was born in a small mining town in Idaho and had a normal middle-class childhood, before going to the University of Pennsylvania, where he met his life-long friend, the poet William Carlos Williams. He left knowing Latin, Greek, French, Italian, German, Spanish, Provençal and Anglo-Saxon. After a brief teaching career in America, Pound departed for Europe, where he was to spend most of his wandering life. In September 1908 he settled in London, where he met W.B. Yeats and joined, then led, the imagists. Three books of his own poetry were quickly published as he continued his editing career.

After the First World War Pound moved to Paris and wrote one of the most highly praised poems of the 20th century, *Hugh Selwyn Mauberley* (1920), a portrait of contemporary British literary culture. By this time his verse had developed a style distinguished by economy, brevity and clarity, in which concrete details and exact visual images were used to capture intense moments of experience. Like T.S. Eliot, Pound wanted a modernism that brought back to life the highest standards of the past, while forging into the new. His longest, most famous work is *The Cantos*, which he wrote on and off from 1925 in Italy, where he lived for most of the rest of his life. *The Cantos* is a logbook of Pound's own private journey through Greek mythology, ancient China and Egypt and many other periods and subjects. The verses are highly readable and contain odd moments of perfect beauty.

During the Second World War Pound was imprisoned for his fascist, anti-American views, and when the war ended he was declared 'insane and too mentally ill to stand trial'. He spent 12 years in a mental hospital in Washington, D.C., before being released in 1958. Pound returned to Italy, dividing his time between Rapallo and Venice.

monologues. The work is elegaic, insistent and often painfully moving in its juxtaposition of the banal, arid world we inhabit and the spiritual wholeness that pervades his poetry.

The Waste Land

Written in five separate parts, *The Waste Land* uses a mosaic of quotations from Spenser, Dante, Baudelaire, Wagner and Shakespeare to provide a rich background to the voices of the present-day characters we hear bickering, joking and wondering about their lives. Edgell Rickword has correctly written that Eliot was concerned 'to explore and make palpable the more intimate distresses of a generation for whom all the romantic escapes had been blocked'. In place of Cleopatra, Desdemona and Ophelia, for example, he gives us a neurotic woman whose 'nerves are bad tonight', an exhausted typist and a fed-up war bride in a pub. Everywhere is the contrast between an abundant past and a sterile present. A people whose lives have been effectively laid waste in the aftermath of the war is minutely, but sympathetically, dissected.

Modern -isms in Europe

The changing sensibility of Europeans during the first quarter of the century was largely due to the increasing mechanisation of all aspects of life. Cars, aeroplanes, speed, noise, and specifically the violent machinery of war inspired Wyndham Lewis' vorticist movement and Tristan Tzara's Dadaists to experiment with extreme fragmentation in print. André Breton meanwhile developed his theories of 'surrealism', which allowed the chaos of the unconscious mind to seep onto the surface of the page.

VORTICISM

The imagist movement did not hold Pound's attention for long. After it was hijacked by the cigar-chewing Amy Lowell (Pound felt that she had changed the movement to 'Amygism'), he left and forged a bond with the exuberant poet-cum-cultural agitator, Wyndham Lewis (see page 57), and together they developed vorticism, publishing their manifesto in July 1914 in the first edition of Lewis's magazine, *Blast: The Review of the Great English Vortex*.

> BLAST first (from politeness) ENGLAND
> CURSE ITS CLIMATE FOR ITS SINS AND
> INFECTIONS ...
> VICTORIAN VAMPIRE, THE LONDON
> cloud sucks the TOWNS heart.

Although Wyndham Lewis later denied it, his ideas had been formed largely by the Italian futurist movement, begun around 1911 by F.T. Marinetti. The futurists were intoxicated by the idea of speed, by the 'ivresse of travelling at one kilometre an hour' in one of the newly invented automobiles, planes or trains. The idea that nothing could be regarded in the same way once it had been viewed as one sped past it inside a machine was central to both futurism and vorticism, and it gave rise to huge abstract paintings and much dislocated use of typography and punctuation.

In March 1912 the futurist exhibition in London was 'a colossal success', and Wyndham Lewis decided that he was not interested in speed alone but also in breaking – blasting – open the surface of everything represented in words or pictures to make a huge, explosive 'English vortex' of energy. The surface of everything must be imploded and made new. 'There should be a bill passed in Parliament at once FORBIDDING ANY IMAGE OR RECOGNIZABLE SHAPE TO BE STUCK UP IN ANY PUBLIC PLACE,' he wrote. London had recently for the first time been exposed to various contemporary European artists, and Wassily Kandinsky, Constantin Brancusi and the post-impressionists had all been exhibited to tremendous acclaim.

Instrumental to all this energetic rhetoric was the First World War and the raging machines of destruction involved in that catastrophe. Like all the modern -isms springing up in Europe at this time, vorticism was as much an angry reaction to the violent end of Europe's physical coherence as anything else.

In fact, translating the theories of the explosive 'vortex' to literature was an unrealistic aim. Apart from using typefaces and punctuation in novel, jagged ways, there was not much that words on paper could do to express speed or violence. *Blast* survived for only two issues (1914 and 1915), and the movement had lost its momentum by 1920. Lewis's experimental play, *Enemy of the Stars*, and his funny, disjointed novel *Tarr* (1918) survived vorticism, however, and can still surprise the reader with their violent exuberance.

DADAISM

One evening in 1916, as legend has it, Tristan Tzara, Jean Arp, Marcel Janco, Hugo Ball and a few more burgeoning Dadaists who were in the Café de la Terrasse in Zurich decided on their movement's name by sticking a knife into a French-German dictionary. Dada was the word they stuck into. It means nothing, effectively, which is at the heart of Dadaism. Disgusted by the war and the bourgeoisie of Europe who were profiting from it, they embarked on a career of promoting precisely nothing. Poetry readings would be held, with no poetry. Walks around Paris would be arranged, with no guide.

The cover of the July 1915 issue of Wyndham Lewis's *Blast* magazine, which was the mouthpiece of the Vorticist movement for a brief but extraordinarily energetic period of English experimentation.

Art exhibitions would be held in which the objects on display were simply things found on the street – Marcel Duchamp's *Bicycle Wheel* (1913) was among the most famous of these *objets trouvés*.

Although not really a literary movement – producing 'literature' would be against the principles of its members – Dadaism was enormously influential to the century's developing sensibility, and it flourished in Zurich, New York, Berlin, Cologne, Paris and Hanover for a few volatile years. The last Dada periodical, *291*, was published in 1924.

SURREALISM

Surrealism was, in effect, the child of Dadaism, building on Dadaism's insistence on the irrational in the face of a world gone mad. The French poet and critic André Breton (1896–1966) published the first surrealist manifesto in 1924, in which he explained that the movement was concerned to find a means of reuniting conscious and unconscious realms of experience. When this was achieved, there would be no boundaries between the world of dreams and fantasies and the everyday, ratio-nal world. A vast and untapped ocean of potential would be available to everybody. The logical and rational would be seen for what they really are – petty limitations on a life fully lived.

Although its major influence was in the field of painting, surrealism manifested itself in literature in a juxtaposition of words, which startled because there was no logical thought behind them. Breton and his followers experimented with 'automatic writing', in which people wrote in a trance – an early version of the stream of consciousness – which psychoanalysis had, in part, made possible. The aim of this was to force readers to surrender themselves to an inherent 'sense' in the words they read, forcing them to make jumps in their understanding and to make connections where no sensible connection existed, and thereby enhancing their capacity to experience the world.

My wife with shoulders of champagne
And of a fountain with dolphin-heads beneath the ice
My wife with wrists of matches
My wife with fingers of luck and ace of hearts
With fingers of mown hay.

ANDRÉ BRETON, '*Freedom of Love*'

American moderns

The intense groupings (and re-groupings) of radicals in Europe had profound reverberations in America, but here, instead of movements, there tended to be experimental individuals who absorbed the innovations of their European contemporaries and combined it with their own recent naturalist tradition. Slowly but surely a handful of American writers came close to the centre of an international and revolutionary modernist spirit.

HART CRANE (1899–1932)

Born in Ohio of parents whose violent disagreements undoubtedly damaged him psychologically, Harold Hart Crane was to become one of the first poets of his generation to find new ways of expressing 'all this that balks delivery through words'. During his brief but troubled adult life Crane was concerned with 'pouring' out words to work against the rigidities of logical thinking. He absorbed Walt Whitman's work at an early age – he later wrote '–No never to let go/my hand/in yours/Walt Whitman–/so–' – and read T.S. Eliot, who much impressed him, although he found the 'pessimism' of *The Waste Land* inappropriate. His aim, he claimed, was to write 'towards a more positive ... ecstatic goal'.

By 1923 Crane was living in Greenwich Village, New York. Alcoholic and homosexual, he started writing poems whose words slid freely into each other, driven not by logical but by emotional, associative connections. His first collection, *White Buildings*, was published to slight acclaim in 1926, after which he visited London and then Paris. His most famous poem, 'The Bridge', was published in 1930. He suffered from a lack of public and private affection and – having failed in his own, and society's, terms – drowned himself two years later.

E.E. CUMMINGS (1894–1962)

Edward Estlin Cummings was born in Cambridge, Massachusetts. He took a BA and an MA at Harvard, served in the First World War as an ambulance driver and was interned for some months in a French detention camp, which provided him with material for his autobiographical novel, *The Enormous Room* (1922). His first book of poems, *Tulips and Chimneys*, appeared the following year, beginning his experiments with the typography and structure of poetry that were to concern him for the next 40 years.

For cummings (who never spelt his name with capitals), a poem consisted of the poem plus its typography – the words and the way they appear being inextricably linked. He used lower case letters, brackets (splitting up parts of single words as well as phrases), odd capital letters, erratic margins and anything else he could think of to break up – or smash open – the poem's surface. 'Like the burlesk comedian, I am abnormally fond of that precision which creates movement,' he wrote. His placing of words in evocative shapes on the page anticipated the work of the concrete poets years later.

life hurl my
yes, crumbles hand(ful released conarefetti)ev
eryflitter,inga.where
mil(lions of aflickf) litter ing brighmillion ofS
hurl; ...
(One XL, is 5, 1926)
is a typical beginning.

Cummings is often criticized for his whimsicality, but at its best his poetry communicates a sheer delight in the present – a lyric celebration of being alive.

WILLIAM CARLOS WILLIAMS (1883–1963)

'A poem is a small (or large) machine made of words as [the poet] finds them inter-related about him and composes them ... into an intense expression of his preoccupations and ardours that they may constitute a revelation,' Williams wrote.

His first book, *Al Que Quiere!* (*'To Him Who Wants It!'*, 1917), established a style that was distinct and new: clear images and spacious layout, with practically no punctuation but a wide range of information in each poem – scattered and intense.

'I have eaten/the plums/that were in/the icebox', is the well-known first verse to a poem, 'This is just to say', which is incredibly simple yet strong. The poet is sorry he ate the plums, but his words, in effect, replace them, so the cycle of affectionate exchange is continued through his writing of the poem that mourns them.

Williams met Pound and Joyce in Europe in 1924 and took from imagism the idea that poetry must find new beginnings in things, rather than ideas – 'no ideas but in things,' he once famously said. In 1931 he founded the objectivist group to further his aim of writing sparse, unrhyming, unmetred verse that concerned itself with clarity of description. His longest work was the five-volume *Paterson*, written between 1946 and 1958, in which he considered the idea of a city on the shores of a river, which, in its changing complexity, represents the complexity of man. His lines were always short – 'because of my nervous nature,' he said – and the breaks in them are there to interrupt, rather than to contain, the flow of the thoughts they contain. In this way Williams achieved an enormous range of emotions in plain and simple language.

Above: e.e. cummings re-wrote the rules of grammar and punctuation, leading the way for later developments in language and presentation – particularly influencing the American Beat poets of the fifties.

Left: The sparse beauty of William Carlos Williams' verse had at its centre the imagists' notion that ideas must be evoked through detailed descriptions of everyday things.

4 The new novel

Virginia Woolf, critic, novelist, and a leading light of the Bloomsbury Group. Her essay 'A Room of One's Own' made her an enduring figurehead for the feminist movement.

Critical opinion is rarely stable. Few writers of the 20th century can be spoken of in the same breath as the greats of the 19th. Flaubert, Dickens, Tolstoy, Mark Twain – to mention just a few – are assured of their place in the canon, but the only undisputed giants of the 20th-century novel are Joyce, Kafka and Proust. More than anyone else they redefined the possibilities of fiction. Virginia Woolf and D.H. Lawrence are also tremendously significant figures, although their visions were more personal and their reputations are still in flux.

Virginia Woolf (1882-1941)

VIRGINIA WOOLF'S STATUS as a great writer has been subject to more controversy than that of any other leading English novelist. At the time of her death, she was recognized as the foremost exponent of modernist techniques in the novel and as the English writer who went furthest in rejecting the principles of conventional realism. She is now better known as an essayist and one of the founders of feminist literary criticism. Her essay, 'A Room of One's Own' (1929), which discusses the predicament of women writers in a world dominated by men, was – and still is – enormously influential for the women's movement. Critical attention has focused on the technical innovations in her novels, while questioning their status as important works.

She was the daughter of a distinguished Victorian man of letters, Sir Leslie Stephen (1832–1904), and was educated at home with her sister, the painter and designer Vanessa Bell (1879–1961). Much of the popular interest in her has centred on her position as a key figure in the Bloomsbury Group rather than her achievements a writer. This was a circle of mainly upper-class English writers, intellectuals and artists who met or lived in the Bloomsbury district of London. The great fascination with the Bloomsbury Group in recent years concentrates on their semi-bohemian lifestyles and their colourful and unconventional sexual relationships. Only Virginia Woolf and the economist John Maynard Keynes (1883–1946) have achieved lasting fame.

In 1905 Virginia Woolf began writing for the *Times Literary Supplement*, and she continued to write essays and criticism for the rest of her life. Her first novels – *The Voyage Out* (1915) and *Night and Day* (1919) – were conventional works, dealing with family relationships in a fairly straightforward way. With *Jacob's Room* (1922), however, she began to experiment, and her fiction turned away from charting the observable actions of characters to registering their private thoughts and feelings. She wanted to capture the continuous flow of experience from a totally subjective viewpoint. Traditional fiction, with its concentration on external events and clearly defined characters, no longer interested her. Life, she said in a famous essay in 1919, was 'a luminous halo, a semi-transparent envelope surrounding us from the beginning of consciousness to the end'. It was with this 'semi-transparent envelope' that she now concerned herself.

Although she had disliked Joyce's *Ulysses* in 1921, describing it as a disaster, his stream-of-consciousness technique was central to the construction of her first important novel, *Mrs Dalloway* (1925). The book takes one day in the life of Clarissa Dalloway, who moves from preparing a party in the morning to watching her guests leave at the end of the evening. In the course of her day she reflects on the various choices she might have made that could have changed her life. But nothing does change throughout the novel, except the thoughts Clarissa has about herself. This method of constructing a novel around an interior monologue, so that the 'action' is the sum of a person's changing mood, shapes all Woolf's subsequent work, being most successfully applied in *To the Lighthouse* (1927). With *The Waves* (1931), in which the plot follows the movements of the changing sea rather than the relations between the characters, the method had perhaps reached the limits of its creative possibilities. Some critics regard *The Waves* as her finest work, but it is more commonly seen as the product of an over-refined sensibility, too delicate and subtle, and, above all, too far removed from coarse-grained reality to engage the reader's interest. Virginia Woolf suffered from bouts of mental instability, and in 1941, in a state of extreme depression, she committed suicide by drowning herself.

Marcel Proust (1871-1922)

PROUST DEDICATED most of his life to a single work, *À La Recherche du Temp Perdu* (*Remembrance of Things Past*, 1913–27). What many consider the greatest novel of the 20th century is the least easy to summarise. The French title can be translated literally as 'in search of lost time'. It has become a cliché to say that the central concern of this vast book of over 3,000 pages is the relation between time and memory. In fact the book covers a great diversity of themes and subjects which Proust's supreme artistry weaves together in a harmonious whole. Everything about this unique work resists critical labels.

The first volume was printed at the author's own expense after it had been rejected by a publishing house whose director was the novelist André Gide; it was later accepted when Gide realized the enormity of his mistake. Until then, Proust had been known as a dilettante and social butterfly, who assiduously pursued the leading hostesses of smart Paris society. He was an occasional journalist and the author of a collection of short stories and some parodies of the French writers he most admired. To contemporaries such as Gide, he seemed more at home in fashionable society than in literary circles. His father was an eminent Parisian doctor, and his mother, a highly cultivated woman to whom he was passionately devoted, came from a wealthy Jewish family. In 1907, two years after his mother's death, he became a semi-recluse and remained so for the rest of his life, withdrawing to a sound-proofed, cork-lined room to write his masterpiece.

'For a long time I used to go to bed early.' This famous opening sentence of C.K. Scott Moncrieff's translation of *Du côté de chez Swann* (*Swann's Way*, 1913) introduces the first person narrator, Marcel, who is referred to by name only once. His life and consciousness provide the book's common thread, as he moves through the glittering world of Parisian high society. The idea of lost time regained is just one strand. Proust's genius was to combine a sensibility of the highest order – a heightened awareness – with an extraordinary analytical intelligence. Among many other things, the novel contains profound analyses of snobbery and social rank, and of the nature of love, both heterosexual and homosexual, which he sees in terms of sexual jealousy. The section entitled 'Swann in Love' runs for more than 200 pages and could stand as a novel in its own right. The narrator describes the torments of jealousy suffered by a man of fashion who is in love with a courtesan. Charles Swann is one of the many people who reappear at different stages in Marcel's life and who together form the greatest gallery of characters in 20th-century literature. The most fascinating of them is the predatory homosexual, Baron de Charlus, a tragi-comic figure of heroic proportions. Charlus was modelled on the eccentric aristocrat Comte de Montesquiou, who once described the young Proust as 'a hysterical little flatterer'.

Remembrance of Things Past

À la recherche du temps perdu has the reputation of being dauntingly highbrow, the kind of book people feel they should read but never actually manage to. It is true that there are passages that strain the most devoted reader's attention – notably in the sixth volume, *La Prisonnière* (*The Captive*, 1923), where the narrator analyses his relationship with his lover Albertine in obsessive detail – but large stretches of the novel are taken up with the portrayal of social activity in salons and drawing rooms, at dinner parties, in restaurants and

Born to exceptional wealth, Proust seemed to his contemporaries to be devoting his life to leisure and pleasure. Not until the last years of his life did they recognize supreme artistic intelligence and honesty.

at all sorts of other gatherings, and these episodes are brilliantly comic. They are also masterpieces of social and psychological dissection. Proust's understanding of human nature has never been equalled, and far from being the over-sensitive aesthete he is sometimes depicted as, he caught the spirit of the times as no one else. The German critic Walter Benjamin paid an eloquent tribute to this dimension of his work: 'The nineteenth century did not reveal itself to Zola or Anatole France, but to the young Proust, the insignificant snob, the playboy and socialite who snatched in passing the most astounding confidences from a declining age as from another, bone-weary Swann.'

The key to the search for lost time is the notion of involuntary memory. This arrives fortuitously, triggered by sensations like taste and smell. It contrasts with the memories we recall at will through its infinitely greater immediacy and sensuous reality. When the narrator tastes a madeleine cake he has dipped in his tea, he is overpowered by a childhood memory. Memory of this kind does more than replay experience: it transforms the past and, through the past, consciousness of the present. Proust sees art as capable of serving a role that is analogous to involuntary memory. At the end of the book, the fictional Marcel commits himself to art (mirroring the author's trajectory) and so resolves his disenchantment with the aridities of social existence and his own life.

Proust once said that he would like the book to be printed as a continuous flow of prose running over two columns with no paragraphs. As it is, the rhythms and cadences of his prose – even more fluid in French than in Scott Moncrieff's superb English translation – have an almost hypnotic effect. Jean Cocteau described the intonations of his written voice as 'obeying the laws of night and honey'.

'... he cried out in his heart: "To think that I have wasted years of my life, that I have longed for death, that the greatest love that I have ever known has been for a woman who did not please me, who was not in my style!"'

MARCEL PROUST, 'Swann in Love'

Franz Kafka
(1883-1924)

FEW NOVELISTS HAVE provoked more varying interpretations – and more misunderstanding – than Franz Kafka. The adjective 'Kafkaesque' is used in dozens of languages for a nightmarish and oppressive atmosphere in which the individual is the victim of forces beyond his control. Yet he was a writer of astonishing power, and his work is often lyrical and even playful. The poet W.H. Auden wrote: 'Had one to name the author who comes closest to bearing the same relation to our age as Dante, Shakespeare and Goethe bore to theirs, Kafka is the first one would think of.'

Kafka was born into a middle-class Jewish family in Prague, Czechoslovakia. After studying law at university, he worked in an insurance office and wrote in his spare hours, sometimes late into the night. An acutely sensitive individual, he lived with his parents and was overshadowed by a father whom he saw as impossibly domineering. Not until the last year of his life, when he was dying of tuberculosis, was he able to move out of the family home to live with a woman – a step he referred to as 'a reckless move which can only be compared to some great historical event, like Napoleon's Russian campaign'. Kafka was little known in his lifetime. Only a few of his stories were published before his death, and in his will he instructed his friend, the Austrian writer Max Brod, to destroy all his writings. Brod ignored his wishes and published the remaining short stories as well as the novels – *Der Prozess* (*The Trial*, 1925), *Das Schloss* (*The Castle*, 1926) and the unfinished *Amerika* (*America*, 1927).

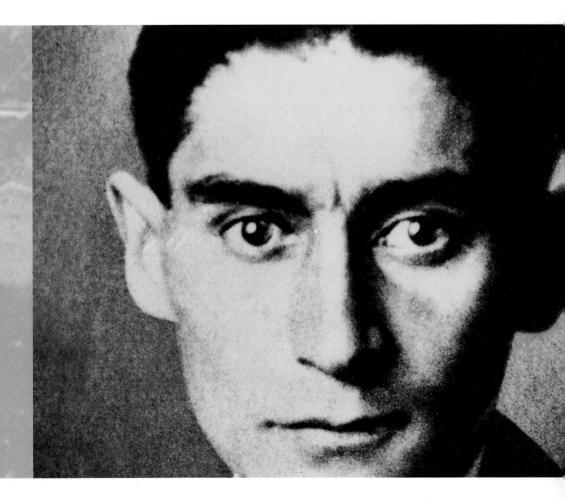

Right: The last photograph of Franz Kafka, taken in Kierling Sanatorium. In his will, he asked his friend Max Brod to burn his unpublished novels; fortunately Brod ignored his request.

Far right: A window display in the Kafka Bookshop in Prague. Virtually unknown at the time of his death, within ten years Kafka was recognized as one of the supreme prose writers of the century.

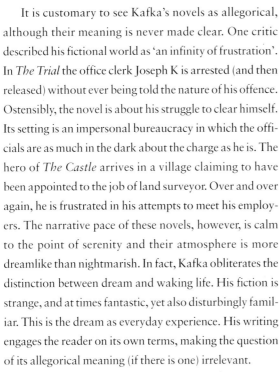

It is customary to see Kafka's novels as allegorical, although their meaning is never made clear. One critic described his fictional world as 'an infinity of frustration'. In *The Trial* the office clerk Joseph K is arrested (and then released) without ever being told the nature of his offence. Ostensibly, the novel is about his struggle to clear himself. Its setting is an impersonal bureaucracy in which the officials are as much in the dark about the charge as he is. The hero of *The Castle* arrives in a village claiming to have been appointed to the job of land surveyor. Over and over again, he is frustrated in his attempts to meet his employers. The narrative pace of these novels, however, is calm to the point of serenity and their atmosphere is more dreamlike than nightmarish. In fact, Kafka obliterates the distinction between dream and waking life. His fiction is strange, and at times fantastic, yet also disturbingly familiar. This is the dream as everyday experience. His writing engages the reader on its own terms, making the question of its allegorical meaning (if there is one) irrelevant.

Kafka is as much esteemed for his short stories as for his novels. Some of the early stories, such as 'Children in a Country Lane', have a remarkable and seemingly effortless lyricism. The later ones are often fables or parables, as he sometimes called them. Again, they seem to defy interpretation and this somehow contributes to their resonance. Works like 'Confessions of a Hunger Artist', 'The Bucket Rider' and 'A Country Doctor' have an almost mythic power in the way they combine mundane details of everyday life with strange and sometimes horrific events. 'In the Penal Colony' describes a terrible punishment apparatus, which uses needles to inscribe the details of the prisoner's crime on his back. Surreal events are related in a matter-of-fact manner, made all the more effective by Kafka's exceptionally lucid prose.

Metamorphosis

His most famous story is 'Die Verwandlung' ('Metamorphosis' or 'The Transformation', 1916), which begins: 'As Gregor Samsa awoke one morning from a night of uneasy dreams he found himself transformed in his bed into a gigantic insect.' It is characteristic of Kafka that Samsa's main concern is how he is going to get to work, rather than why he should have changed into an insect. He fights to make his family understand that he has not really changed, although he is now repellent to them. By the end of the story he is dead, his anguish dismissed as his family takes a trip to the country, relieved to be rid of him.

Among his fellow Czechs Kafka is regarded primarily as a comic writer. Many critics see his writing as the purest expression of contemporary alienation. Yet another school of thought regards him as a visionary who foresaw the age of the concentration camp and totalitarianism. There are elements in his fiction supporting all these interpretations. For example, the first sentence of *The Trial* – 'Someone must have been telling lies about Joseph K., for without having done anything wrong he was arrested one fine morning.' – could be taken as a prophetic description of an experience that was to become all too familiar for people living in Stalin's Russia and Nazi Germany: the knock on the door by the secret police. But it may be that the truest reading of Kafka is the one that treats him ultimately as a realist, 'the most precise realist of this century'.

James Joyce (1882–1941)

Probably no writer has had a greater influence on modern English fiction than the Irishman James Joyce. The paradox of this is that, outside of higher education, Joyce's most important work, *Ulysses*, is seldom read today. Indeed, for many people stretches of what is often labelled the 'Novel of the Twentieth Century' are largely unreadable.

Joyce was born in Dublin, and although he spent most of his adult life away from Ireland his fiction revolves around his native city. His first novel, *A Portrait of the Artist as Young Man* (1914–15), was started before he left Dublin and completed 12 years later in Trieste, Italy, where he lived for ten years, supporting his wife and family as an English teacher. This autobiographical novel follows the development of Stephen Dedalus from childhood, through a crisis of religious faith, to his student days. By the end of the book Stephen has comes to embrace his destiny as a writer, committed to exile in order to 'encounter ... the reality of my experience and to forge the uncreated conscience of my race'. Within a relatively conventional form, the novel is striking for the way it employs a variety of styles, each appropriate to the different stages of Stephen's life. Joyce had an almost preternatural mastery of language. In his book of short stories, *Dubliners* (1914), he adopted a more transparent, naturalistic style. Each of these stories about the lives of ordinary Dubliners focuses on a moment of truth – what Joyce called an 'epiphany' – in which the character's hopes and expectations are revealed as illusory.

Ulysses

Ulysses (1922) was published in Paris only after it had been rejected 87 times, and it was at first banned for obscenity. Rather than a novel, it could be regarded as a vast fictional laboratory in which Joyce explores the resources of the English language to their utmost. Buried within it is a great naturalistic novel based around Leopold Bloom, a Jewish advertisement salesman, his

James Joyce in Paris, 1920, with Sylvia Beach who was the proprietor of a bookshop called Shakespeare & Co. and also the first publisher of Joyce's masterpiece *Ulysses*.

O'Connell Street, Dublin. Although he lived most of his adult life abroad, all of Joyce's fiction is set in Dublin, the city he grew up in.

unfaithful wife, Molly, and Stephen Dedalus, the protagonist of Joyce's *A Portrait of the Artist as a Young Man*, who is now a young poet. The episodes in the book roughly correspond to the adventures of Homer's *Odyssey*, in which Odysseus is reunited with his wife after years of wandering. All the events take place in Dublin over a single day. Joyce uses the technique of 'interior monologue' to reveal Bloom's innermost thoughts and feelings as he wanders from place to place – a pub, a library, a newspaper office, a maternity hospital, a brothel – before returning home. The celebrated final section presents Molly's stream of consciousness in a continuous outpouring of prose, uninterrupted by punctuation and ending in a joyous affirmation of feeling for her husband: '... and yes I said yes I will Yes.'

'Some of my methods are trivial, some are quadrivial,' Joyce said with characteristic verbal playfulness. Despite the immense vitality and warmth of his portrayal of the central characters (and through them the people of Dublin), the greater part of *Ulysses* reflects his preoccupation with language. The commonplace and unheroic figure of Leopold Bloom is a wonderful creation, made more real to us than any other character in fiction, but as the book progresses Bloom's own voice dwindles as Joyce's narrative voice – or rather multiplicity of voices – predominates. The novel experiments with every conceivable literary technique, including a systematic parodying of English literary styles from *Beowulf* onwards. It also absorbs all sorts of other uses of language from the worlds of journalism, commerce, science and popular culture. For instance, the extended conversation between Bloom and Stephen Dedalus (who takes the role of a sort of spiritual son) parodies technical English through a series of questions and answers, such as 'What were Stephen's and Bloom's simultaneous volitional quasisensations of concealed identities?' These aspects of the book have made it an inexhaustible source of inspiration to other writers, while rendering much of it inaccessible to readers.

Finnegans Wake

'Aren't there enough words for you in English?' Joyce was once asked. 'Yes,' he replied, 'there are enough, but they aren't the right ones.' In *Finnegans Wake* (1939) Joyce tries to convey the dream consciousness of a Dublin inn-keeper, Humphrey Chimpden Earwicker, over the course of one night. For this purpose, he invented what amounts to a new dialect of English. It is composed of neologisms, puns, words joined together, portmanteau words, phonetic spellings and words and phrases from 65 other languages, as well as being packed with literary and other allusions. Without a guide, the book is impossible to follow, although parts of it have a great poetic beauty. Joyce laboured over *Finnegans Wake* for 17 years, during which he underwent ten eye operations and was deeply troubled by his daughter's developing schizophrenia. As an attempt to extend the limits of language, the book must be considered a failure: it is too obscure and too dense with private references. But even in his failures Joyce remains an exemplary figure. On the centenary of his birth, his friend Samuel Beckett wrote the moving tribute: 'I welcome this occasion to bow once again, before I go, deep down, before his heroic work, heroic being.'

'Once upon a time and a very good time it was there was a moocow coming down along the road and this moocow that was coming down along the road met a nicens little boy named baby tuckoo'

JAMES JOYCE, *A Portrait of the Artist as a Young Man* (1914–15)

D.H. Lawrence (1885-1930)

A WORKING-CLASS BOY from Nottinghamshire, David Herbert Lawrence was to be one of the most controversial writers of his century. 'Filth. Nothing but obscenities,' Joseph Conrad decided. 'That man really writes very badly,' thought James Joyce. Yet for E.M. Forster he was 'the only prophetic novelist writing today', and the critic F.R. Leavis believed him to be the greatest writer of his time. His books were ridiculed, misunderstood and banned, *Lady Chatterley's Lover* remaining so for over 30 years. His vision of 'the original self' and his certainty that 'the solar plexus of the blood' was the only possible directive in the newly industrialized and 'dead' world, which he hated, have enthralled and irritated in equal measure since he first was published in 1911.

The fourth child of a coal-miner and of a former teacher, who considered herself intellectually and socially superior to her husband, Lawrence won a scholarship to Nottingham High School in 1898. When he was 16 years old he left school to work in a factory, but had to leave after his first severe attack of pneumonia. He began visiting the nearby Haggs Farm and started an intense friendship with Jessie Chambers, the daughter of the farmer, and she sent some of his poems to Ford Maddox Ford at the influential *English Review*. Following the publication of these, Lawrence started work on his first novel, *The White Peacock* (1911), while he was studying for a teacher's certificate. In 1912 he met Frieda Weekley, the wife of one of his professors and the mother of three, who was six years older than himself. Like Lawrence, she was suffocated by life in Nottingham. They fell in love and eloped to Germany, beginning an impoverished, stormy and nomadic existence, which lasted the rest of Lawrence's life.

Lawrence now completed his third novel, *Sons and Lovers* (1913), which depicts his own early life with vivid realism, focusing on the triangular relationship between his fictionalized self (Paul Morel), his two lovers – Miriam and Clara – and his bitterly possessive, watchful mother, who essentially stunts his ability to love anyone but herself. Apart from the compelling portrait of the passion between himself and his mother ('my first great love,' he later wrote), *Sons and Lovers* explores Lawrence's philosophy of the need to resist the deadening processes of industrialization. He sees the systematic destruction of the vital passion of human relationships through the mechanical standardization that machine-made 'progress' imposes. Humanity is diminished when there is no sense of mystery in its culture. 'The visible world is not true,' he wrote in a letter about this time. 'The invisible world is true and real. One must live and work from that.' Lawrence was, nevertheless, a great lover of the visual world; his novels, poems and stories are full of flowers, landscapes, colour and scent, which serve to represent the emotions of his characters and build up particular symbolic maps in each major work.

His writing is relentlessly intense and sexually frank, with one or several tortured relationships forming the core of each novel, generally expressing oppositional and irreconcilable attitudes to life, creative work, money and sex – 'mighty opposites', as Lawrence termed them. *Lady Chatterley's Lover* (1928) positions the passionate Constance between her intellectual, upper-class husband, who has been paralysed from the waist down by a war wound, and the earthy, classless gamekeeper, Mellors, who liberates Constance into a vital 'phallic consciousness'. Lawrence's characters are anguished, intense and emotionally convoluted, yet in some ways very straightforward. They feel profoundly, with a stark immediacy that can be cumulatively exhausting to read: 'The battle that raged inside him made him feel desperate'; 'He had denied the god in him'; 'Gudrun was as if numbed in her mind by the sense of the indomitable soft weight of the man ... enclosing and encompassing the mare heavily into unutterable subordination, soft-blooded subordination, terrible'.

His poetry is equally palpitating. 'In free verse we look for the insurgent naked throb of the instant

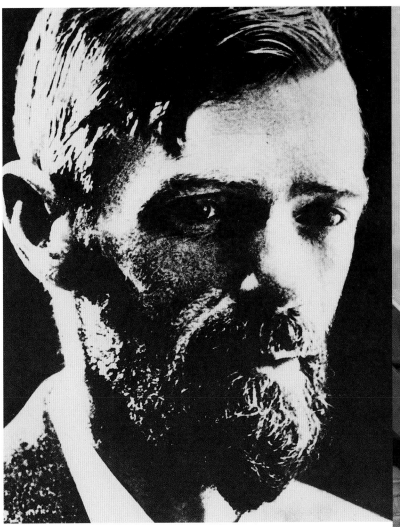

moment,' he explained in an introduction to *New Poems* (1918). But this fervour was in the service of Lawrence's vision, his insistence on a reawakening of 'reverence' in life, to be achieved through the renewal of human vitality and through 'man's physical rootedness in the natural order'. Christian civilization, he felt, was in ultimate decay, and, like Yeats, he wanted new gods to appear and to initiate a fresh cycle of civilization.

A productive talent

Lawrence's output was remarkable, considering his unsettled life, poor health and fraught relationship with Frieda (whom he married in 1914). Hounded out of Cornwall during the war, they travelled to Ceylon, Australia, America and Mexico, where they finally settled. He wrote *Kangaroo* (1923) in six weeks, while they were visiting Australia, and·*The Plumed Serpent* (1926) was completed while they were visiting Mexico. Three collections of short stories were published during his lifetime, and the *Collected Stories*, which some critics consider his

supreme achievement, appeared posthumously in 1955. He wrote two books of travel writing – terrifically vivid evocations of atmosphere and physical beauty – of which *Mornings in Mexico* (1927) is probably the best. His *Complete Poems* were published in 1957; his 'unsurpassable' collected letters are also in print. He died in the south of France, to where he and Frieda had moved when his terminal tuberculosis was diagnosed. He was buried in Venice, but his ashes were later returned to Taos, Mexico, where he had organized his own alternative community, shaped by primitive mysticism and political authoritarianism, shortly before his final illness.

chapter 5

The First World War and its aftermath

The Mule Track by Paul Nash, one of the official war artists of the Great War. Over eight million men died in the nightmare of trench warfare. The poetry of Owen, Sassoon, Rosenberg and others is an enduring legacy.

The Great War transformed the rhythm of European life for four futile years and altered the consciousness of Europeans forever. Gone were the certainties of personal development and political stability. Countries were torn apart and people who would not previously have met were thrown together; Siegfried Sassoon met Wilfred Owen in a sanatorium, for example. Creative work was overwhelmed by the practical realities of living under emotional and physical siege, but writers did not stop writing; rather they wrestled to make meaning of the horror – to provoke, to consider, to console.

The war poets

The war poets are so called because they wrote specifically in reaction to their experience in the trenches, leaving all other subject matter behind. All except Siegfried Sassoon lost their lives before their poetry could be collected and published, but it remains as a lament for, and a warning of, the atrocities in which they were involved.

ISAAC ROSENBERG (1890–1918)

Born in Bristol but brought up in the East End of London, Rosenberg enlisted in 1916 and was sent to France, where he fell in action two years later. He was the only poet of the war who set out to devise a language to engage directly with the violence of the experience. The poet, the language and the horrific material are one. His images stand as themselves, rather than being attached to ideas, so that in 'Dead Man's Dump' we read: 'A man's brain spattered on/A stretcher-bearer's face.' Having trained as an artist, he was concerned to present a stark picture of the slaughter he saw – to bring an individual human situation into close-up in each poem.

WILFRED OWEN (1893–1918)

Owen enlisted in the Artists' Rifles in 1915 and was soon commissioned in the Manchester Regiment. He had already been writing poetry for some years, but the experience of trench warfare quickly focused his work, giving it a taut new power. Poems written after January 1917 – when he reached the Front – are full of anger at the war's brutality and an elegiac pity for 'those who die as cattle'. His work was revolutionized by a chance meeting with Siegfried Sassoon in a sanatorium near Edinburgh. He became more driven by his mission to describe the trenches to those at home and to explain how fear and death and suffering numbed men or drove them mad. His work achieves its particular poignancy by his use of terms previously reserved for the beautiful in life to describe the hideous world he saw: to describe 'the truth untold/The pity of war, the pity war distilled'.

SIEGFRIED SASSOON (1886–1967)

Sassoon started writing poetry when he was in the trenches and, like Owen, his theme was to make the civilian population aware of its responsibilities to the soldiers at the Front. His protests against the war were at first attributed to shell-shock, and he was sent to a sanatorium. From his sick-bed he organized a public protest against the war. His verse is filled with a bleak realism and a contempt for war leaders, describing the bewilderment of individual young men 'crouched and flinched, dizzy with galloping fear ... While posturing giants dissolved in drifts of smoke.' He lived to enjoy his growing reputation, which was consolidated with his second collection, *Counter-Attack*, in 1918.

If you could hear, at every jolt, the blood
Come gargling from the froth-corrupted lungs,
Obscene as cancer, bitter as the cud
Of vile, incurable sores on innocent tongues, –
My friend, you would not tell with such high zest
To children ardent for some desperate glory,
The old Lie: Dulce et decorum est
Pro patria mori.

WILFRED OWEN, *'Dulce Et Decorum Est'*

The lost generation

It was not, in fact, Gertrude Stein, but the man who ran the garage that serviced her car, who coined the phrase 'une génération perdue'. He was referring to one of his mechanics. When the remark was repeated to Ernest Hemingway, he understood its resonance for himself and the fast-living, hard-drinking, disillusioned writers he associated with in Paris at the time, and he used the line as an epigraph to his novel *The Sun Also Rises* (1926), published in Britain as *Fiesta* (1927).

In the United States President Harding's 'back to normalcy' policy seemed provincial, materialistic and spiritually barren, and many American writers remained in Europe after the war. Their work is characterized by its commitment to emotional honesty – an acceptance that Europe had, indeed, lost its inherited values, but that it was necessary to write about the moral consequences of the war.

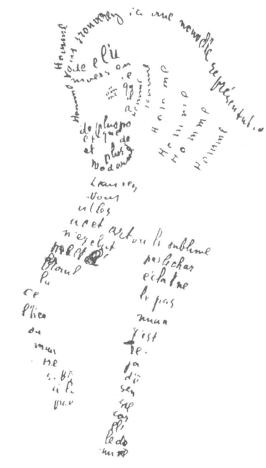

GERTRUDE STEIN (1874–1946)

'It was easy to get into the habit of stopping in at 27 rue de Fleurus late in the afternoon for the warmth and the great pictures and the conversation.' So wrote Hemingway, in his memoir of life in Paris in the 1920s, *A Moveable Feast* (1964). In her own reminiscence of the same period, *The Autobiography of Alice B. Toklas* (1933) – Alice being her lifelong companion and lover – Gertrude Stein shows us why young American writers were drawn to her flat. The Pennsylvania-born writer had been living in Paris since 1903. She had bought pictures by, and become friends with, struggling young French and Spanish painters – including Picasso, Braque and Matisse – and, through their revolutionary, cubist perspective, devised a new theory of writing. The nub of her theory was that language could be used as the cubists used paint. Literature should not be constrained by notions of past, present and future, any more than a picture should represent only one aspect of the thing it represented. 'The composition in which we live makes the art we see and hear,' she wrote.

In order to give the impression of a 'continual present', she devised her own, repetitive, circular rhythm of constructing phrases. *Tender Buttons* (1911) is a collection of still-life studies of objects, which came closest to her ideal of language as painting, being an attempt to make us look at something 'until something that was not the name of that thing but in a way was that actual thing would come to be written'. Because words, unlike brush strokes, must be read one after the other, however, she did run into difficulties with her experiments. Her effects were more influential on poetry than prose, but certainly Ernest Hemingway could not have written as he did without Stein's guidance and advice.

GUILLAUME APOLLINAIRE (1880–1918)

Like Gertrude Stein, Apollinaire's influence on the 20th century was not so much as a result of what he himself produced – although his poetry is both innovative and moving – as for his capacity to understand and shape what others were discovering for themselves. Like Stein, he was as much at home with painters as with writers, and he was a friend of Picasso, Braque and Max Jacob, with whom he started a 'central laboratory' of the arts in Montmartre. It was he who first named the cubists (he described their work as being made up of 'little cubes') and who identified a 'surrealist' movement, in a review in May 1917. He, too, saw connections between painting and writing, and was particularly interested in what he called 'simultanism', when a picture or a poem is experienced simultaneously as a physically pleasing construction and also as something that describes a

Left: One of Guillaume Apollinaire's 'ideogrammes' – part poetry, part drawings, they were symptomatic products of a time when the mood was one of dissatisfaction with conventional forms of expression.

Below: Gertrude Stein's apartment in Paris was a regular meeting place for painters and writers. Stein would talk to the 'geniuses', while her lover Alice B. Toklas entertained their wives.

recognizable object in new ways. His best known work is the collection *Alcools* (1913), consisting of poems written between 1898 and 1913. When he saw the proofs, he decided that the punctuation was unnecessary. 'I cut it out,' he said, 'The rhythm itself and the division of the lines are the real punctuation.' This daring notion was responsible for much later experimentation with poetic form, as was his idea that a poem about rain might be shaped like rain on a page, for example – an idea that was effectively the beginnings of concrete poetry.

He was wounded during the First World War, which he likened to 'being at the opera all the time', and never completely recovered his health, dying of pneumonia in 1918. In 1951 a street in St Germain des Pres in Paris was renamed Rue Guillaume Apollinaire in his honour.

FORD MADOX FORD (1873–1939)

Born Ford Hermann Hueffer, Ford was in Britain when war broke out, and he is known as a member of the group of writers called 'the men of 1914', the British equivalent of the 'lost generation' in Paris. His work, like theirs, offers a bleak vision of shattered civilization and is filled with the tensions and contradictions of a social order gone mad. Issues of sex, class, money and politics weave uneasily through his stories of Edwardian aspirations that are undermined by corruption and moral failure.

His undisputed masterpiece, *The Good Soldier*, was published in 1915 and remains unrivalled as an exploration of the disintegration of the 'good people' of Europe. 'This is the saddest story ever told,' the novel begins, and it is, indeed, a pitiful tale of betrayal, sexual manipulation, insanity and loss. What makes it remarkable – and alarming in a particularly 'modern' way – is that we are never sure whether the American narrator, John Dowell, is himself half-crazy or not. The story he is relating is 'a sort of maze', he tells us, but he consoles himself 'with thinking that this is a real story and that, after all, real stories are probably told best in the way a person telling a story would tell them. They will then seem most real.' This type of reflection has the effect of making Dowell's story strangely unreal. It also necessitates the uneasy realization that, of course, events become stories only because they are told – which much modern writing has since been concerned to make its subject.

Moveable feasts

By the time the war was over it was clear that modernism was an international movement, reaching from Moscow to Chicago – from Henrik Ibsen and Edvard Munch in Scandinavia to Emilio Marinetti and Luigi Pirandello in Italy. It had many centres, but the focus of all these was Paris. Poetry, drama, music and painting flourished together there in a quick succession of new movements. American writers came and often stayed: 'We always returned to it no matter who we were or how it was changed', wrote Ernest Hemingway. 'Paris was always worth it and you received return for whatever you brought to it.'

ERNEST HEMINGWAY (1899–1961)

Perhaps more than any other novelist of the century, Ernest Hemingway changed the way writers use words. And although he has been more imitated than anyone, it would be impossible to mistake a few paragraphs of his for the work of anyone else. He was 25 years old when his writing career began seriously. He had been a newspaper reporter in Kansas City; he volunteered as an ambulance driver and was wounded in Italy in 1917. He then served with the Italian infantry and was twice decorated for his voluntary services. After the armistice he reported on the Graeco-Turkish war of 1922, but gave up journalism two years later, when he made his way to Paris, renewed his friendship with Gertrude Stein and Ezra Pound and began to work full time on his fiction.

But post-war Europe was a place where, as Sherwood Anderson had remarked, words were extremely suspect. During the war, Anderson explained, every government had been in 'the advertising business, selling the war to the young men ... by the same noble words advertising men used for the sale of soap or automobile

Right: Ernest Hemingway invented a sparse yet lyrical prose style that captured the anxiety of his time, and influenced most subsequent novelists.

Far right: Gary Cooper, who played Hemingway's tragic hero, a soldier who marries a nurse who dies in childbirth in the seminal war story *A Farewell to Arms.*

tyres'. The lost generation was lost for words, as much as anything else.

'The greatest difficulty, aside from knowing truly what you really felt, rather than what you were supposed to feel ... was to put down what really happened

in action; what the actual things were which produced the emotion,' was how Hemingway put it. Having identified this 'difficulty', he began his life's struggle to overcome it and in doing so created a new school of writing – a blending of precise but rhythmic lyricism with exact physical detail.

When Hemingway first showed his stories to Gertrude Stein she told him to 'begin over again – and concentrate'. Concentration thereafter became his main fictional aim. 'All you have to do is write one true sentence,' he says he told himself. 'Write the truest sentence that you know.' His tight style was first in evidence in a collection of stories, 'In Our Time' (1924). Like the tales in Men without Women (1927), these are tales of war-

exhausted, sleepless men, living at the limits of pain, action and experience. The stories are characterized by lifestyles that Hemingway described as 'grace under pressure' lived in a world of dislocated encounters and historical loss, and Edmund Wilson described them as always having in them 'the undruggable consciousness of something wrong'.

His first novel was The Sun Also Rises (1926), which was published as Fiesta (1927) in Britain. Here, typically, the narrator's war wound, which has rendered him impotent, becomes a metaphor for the 'wound' of contemporary Europe, where personal happiness is somehow impossible in the face of a larger awareness of futility. Hemingway uses his rootless narrator to illustrate how a sense of anguish and futility need not destroy a man, but rather gives him the opportunity to learn a new and individual 'grace'. 'I did not care what it was all about,' Jake Barnes tells us. 'All I wanted was to learn how to live in it. Maybe if you learned how to live in it you learned from that what it was all about.'

The function of Hemingway's heroes – and there are only heroes for him, not heroines – is primarily to illustrate the possibility of living one's life with nobility and courage, no matter how hopeless the physical facts of that life may be.

A Farewell to Arms (1929) was his second and most masterly book. Like much of Hemingway's later fiction it concentrates on a sense of direct encounter between struggling man and an implacable universe; here a doomed love affair between an American volunteer in the Italian army and the nurse who dies giving birth to his child. 'That was what you did. You died,' Lieutenant Henry observes.

Hemingway's fundamentally tragic vision intensified as he aged, leaving him a man of action battered by action into the final desperate act of suicide. 'We have lost a Titan,' Cyril Connolly wrote in 1961. 'He had the energy, the endurance, the personal grandeur of the Balzac, Stendhal, Flaubert, Tolstoy category.'

❛ I went over to the side of the bed. The doctor was standing by the bed on the opposite side. Catherine looked at me and smiled. I bent down over the bed and started to cry ... "I'm going to die," she said; then waited and said, "I hate it" ... Then a little later, "I'm not afraid. I just hate it. ❜

ERNEST HEMINGWAY, A Farewell to Arms (1929)

The jazz age

While the post-war novel in Europe was dominated by a sense of war as an apocalyptic metaphor for a changed world, the novel in America was concerned with its own particular sense of decadence, cultural emptiness and political failure. The 1920s was a decade that modernized America, sweeping away the values ordinary people thought central to the meaning of national life. Credit ran free, and new technology boomed. Psychoanalysis, flappers, jazz and film tumbled into the urban scene in a new spirit of hedonism and reckless pleasure.

F. SCOTT FITZGERALD (1896–1940)

No American writer explored the mixture of excitement about the new and anxious awareness of historical loss more completely than Francis Scott Fitzgerald. He was born in Minnesota, went to Princeton in 1913 and trained as an army officer, but he did not get to France until 1920, when the expatriate season was in full swing. Unlike his compatriot Sinclair Lewis, whose analysis of puritanical Middle America, *Main Street*, was already a bestseller, Fitzgerald was obsessed by East Coast wealth and charm. The hero of his first novel, *This Side of Paradise* (1920), was a blueprint for the central characters of all his subsequent work. A 'golden boy', named Amory Blaine, 'hallowed by his own youth', chases wealth, beauty and religion. A 'romantic egotist', he is involved in a doomed love affair, which was actually based on Fitzgerald's own first love at Princeton. The theme of waste and the need for responsibility is central here, as is Fitzgerald's fascination with money and its corrupting power.

For Fitzgerald, the rich were, as he put it 'different from you and me', and unless you understood their otherness, you would not understand their ability to defile, to corrupt and to destroy. 'They possess and enjoy early,' he explained, 'and it does something to them, makes them soft where we are hard, and cynical where we are trustful in a way that, unless you were born rich, it is very difficult to understand.' By the time he finished his second novel, *The Beautiful and Damned* (1922), Fitzgerald, too, was rich. And with his famous marriage to the unstable, glamorous, hard-drinking Zelda, he was drawn into the heart of the world he wrote for and about. Like the exotic couple in that novel, Zelda and Fitzgerald wanted to make their marriage a 'glorious glamorous

F. Scott Fitzgerald's marriage to Zelda was laced with tragedy. Her instability and eventual breakdown formed the material for his semi-autobiographical masterpiece *Tender is the Night*.

performance' – a performance that ultimately led to Fitzgerald's alcoholism, breakdown and early death.

Fitzgerald's reputation was consolidated in 1925 with the novel that 'invented a generation' – his masterpiece of romantic disillusion and moral carelessness – *The Great Gatsby* (1925). For Jay Gatsby, 'divided between power and dream', who devotes his world to his obsession with the exquisite but shallow Daisy, stands as a metaphor for America itself. His story, which is told by Nick Carraway, takes place in the valley of ashes, watched over by the disembodied eyes of an ophthalmologist's huge advertisement. Like Fitzgerald, Carraway is both enchanted and repelled by the inexhaustible variety of social life. He goes to Gatsby's impossibly glamorous, chaotic parties, becomes an uneasy friend and watches as Gatsby's dream of the Daisy he once loved becomes a chilling, misunderstood reality, which ends in death and murder. The tragedy of the novel is that neither Daisy nor anyone else could be 'commensurate to [Gatsby's] capacity for wonder', just as nothing in modern America is commensurate to the great dream of the Founding Fathers. 'Gatsby believed in ... the orgiastic future that year by year recedes before us,' Carraway explains. That his dream was impossible is 'no matter'. 'We beat on, boats against the current, borne back ceaselessly into the past.'

Fitzgerald's drinking, dissolute lifestyle and tortured relationship with the increasingly unstable Zelda, meant that his output was limited after *The Great Gatsby*. *Tender is the Night* (1934), a flawed masterpiece with which he was never happy himself, took him nine years to complete. This novel is more personal, more violent, in some senses more poignant than *The Great Gatsby*. It tells of the disintegrating marriage of Dick Diver, a psychiatrist – 'a spoiled priest' – whose family effectively pay him to care for his unbalanced wife, Nicole.

The Divers live an apparently charmed life on the French Riviera, throwing parties, swimming, delighting the world. They were, for their creator, the representation of 'the exact furthermost evolution of a class'. Their class is a doomed one, however. Dick loses his integrity, tainted by the wealthy expatriate world, and becomes a corrupted healer, who degenerates and eventually goes back to waste in the ultimate degenerating force that is America itself.

It was in the end Fitzgerald's own impassioned romanticism that intensified his disgust at how material wealth corrupted the 'American dream', just as it was his increasing disgust at his own collusion with it that led him to his tragic last years. When he died in 1940, none of his books was in print.

> 'Her voice is full of money,' he said suddenly.
> That was it. I'd never understood it before. It was full of money – that was the inexhaustible charm that rose and fell in it, the jingle of it, the cymbals' song of it ... High in a white palace the king's daughter, the golden girl ...'

F. SCOTT FITZGERALD, *The Great Gatsby* (1925)

Expatriates

It was not only to Paris that the rootless post-war intelligentsia flocked. Europe was everywhere more open to experiment, more direct in its sexual mores, more keen to party and cheaper to drink in than London, Dublin or New York (where Prohibition made alcohol difficult and expensive to obtain). *Ulysses* ends with the words 'Trieste – Zurich – Paris 1914–21', and many lesser writers than Joyce enjoyed the new fluidity that the war had made possible – indeed necessary – for their wandering generation.

HENRY MILLER (1891–1980)

Born in Brooklyn, Henry Valentine Miller took a variety of jobs before ending up as an employment manager for the Western Union telegraph company. In 1924 he left his job to write on a full-time basis, and in 1930 he left America and a disintegrating marriage to live a bohemian life in Paris. After nine years he moved to Greece and ten years later he returned to California, where he lived in Big Sur until his death.

Miller's first novel, *Tropic of Cancer* (1934), was hailed by Samuel Beckett as 'a momentous event in the history of modern writing'. A sexually frank, fictionalized account of his adventures among the prostitutes and pimps, penniless painters and writers of Montparnasse, the book was banned in all English-speaking countries as soon as it was published. Miller has also been attacked for his sexual misogyny, his nihilism and his self-indulgent sentimentality, but *Tropic of Cancer* and its companion *Black Spring* (1936) were important books, struggling to realize the limits of the specifically American dream of absolute freedom. Miller's freedom involved an abdication of morality and responsibility, but it is nonetheless affirmative and was a major influence on the Beat Generation in America. He wrote 20 books during his long life. They are all 'self-unravellings': boisterous celebrations of his erotic imagination – often flawed, but always vibrant attempts to tell the whole truth about the life he lived.

LAWRENCE DURRELL (1912–90)

Lawrence George Durrell was born in India, sent to school in Canterbury and moved to Paris then Cairo, where he was posted to the British Information Office during the Second World War. Like Miller, who said he 'first heard the sound of [his] own voice in Durrell', his first novel, *The Black Book: an Agon* (1938), was banned for its sexual explicitness. His most successful work was the *Alexandria Quartet*, set in the city that Durrell thought 'always hovered between illusion and reality, between the substance and the poetic images which its very name aroused'. In four skilfully plotted novels, he tells and retells the same stories from different characters' viewpoints and in varying historical time. The writing is lush and the relationships intensely erotic. L.G. Darley, a schoolteacher (and secret agent) is involved with Justine, then Clea, who, in turn, are indirectly involved with smuggling arms. The interweaving of a spy plot with a shifting pattern of sexual liaisons is masterly, although Durrell has been accused of being self-indulgent and pretentious in the laboured philosophical ideas he feels the need to explore on the page.

ROBERT GRAVES (1895–1985)

'My theme was always the practical impossibility, transcended only by a miracle, of absolute love continuing between a man and a woman,' wrote Robert Graves in 1965. He began his long career as an expatriate poet when the war interrupted his Oxford education. While serving in France he read his own obituary in *The Times*, just before his 21st birthday, and there is something in his work of a voice speaking from some other place – outside known frameworks – almost eerily from the past. He was not interested in formal experimentation, although his romantic love poetry has its own contemporary authenticity and a modern, pared-down style. He owed much of his poetic education to the American poet, Laura Riding (1901–91), with whom he fell in love in 1926 and lived with on Majorca for ten years. He admired 'the strong pulling of her bladed mind' (as,

later, did W.H. Auden, Ted Hughes and John Ashbery), and he was led by her insistence that a poet must 'tell the truth and nothing else'.

His love of the Mediterranean and rejection of the dehumanizing effects of technology and industrialization led him to leave his native London, where he wrote his early biography *Goodbye to All That* (1929), and start an 'old habit of non-residence'. He saw being a foreigner as essential to his clarity of vision. As he developed, he was concerned to explore the possibilities of a world without 'the blood sports of desire'. His idea of love 'walking a knife edge between two different fates' was embodied in the twin notions of a physically satisfying 'white goddess', and a more difficult but rewarding 'black goddess'. His engagement with language always delights, and his poems are intensely alive with the tension between the 'practical impossibility' and the 'miracle' of love.

6 Between the wars

Below: A scene from the film version of E.M. Forster's *A Passage to India*. After this novel, Forster gave up writing fiction and pursued a life as a critic and journalist.

Right: E.M. Forster. One of England's chief representatives of liberal humanism, Forster once said his main reason for writing novels was to give pleasure to his friends.

It is tempting to define the literature of the 1920s and 1930s entirely in relation to its position between the two world wars: to see disillusionment alongside a desperate gaiety as characteristic of the writing of the 1920s and the committed writing of the 1930s as a precursor to the Second World War. But few artists fit neatly into such categories. As in any other era, the writing of this period is distinguished by its variety and coloured as much by particular national concerns as anything else.

Forster and Lewis

E.M. FORSTER (1879–1970)

It is hard for us now to grasp the impact of the First World War. One in every ten British men under the age of 45 died in the war, and two more were wounded. For British writers living through that period, the effect was a devastating loss of faith in their own civilization. D.H. Lawrence conveyed a widespread feeling when he wrote in a letter: 'Something very good, and poignant to remember, now the whole world of it is lost.'

The four novels Edward Morgan Forster wrote before 1914 – *Where Angels Fear to Tread* (1905), *The Longest Journey* (1907), *A Room with a View* (1908) and *Howard's End* (1911) – are marked by his commitment to pre-war liberal and humanist values. 'Only connect', the epigraph to *Howard's End*, expresses his belief in the supreme importance of personal relations. 'I hate the idea of causes,' he wrote in 1951, 'and if I had to choose between betraying my country and my friend, I hope I should have the guts to betray my country.' *Howard's End* tries to reconcile the opposition between inward feeling and outward behaviour – represented by two families, the artistic and intellectual Schlegels (with whom his sympathies lie) and the action-driven, business-oriented, male-dominated Wilcoxes. Forster's wistful endorsement of the life of feeling, his powers of psychological observation and his ability to extract drama from small-scale social collisions give the early novels considerable charm.

His finest achievement, the post-war novel *A Passage to India* (1924), shows a bleaker view of human relations. Set in India under British rule, it explores the failure to connect. The tragic misunderstandings that arise between the English and the Indians do so despite the good intentions of both sides. After this, Forster fell silent, declaring that he had nothing more to say in fiction. He continued to write essays and critical works, notably *Aspects of the Novel* (1927) with its celebrated remark: 'Yes – oh dear yes – the novel tells a story.'

WYNDHAM LEWIS (1882–1957)

Lewis repudiated D.H. Lawrence and what he caricatured as his philosophy of 'hot, unconscious "soulless" mystical throbbing'. But he would have shared the same sense of a world shattered by war. 'How calm were those days before the epoch of wars and social revolution,' he once wrote. Lewis's novels are violent satires that voice contempt for almost every aspect of the modern age, and they are particularly savage towards his contemporaries in the arts. *The Apes of God* (1930) attacks the world of painting and literature of London in the 1920s, presenting the arts as a fashionable racket. An earlier book, *The Childermass* (1928), is set in a wasteland outside Heaven, where the 'emigrant mass' of humanity awaits judgement by the Bailiff.

Lewis was also a gifted painter – he was a founder of the literary and artistic movement known as vorticism (see page 32) – and his prose shows some of the same qualities as his paintings with their striking colours, bold lines and sharp angularity. The novels portray humanity with a mixture of comic energy and cool derision. A characteristic technique is to describe behaviour in such a way as to defamiliarize or dehumanize it. Lewis's highly original style has won him some distinguished admirers, but the extremity of his vision – coupled with his support of fascism in the 1930s – made him an isolated and neglected figure.

English disaffections

The British literary world of the 1920s and 1930s was a peculiarly intimate one. Most of the leading writers shared the same background – all four writers discussed here were educated at public schools and Oxbridge – and in many cases belonged to the same social set. Their attitudes were not radical, either politically or artistically, but their work reflects the prevailing sprit of uncertainty and pessimism, despite its often ebullient sophistication.

Left: Evelyn Waugh's serious expression here might surprise anyone who reads his diaries, which give an entertaining account of his high-spirited and rumbustious (and hard-drinking) social life as a young man.

Right: A caricature of Aldous Huxley, whose brilliantly imagined picture of the future, *Brave New World*, assures him a lasting place in the English literary canon.

EVELYN WAUGH (1903–66)

A friend of Evelyn Waugh described him as speaking in perfectly formed sentences. The comic novels he wrote before the Second World War are likewise perfectly judged in their phrasing and timing. In a deadpan, apparently 'objective' manner, he mixes farce and fantasy with an implicit disdain for conventional pieties. The Waugh hero is usually an innocent fool abroad in an amoral world. His immensely successful first novel, *Decline and Fall* (1928), traces the chequered career of a young man after he has been sent down from university,

the victim of a drunken prank. *Vile Bodies* (1930), which is set among the 'bright young things' of London's Mayfair, *Black Mischief* (1932), *A Handful of Dust* (1934) and *Scoop* (1938) confirmed his status as a master of high comedy and satire, the brilliance of the comedy tending to disguise the extent of Waugh's satirical vision. In the best of these, *A Handful of Dust*, the hero, Tony Last, loses his wife, his son and the family home and goes off to South America where he is trapped in the jungle by a mad old recluse, Mr Todd. The final chapter – at the same time wildly funny and horrific –

sees him held captive, being forced to read Dickens to his host – 'May I trouble you to read that passage again? It is one I particularly enjoy.'

Apart from *The Loved One* (1948) – a biting satire on Californian funeral practices – his later novels were in a more realistic vein and largely eschewed comedy. *Brideshead Revisited* (1945) is about the narrator's involvement with the self-destructive, alcoholic, younger son of an aristocratic English Roman Catholic family. Its dominant tone is one of romantic nostalgia, conveying the sense of glamour attached to a way of life now in decline. Waugh later came to dislike the novel and conceded it was marred by sentimentality.

ALDOUS HUXLEY (1894–1963)

Huxley's early novels present an elegant, witty, ironic and sometimes malicious commentary on the attitudes of the English literary and intellectual coteries of his time. These works – in particular *Those Barren Leaves* (1925) and *Point Counter Point* (1928) – rely heavily on the technique of the conversation piece, in which the principal characters discourse with enormous brilliance and learning. Beneath the glittering talk lie attitudes of despair or cynicism. One of the few exceptions is the admiring portrait of D.H. Lawrence as Rampion in *Point Counter Point*, to which Lawrence responded: 'Your Rampion is the most boring character in the book – a gas bag.'

Huxley is often charged with having written novels that are too cerebral and lacking in warmth, but after he moved to California in 1937 he embraced a kind of mysticism, which he explored in his last novel *Island* (1962) and in a series of non-fiction works. Notable are the classic studies of the connection between drug experiences (with mescaline) and mysticism, *The Doors of Perception* (1954) and *Heaven and Hell* (1956).

In his best known novel, *Brave New World* (1932), Huxley applied his exceptional intelligence and erudition to a deeply pessimistic view of the future. This is a science fiction fable about a world state in which technology, in the form of social conditioning and genetic engineering, is used to manufacture happiness for all at the cost of individuality. As a picture of a dystopian future, it can be compared to George Orwell's equally grim *Nineteen Eighty-four*, with the difference that many people see the predictions Huxley made over 60 years ago as closer to today's reality than Orwell's view.

CHRISTOPHER ISHERWOOD (1904–86)

Isherwood met the poet W.H. Auden (see page 81) when they were students at Oxford and collaborated with him on three verse dramas, among them *The Ascent of F6* (1936). In 1939 he and Auden moved to America, where he settled in California. But it was his experience of living in Berlin, between 1929 and 1933, that supplied him with the material for his best known novels, *Mr Norris Changes Trains* (1935) and *Goodbye to Berlin* (1939). These are portraits of dubious and eccentric characters living amid the decadence and frivolity of pre-war Germany. 'I am a camera with its shutter open, quite passive, recording,' says the narrator in *Goodbye to Berlin*. Isherwood's prose is, indeed, neutral and detached, but he treats his characters with a great deal of affectionate humour. Mr Norris is an engaging con-man, involved in the criminal and political underworld. The most memorable figure in the second novel is the charming and feckless cabaret artist, Sally Bowles, later the inspiration for the musical *Cabaret*.

HENRY GREEN (1905–73)

Very much a 'writer's writer', Henry Green has been much admired by other authors, including John Updike, for his stylistic innovations. In his three major novels – *Living* (1929), *Party Going* (1939) and *Loving* (1945) – he developed a highly idiosyncratic and economical style, which draws on the phrasing and intonation of colloquial speech. For example, it often leaves out articles after the pattern of working-class speech in the North of England – 'They sat round brazier in a circle' – but does so in narrative as well as in dialogue. Green had worked on the shop floor in his family's engineering firm before becoming the managing director, and he wrote about working-class factory life in *Living*. In his best novel, *Party Going*, a group of young socialites on their way to France find themselves trapped by fog in a station hotel.

American fiction

Not all novelists between the wars chose to write in avant-garde modes. In the United States the traditional virtues of strong characterization and plotting served the purposes of those whose main subject was America itself – its dreams and aspirations, its failures and guilt. In the work of Nathanael West this examination is shot through with dark humour and a bitter pathos. Other novelists, such as Sinclair Lewis and Thornton Wilder, concentrated on small-town life, often finding redeeming and peculiarly American virtues there. And even Thomas Wolfe's autobiographical novels take his own story as emblematic of the American experience.

SINCLAIR LEWIS (1885–1951)

The first American to win the Nobel prize for literature, Lewis worked as a journalist before achieving fame with the novel *Main Street* (1920), a satirical portrait of life in a small Midwestern town, which exposes the narrow-mindedness and provincialism of the town's citizens. His next book, *Babbitt* (1922), made him one of the most widely read and controversial American authors of his time. Also set in a Midwestern town, it is the story of a self-satisfied, self-congratulatory businessman, George Babbitt. The portrait struck a familiar chord with the American reading public, and the terms Babbitt and Babbittry have now passed into general usage to describe excessive complacency and materialism.

Lewis has been criticized for turning literature into a branch of superior journalism – for writing with the 'cynical expertise of the star reporter' – and it has also been pointed out that the satirical intent in *Main Street* and *Babbitt* is ambiguous. The author himself said, 'I

Sinclair Lewis, 1930. Now regarded as a comparatively minor figure, Lewis was feted as one of America's greatest authors during his lifetime.

wrote *Babbitt* not out of hatred for him but out of love,' and it is not always clear whether he means to bury Babbitt or praise him.

Elmer Gantry (1927) is perhaps Lewis's only unalloyed triumph. This is still topical, with its theme of sham religions and story of a crooked evangelical preacher who defrauds his followers.

NATHANAEL WEST (1903–40)

If the impact of Sinclair Lewis's satires has lessened in recent years, the reputation of Nathanael West's novels has risen steadily. He has been hailed as the most modern of American writers in the 1930s and as the great precursor of black comedy. He was virtually unrecognized in his own lifetime – a not uncommon fate for truly original writers – and only attracted attention after his second novel, *Miss Lonelyhearts* (1933), was translated into French.

West was born Nathan Wallenstein Weinstein in New York, the child of Jewish immigrants. After a spell in Paris, where he wrote his first novel, he returned to New York and worked as a hotel manager for some years before eventually landing a job as a screenwriter in Hollywood. *Miss Lonelyhearts* is about an agony column writer who becomes overwhelmed by the sufferings of his correspondents. The story is told with bitter irony in a sparse and highly charged prose.

West's last and best novel, published shortly before his death in a car crash, was *The Day of the Locust* (1939). This is a satire on Hollywood, but it is concerned less with the film industry than with the dreams and aspirations it fostered – with the bizarre lifestyles and sometimes squalid existences of the people surrounding it. Its protagonist is a painter who falls in love with a second-rate starlet.

THOMAS WOLFE (1900–38)

In his short life, Thomas Wolfe wrote four massive novels – *Look Homeward, Angel* (1929), *Of Time and the River* (1935), *The Web and the Rock* (1939) and *You Can't Go Home Again* (1940), the last two published posthumously – which form a continuous autobiographical fiction. Wolfe came from the South, the son of a stone-cutter in North Carolina, and moved to New York, where for a time he taught English at New York University. His output was vast, and the novels, large as they are, were only published after heavy editing. He conceived of his fiction on an epic scale, noting in a letter: 'There are few heroic lives; about the only one I know a great deal is my own.' The novels seek to create a romantic and heroic myth from the story of the writer's life and turbulent upbringing, but the writing is too undisciplined and lacking in control to be wholly successful. At its best – in *Look Homeward, Angel* – though, it contains passages of considerable vividness and emotional power.

THORNTON WILDER (1897–1975)

Wilder's plays and fiction have achieved enormous popularity, largely by appearing to be deeply philosophical while actually entertaining their readers and giving them the bonus of thinking they are reading something highbrow. As one critic has said: 'They can think they are worried, but are not really.' Wilder's first popular drama was *Our Town* (1938), a play that had all the trappings of avant-garde theatre – a bare stage, a garrulous stage-manager who chats to the audience and analyses the characters – but that is, in fact, fairly mundane in its preoccupations and has a final message that there is 'something way down deep that's eternal about a human being'.

His first success in fiction was *The Bridge of San Luis Rey* (1927), which traces the fortunes of various people eventually killed when a South American bridge collapses. This is effortlessly well organized and beautifully told, but insubstantial compared with his later novel, *Heaven's My Destination* (1935). With this tale of a book salesman, George Bush, Wilder found an authentic voice to satirize movingly the clash of materialism and evangelism in America.

> It is hard to laugh at the need for beauty and romance, not how tasteless, how horrible, the results of that need are. But it is easy to sigh. Few things are sadder than the truly monstrous.
>
> NATHANAEL WEST, *The Day of the Locust* (1939)

American modernism

The extraordinary transformation of the arts that passed through the West from the 1890s onward began somewhat later in America – around 1912–13 – but was then implemented with remarkable speed – and much more tolerance than elsewhere – assimilating not only the European modern movement but also elements of a specifically American past. The naturalism of the 1890s combined with technical experimentation to produce outstanding writers in the 1920s, Anderson, Fitzgerald, Hemingway, Faulkner and Dos Passos being the major figures of their generation in fiction.

WILLIAM FAULKNER (1897–1962)

Faulkner was born in Albany, Mississippi, and his family had lived in the region for generations. His work is a taut intermeshing of new (and European-coloured) literary forms, and a very definite – often Gothic – sense of history and place. His upbringing was characteristic of a Southern white boy of middle-class parents: ponies, guns, hunting and fishing. After a sketchy education, he took an assortment of jobs, ending up as a journalist in New Orleans, where he met Sherwood Anderson, who knew Hemingway and other expatriate writers. Anderson encouraged Faulkner to continue with the novel he was working on at the time, and *Soldier's Pay* was published in 1926. A second novel, *Mosquitoes* (1927), was also accepted, but the third was not and nor were his short stories, so Faulkner wrote *Sartoris* in 1929 specifically to attract commercial success.

Meanwhile, he had 'written his guts' into an intense, technically ambitious and emotionally sophisticated work, which he presumed would never be published. Despite its baroque, sometimes demanding style, *The Sound and the Fury* was published in 1929. Faulkner had read and been impressed by Joyce, and he experimented with the stream of consciousness, using the voices of four different characters to tell the story of the Compson family. The most disorientating of these is Benjy, one of three sons, and we slowly come to understand that he is simple. His brothers are the twisted and sinister Jason, and the sensitive Quentin, who finally kills himself over his tortured desire for his sister, Caddy. The last section of the novel is told by Dilsey, the Negro servant, whose straightforward goodness contrasts with

William Faulkner's portrayal of the American South is lyrical beauty laced with tragedy. The technical brilliance of his prose earned him the Nobel Prize in 1949.

New York in the 1920s. The energy and vibrancy of the city is captured in John Don Passos's *Manhattan Transfer*. He uses multiple narrators and collaged newspaper clippings to give an authentic urban feel.

his employers' mutual manipulation. The contrast between how Negroes are, and how they are treated by whites, was to be a constant theme in Faulkner, as was his interest in convoluted family relationships.

His novels are generally brooding and dark, but they have a quirky humour, too, which is most consistently present in *As I Lay Dying* (1930), a book that charts the attempts of her family to bury poor, white (and dead) Addie Bundren in Jefferson, which was her last wish. The malodorous coffin lurches through the novel, eventually landing in Jefferson, where her widower finds a new wife, and new teeth, too. Entirely narrated by the Bundren family, this is Faulkner's most systematically multi-voiced work, and, although difficult reading, his books slowly achieved popularity.

He was now able to sell short stories to well-paying magazines – they were collected in two volumes in 1931 and 1934 – and to live in comparative affluence, which increased the drinking habit that finally killed him. He bought a plane, in which his brother was killed, and this personal tragedy certainly fuelled the emotional intensity of his supreme 'modernist' novel, *Absalom, Absalom!* (1936), a tale of incestuous passion and murder, which ends with a killing with a scythe and the family home being razed to the ground.

Later works continued to explore themes of racial, sexual and environmental exploitation, while refining his long, intricate sentences and his use of the interior monologue as a central storytelling device. Faulkner's world is evil, but it is not an evil without guilt or without end. As he said in his Nobel prize acceptance speech in 1949: 'Man will not merely endure, he will prevail ... because he has a soul, a spirit capable of compassion.'

JOHN DOS PASSOS (1896–1970)

Chicago-born Dos Passos graduated from Harvard in 1916 and then, like Hemingway, served as an ambulance-driver until the end of the war, which provided the subject of his first, autobiographical, novel. *Three Soldiers* (1921) is an unusual book in that it described the horror of war as it really was but has none of the technical innovation that marked Dos Passos's later work. During the post-war years he travelled in Europe as a newspaper correspondent, exposing himself to both writing and life that sharpened his social and artistic perceptions and confirmed his radical sympathies. He also translated Brazilian, Mexican and French writers during this period.

His second novel, *Manhattan Transfer* (1925), is a study of the teeming metropolis of New York as seen through the lives of various characters. Their stories are told in parallel, sometimes overlapping episodes, intercut with newspaper clippings, snatches of popular songs and the 'camera eye' of the narrator, who records his omnipotent view in impressionistic passages of prose poetry and stream of consciousness reflection. This novel and his next work, *USA*, which was written in three volumes, *The 42nd Parallel*, (1930), *1919* (1932) and *The Big Money* (1936), established his reputation as an experimental 'modernist' writer. Dos Passos has been accused of an inability to imagine or develop character and of failing to engage the reader in any human emotional conflict or depth. His novelistic strengths are certainly limited, but his radical techniques and the energy with which he explored them were themselves an enormous achievement, paving the way for many formal developments in later American writing.

The novel in France

The genius of Proust had little direct influence on the French novel between the wars. Some novelists chose to experiment with form, as in the harsh language and stream of consciousness used by Céline or in the more playful and philosophical structural games in Gide's *The Counterfeiters*. Sometimes, as in Cocteau's novels, this approach could result in an aestheticism that seemed to turn its back entirely on everyday reality. Other writers, such as Saint-Exupéry and Malraux, used more traditional novelistic techniques to explore individual experience and dilemmas in a manner that prefigures some of the preoccupations of post-war existentialism.

LOUIS-FERDINAND CÉLINE (1894–1961)

Céline, the son of a minor employee in an insurance company, was born near Paris. After being severely wounded in the First World War, he became a doctor, opening a practice in one of the poorer suburbs of Paris. His novel *Voyage au bout de la nuit* (*Journey to the End of Night*, 1934) brought instant fame, establishing him as a writer of genius and one of the major innovators of 20th-century French literature. Written in a vigorous and disjointed style, it describes the experiences of an embittered doctor in a journey, both physical and spiritual, that moves from the First World War, via Africa and America, to the slums of northern Paris. Céline is the denouncer of everything, a writer who sees the world as being in a state of complete decay. This first work seems to be motivated by extremes of disgust and compassion, and at times it achieves a nightmarish, hallucinatory quality.

In spite of his success, Céline continued to practise as a doctor among the poor, writing in his spare time. His next novel, *Mort à crédit* (*Death on the Instalment Plan*, 1936), takes even further the technique of rendering experience in the most immediate and brutal manner. Using language rich in slang and obscenity and virtually abandoning plot, it recounts a nightmare

childhood. The prose – with its welter of broken-off sentences and precipitous pace – gives the impression of total spontaneity, although, in fact, the author worked hard to achieve this tone of voice and thought of himself as a classicist in his writing.

Céline was a difficult and irascible man, and he became increasingly misanthropic in his pronouncements. During the Second World War he sided with the Nazis and fled to Germany with the Vichy government. He was later imprisoned for 17 months as a collaborator. His last works – a trilogy consisting of *D'un château à l'autre* (*Castle to Castle*, 1957), *Nord* (*North*, 1960) and *Rigodon* (1969) – depict wartime existence in Germany. In the eyes of some critics, they are equal in power to the two earlier books for which he is now celebrated.

ANDRÉ GIDE (1869–1951)

Gide's fiction is a rich mix of spirituality and sensuality, expressed in a style that is both fastidiously intelligent and warmly confessional. His rebellion against his strict Protestant upbringing is central to his writing, as is his homosexuality. His first novel, *L'Immoraliste* (*The Immoralist*, 1902), explores these themes through the character of Michel, who takes his new wife to North Africa, where he contracts then recovers from tuberculosis. He also discovers his homosexuality and gradually gives himself over to hedonism, as his wife declines and finally dies from the tuberculosis through which she had nursed her husband. This novel encouraged a generation of French adolescents to question traditional family values and to explore aspects of their lives that were socially repressed or ignored.

Les Faux-monnayeurs (*The Counterfeiters*), which Gide called his 'only novel', appeared in 1926. The aim of this book is to illustrate the unsatisfactory nature of living a 'forged' or second-hand life. Its complex, untidy

structure and the introduction of a hero who is himself a novelist (writing *The Counterfeiters*), anticipates many later developments in the novel. Gide also wrote essays, drama, criticism, and travel and political books as well as his *Journals* (1889–1949), which are thought by some to be his most satisfying work.

ANTOINE DE SAINT-EXUPÉRY (1900–44)

Saint-Exupéry belongs to a long line of literary men of action, and his favourite pastime is the subject of his best novel, *Vol de nuit* (*Night Flight*, 1931). The ruthless head of a South American airline, his mystical chief pilot and the chief's wife are at the centre of this lyrical, semi-autobiographical account of human courage, driven to extremes in the early days of aviation.

Saint-Exupéry had a radiantly happy childhood, which he mined extensively to produce his charming fairy story, *Le Petit Prince* (*The Little Prince*, 1945),

which is ostensibly a children's book but which later achieved cult status as a humanist fable. Other works are a book of meditations, *The Wisdom of the Sands* (published posthumously, 1948) and two books on flying. He died when his plane was shot down while on a reconnaissance flight.

ANDRÉ MALRAUX (1901–76)

Like Saint-Exupéry, Malraux wrote from experience of action. He was an archaeologist, an adventurer, a smuggler and minor revolutionary in Indo-China, a prisoner-of-war, a guerrilla leader and a member of the Spanish Republican air force. During the 1960s he was minister of propaganda, then minister of culture in De Gaulle's governments. As a writer he was always 'engaged', never more so than in his third novel *La Condition humaine* (*Man's Estate* or *Man's Fate*, 1933), which was one of the first 'serious' books of our time to take the form of a semi-thriller. His later novel, *L'Espoir* (*Days of Hope*, 1937), is regarded as the best fictional treatment of the Spanish Civil War.

JEAN COCTEAU (1889–1963)

Cocteau is more famous for his films, theatre, opium habit and extravagant friendships – with Picasso, Diaghilev and Stravinsky among others – than for any substantial body of writing, but everything he turned his hand to has its own distinctive charm. *Les Enfants terribles* (*Children of the Game*, 1929), the second of his two novels, is a classic evocation of adolescence and was later made into a film, as were many of his best works, the results constituting some of the most abiding images of the first half of the 20th century. *La Belle et la bête* (*Beauty and the Beast*, 1946), *Orphée* (1950) and *La Testament D'Orphée* (1961) – in which Cocteau played himself – are among the best of these.

The novel in Germany

The decade following the end of the First World War saw the Weimar Renaissance, which brought the fulfilment of the modernist revolution to Germany and Austria, and Berlin and Vienna became centres of artistic experimentation and innovation. But the 1930s were increasingly overshadowed by the worldwide economic depression. Conditions in Germany were particularly severe and led directly to the rise of National Socialism. Hitler came to power in 1933, and by the beginning of the Second World War almost every leading German artist and intellectual had been forced into exile or had left the country voluntarily.

THOMAS MANN (1875–1955)

Mann is regarded by many as the greatest German novelist of the century. By the end of his life his novels had acquired the status of classics, both in Germany and abroad. His formidable intelligence and learning established him not only as a great writer but also as a leading figure in the intellectual and cultural life of Europe between the wars. Mann's position was one of pessimistic conservatism. With the rise of Hitler, he became more sympathetic to the political left, and in 1933 his steadfast opposition to the Nazis forced him to leave Germany for Switzerland and then America, where he became a US citizen.

Mann's novels constitute a profound analysis of an age that he saw as being in the throes of a cultural crisis. His most persistent concern is the responsibility of the artist in society. *Buddenbrooks* (1901), his first novel, follows the decline of a bourgeois family. It shows how the heir's artistic leanings make him unfit for the practicalities of normal life and result in a lack of the will to live. *Dr Faustus* (1947) tells of a brilliant composer who sacrifices everything for his art and in the end becomes insane. In reworking the myth of Faust (in which Faust sells his soul to the devil), Mann was also presenting his diagnosis of fascism, which he felt was made possible

by irrationalist movements in recent German culture. His best known novel, *Der Zauberberg* (*The Magic Mountain*, 1924) is set in a sanatorium and uses the idea of physical illness as a metaphor for the death of postwar spiritual values.

Mann's prose is complex, finely wrought and demanding. Its characteristic tone is detached and ironic. *Die Bekenntnisse des Hochstaplers Felix Krull* (*The Confessions of Felix Krull, Confidence Man*, 1954) his last novel, strikes a lighter, more relaxed note with the story of an engaging and amorous confidence trickster. Mann was awarded the Nobel prize in 1929.

ROBERT MUSIL (1880–1942)

The Austrian-German novelist Robert Musil represents a type of writer that does not really exist in English fiction: the intellectual novelist whose work explores abstract and philosophical ideas through the lives and reflections of his characters. Marcel Proust and, to some extent, Thomas Mann are similar types: major writers who can also be regarded as major thinkers. Musil was trained as an engineer and had an encyclopaedic knowledge of both the arts and the sciences. All his writings bear the mark of his incisive intelligence (in his diaries he called himself Monsieur le Vivisecteur).

Musil wrote only two novels – *Die Verwirrungen des Zöglings Törless* (*Young Torless*, 1906), a story of homosexuality and sadism set in a military academy, and *Der Mann ohne Eigenschaften* (*A Man Without Qualities*, 1930–32). The latter is a monumental work, with 123 chapters in the first volume alone. In inexhaustible

aLeft: Thomas Mann is regarded by many as the leading German writer of the century. His fiction engages at the deepest level with the central political and moral concerns of the time.

Right: A scene from the film version of Mann's *Death in Venice*. Dirk Bogarde plays the central character, a writer who becomes infatuated with a beautiful boy he meets in Venice.

detail, it follows the life of an introspective intellectual in the year before the outbreak of the First World War. The context is the decaying society of the Austro-Hungarian empire. Along with many intellectuals, Musil was deeply influenced by Oswald Spengler's book *The Decline of the West*, and his wider concern was to analyse what was perceived as the failure of European culture. His hero is without qualities because there are no longer any fixed points or certainties with which he can identify. Musil's books were acclaimed by the critics but ignored by the reading public. He died in exile in Switzerland, bitter and disappointed at his lack of recognition.

ROBERT WALSER (1878–1956)

Walser's novels and short stories could not be more different from those of his contemporaries Mann and Musil. Walser is a true original and unlike anyone else before or since. Kafka greatly admired his novels *The Assistant* and *Jakob von Gunten* (1909), and echoes of his highly distinct style can be found in Kafka's own writing. The influence on Kafka is also evident in the dreamlike atmosphere of his fiction, but Walser is primarily a miniaturist, and his writing has an inimitable spontaneity and freshness. This is most pronounced in the short stories and sketches, in which he is less impeded by conventional ideas of plot. They give the impression of being composed on the spur of the moment in a mood of good-humoured playfulness. For example, one of them starts off: 'The town was beautiful and empty. How concisely put! Can one call this literary writing?' He said himself: 'Not caring about artistic propriety, I simply fired away.'

Walser was born in Switzerland and left school when he was 14 years old to work in a bank. He soon became discontented with this and spent the next 35 years moving from city to city and living an odd-job existence. In 1933 he was diagnosed as schizophrenic and entered a mental hospital, where he remained until his death.

ELIAS CANETTI (1905–94)

Although he was awarded the Nobel prize in 1981, Canetti has never really been given his due as one of the greatest writers of the century. Part of the reason may be that his works do not fit into any single category of literature. He wrote a number of plays, now rarely performed, and just one novel, *Die Blendung* (*Auto-da-Fé*, 1935), the story a professor of Oriental studies who lives only for his library, to which he eventually sets fire. Canetti was born in Bulgaria, the descendent of Sephardic Jews, and grew up in Vienna. When he was six years old, his family moved to Manchester but then returned to Austria. Shortly before the Second World War, he moved to London and for the next two decades devoted himself to the study of crowds. The book that resulted from this passionate interest, *Masse und Macht* (*Crowds and Power*, 1960), is a unique treatise on the behaviour of crowds, which was a genuine contribution to scientific knowledge (although ignored by academics) and at the same time a work of tremendous imaginative and poetic power.

Other European voices

García Lorca, Hasek and Svevo were very different writers, but each reflects in his own subversive way the intellectual and political currents of the time. Hasek's boisterous *The Good Soldier Schweik* – whose central character is one of the worst soldiers in fiction – has been called the 20th century's first anti-war novel. Svevo's analysis of psychoanalysis has never been improved upon, while García Lorca's writing has left a moving testament to a Spain that no longer exists.

FEDERICO GARCÍA LORCA (1898–1936)

Although García Lorca's verse is thoroughly rooted in the traditional poetry of his native Spain, his themes are universal, and he is rightly ranked among the greatest of 20th-century writers. He was the son of a farmer and a schoolteacher mother, who encouraged his musical gifts. When he was a student at the University of Granada he was known as 'the musician' to his friends, but he surprised them when he produced a collection of poetry, *Impressions and Landscapes*, when he was 20 years old. A year later he entered the University of Madrid, where he became friends with the surrealist film-maker Luis Buñuel and the painter Salvador Dali.

During the next two years García Lorca wrote poetry that became known throughout literary circles in Spain, although hardly any was published. 'Verse is made to be recited,' he said. 'In a book it is dead.' In 1921, however, the experimental *Book of Poems* was published. Next came *Canciones* (*Songs*, 1927) and *Romancero gitano* (*Gypsy Ballads*, 1928), which brought him international fame but little happiness, and he moved to the United States following what he called 'one of the most painful states I have ever had in my life'. In America he was overwhelmed by new feelings of horror at the physical world, and the poems he wrote there are bleak, filled with an almost hallucinatory terror. For García Lorca the earth is a terrifying place because we are bound to it but also bound to leave. His ultimate aim was 'to learn a lament that will cleanse me of the earth'. His best poetry achieves an enormous emotional depth by blurring the boundaries between things and feelings – dead leaves weep, while the heart 'bleeds like a fountain'.

García Lorca's theatre contains the same distinctive tone as his poetry, and it ranges from the deliberately grotesque and fantastical, through farce, to rural tragedy, at which he excelled. His three best plays are in this genre, and they deal with the frustrations of rigid social attitudes or with the unnatural role forced on Spanish women by a cultural insistence that they must be always somehow 'other'. *Bodas de sangre* (*Blood Wedding*, 1933) shows the conflict between 'honour' and sexual desire. *Yerma* (1934) tells of a woman who murders her husband because he cannot father a child, and *La casa de Bernarda Alba* (*The House of Bernada Alba*, written in 1936 but not performed until 1945) is a tragedy in which avoidance of scandal leads to hideous tyranny and death. Lorca was murdered by Spanish Nationalists when he was 38 years old.

Left: The great Spanish lyric poet and dramatist Federico García Lorca was shot by the fascists shortly after the start of the Spanish Civil War. Death is the theme of some of his most moving poems.

Above: A scene from a production of Lorca's folk drama *Blood Wedding*, which deals with the tragic story of a bride who flees from her wedding with the man she secretly loves.

JAROSLAV HASEK (1883–1923)

The Czech writer Jaroslav Hasek is credited with 1200 short stories, together with poems and political writings, but his reputation rests entirely on his comic masterpiece, *The Good Soldier Schweik* (1920–23). This unfinished, four-volume novel (he intended it to run to six volumes) is one of the great satirical works of our time, earning Hasek comparisons with satirists such as Rabelais and Jonathan Swift. At its centre is the title character, Schweik, a fat, apparently incompetent and naive, dog-loving Czech, who has been drafted into the Austrian army. He serves as an orderly to a drunken and spectacularly corrupt priest, who loses him in a poker game to an ambitious, lecherous lieutenant. Further escapades and misadventures follow, during which Schweik regularly comes into conflict with his superior officers through his excessive zeal and literal-mindedness in carrying out orders. Eventually, he is certified as an imbecile by an army medical board; he leaves the army and supports himself by selling mongrels under forged pedigrees. Hasek leaves open the question of whether Schweik really is an imbecile or whether he is pretending to be one in order to mock and thwart the authorities. Either way, his antics provide a brilliantly effective device for ridiculing military bureaucracy and other forms of officialdom, and also for demonstrating the futility of war. The book was banned by the armies of three countries (Czechoslovakia, Poland and Hungary) as 'detrimental to discipline'.

Hasek was as anarchic and as subversive of authority as his hero. A heavy drinker, often at loggerheads with the Prague police, he edited the fortnightly magazine *Animal World*, in which he would occasionally publish descriptions of animals he had invented or contribute articles with such titles as 'The Rational Breeding of Werewolves'.

ITALO SVEVO (1861–1928)

If it had not been for a chance meeting with the young James Joyce, the Italian writer Italo Svevo (the pen-name of Ettore Schmitz) would be unknown today. His first two novels, *Una Vita* (*A Life*, 1892) and *Senilità* (*As a Man Grows Older*, 1898), which he published at his own expense, were completely ignored.

He gave up writing and for almost 20 years worked as a businessman in his home town of Trieste. In 1907 he engaged Joyce, then living in Trieste and writing *Dubliners*, as his English tutor. Joyce's tremendous admiration for Svevo's novels encouraged him to return to writing, resulting in his classic work *La coscienza di Zeno* (*The Confessions of Zeno*, 1923), one of the first novels to make use of the ideas of Freudian psychoanalysis and still the most entertaining. Its narrator is a middle-aged businessman, Zeno Cossini, who starts analysis because he wants to give up smoking, among other things. Zeno tries to probe his own weakness of will and his paralysis, but he is, in fact, a master of rationalization. He is endlessly fertile in finding reasons why his 'last cigarette' should not actually be his last. He applies the same ingenuity to justifying his adultery and convincing himself that he still loves his wife. Zeno's convoluted exercises in self-understanding are simultaneously comic, touching and illuminating – and also discomforting in the way they mirror our own capacity for creating fictions about our lives.

Experiments in the theatre

Between them, Pirandello and Brecht were responsible for some of the most important developments in contemporary avant-garde drama. The work of playwrights like Ionesco, Beckett, Genet and Pinter is in many senses a continuation of Pirandello's vision. Brecht's theory of epic drama and his insistence that theatre should not be confined to the stage has influenced both political and popular performance the world over.

LUIGI PIRANDELLO (1867–1936)

Pirandello did not write his first play until he was 40 years old. Before that he had published a number of short stories and novels while he was working as a teacher. His third novel, *Il Fu Mattia Pascal* (*The Late Mattia Pascal*, 1904), marked a sharp turning away from the realism of his earlier work and brought him considerable critical acclaim. It is the story of a man who returns home after reportedly committing suicide but is unable to convince his family that he is still alive. In its concern with questions of identity and its bizarre premise, the book anticipated many of the ideas explored in his drama.

Pirandello was the son of a wealthy businessman in Palermo, Sicily. When his father's firm collapsed in 1903 he was forced to earn a living, abandoning an existence previously devoted to literature and the study of philology. Partly as a result of this financial disaster, his wife went mad and became obsessed with the idea that her husband had seduced not only his pupils but also their own daughter. The experience undoubtedly contributed to Pirandello's central theme – the uncertainty and fluidity of personality. His first important play *Così è (se vi pare)* (*Right You are (If You Think You are)*, 1917) is notable for its wholesale rejection of the idea of objective truth: the truth of the play's events is presented as relative to three different viewpoints.

In *Sei personaggi in cerca di autore* (*Six Characters in Search of an Author*, 1921), his most famous play, the six characters interrupt a rehearsal of another play, complaining that the author has not completed their stories. Refusing to follow stage directions and arguing with the actors, they disrupt the play within the play to such an extent that it breaks down into a series of alternately comic and tragic fragments. For the staging of the play in Paris in 1923, the 'actors' walked down the aisles in everyday clothes and climbed onto a bare stage, while the 'characters' were lowered onto the stage in a blaze of light. This radical break with the conventions of naturalism is common now, but it caused a sensation at the time.

Pirandello called a collection of his leading plays *Naked Masks*. His drama explores the paradoxical idea that people are able truly to reveal themselves only when they are wearing a mask (or adopting a role). In *Six Characters* the characters have a much greater vitality than the actors of the play they interrupt and compel them to question their identity. His other great play, *Enrico IV* (*Henry IV*, 1922) carries the investigation into reality and illusion further with a central character who switches between real and feigned madness.

BERTOLT BRECHT (1898–1956)

The German playwright Bertolt Brecht was a Marxist of a rather unusual kind. In place of Marxist theory and dogmatism, he advocated what he called 'crude thinking'. Brecht's overriding concern was to create a political drama that would actually change the way people thought. His first play, *Baal* (1929), about a charismatic poet-criminal, shows the influence of German

Left: With his theory of epic theatre, Bertolt Brecht (a somewhat unorthodox Marxist) developed an immensely influential and powerful drama for expressing his political concerns.

Below: Pirandello's play *Six Characters in Search of an Author* caused a sensation with its utterly novel exploration of the mystery of human identity.

expressionism but also parodies it. The work that brought him his greatest individual success, *Der Dreigroschenoper* (*The Threepenny Opera*, 1928), written in collaboration with the composer Kurt Weill, is based on *The Beggar's Opera* by the 18th century English writer John Gay. It transposes Gay's highwaymen and thieves, their women and their jailers into characters in the Berlin underworld of the 1920s. Brecht intended the criminal gang to stand for bourgeois capitalists, but the exuberance of the language undermines the opera's political message, and it could equally be taken as a satire on communist revolutionaries.

The aim of 'epic theatre', which Brecht expounded and developed in his later plays and which has had an enormous influence on subsequent drama, is to stir the spectators to action by appealing to their minds rather than to their hearts. In his view, drama that involves the audience emotionally is suspect: its real effect is to turn spectators into harmless members of society by purging them of disruptive feelings. Epic theatre discards the idea that drama should create the illusion of reality and seeks to prevent the audience from identifying with the characters on stage. For this purpose, Brecht developed what has come to be called the 'alienation effect', in which the actors might interrupt themselves by breaking into song, lecturing the audience or holding up placards. It typically uses harsh lighting and leaves the props exposed to view. No attempt is made to conceal the fact that the audience is watching a performance.

Brecht's major plays – *Mutter Courage* (*Mother Courage*, 1941), *Der aufhaltsame Aufstieg des Arturo Ui* (*The Resistible Rise of Arturo Ui*, 1941), *Leben des Galilei* (*The Life of Galileo*, 1943), *Der Gute Mensch von Sezuan* (*The Good Woman of Setzuan*, 1943) *and Der kaukasische Kreiderkreis* (*The Caucasian Chalk Circle*, 1945) – consist of loosely connected scenes with no dramatic climaxes and encourage a highly stylized form of acting.

Brecht went into exile in 1933, living in the United States from 1941 to 1947. He then returned to East Germany where he formed his own theatre company, the Berliner Ensemble. In addition to being a playwright, he was also a very fine lyric poet, and is regarded by many as one of the greatest German poets of the century.

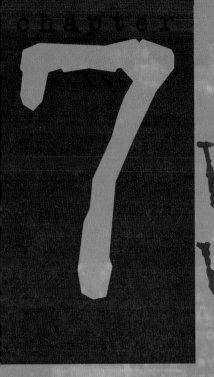

chapter 7

Women on women

Many 19th-century novels depicted the lives of women who were at odds with society, but they had generally been concerned to achieve a 'happy ever after' in which the heroine found herself back in its centre. If she did not kill herself, as Madame Bovary did, she should marry the hero, as Jane Eyre did. In the 20th century a new movement began, and women tried to find different ways to be and to write. Perhaps there *was* something about being female that could not be expressed in the form the novel had taken until then. A far-ranging exploration of different voices started, and what Katharine Mansfield called 'the secret self' began to make itself heard.

Below: An Angel at my Table – Jane Campion's film of the auto-biography of fellow-New Zealander Janet Frame. Frame was saved from a lobotomy when her first book won a prize.

Right: Colette was as enchanted by animals and the natural world as she was with the women and men she devoted her life to loving and writing about.

Colette
(1873–1954)

FEMALE WISDOM

Between 1900 and 1949 Sidonie Gabrielle Colette produced more than 70 novels and stories. She began writing under the pen-name of her husband, Willy, producing the semi-autobiographical 'Claudine' series, in which she described her country childhood and her idealized mother – in effect, the landscape, food, animals, birds and flowers of a world into which sexual passion had not yet intruded.

After leaving the overbearing Willy, Colette was increasingly concerned to describe the quiet desperation of single bohemian woman (she was herself a dancer and mime artist for some years after her divorce in 1906). What irks her heroines is not so much financial need as the longing to be loved, which is always frustrated. Her heroines live in the margins of society. They are outsiders, sometimes lesbians or androgynous misfits, deprived of the comforts of a bourgeois lifestyle. In *La Vagabonde* (*Vagabond*, 1910), for example, the narrator, Renée, is a music-hall dancer, who has to choose between personal freedom and the love of the man to whom she writes throughout the book. The narrative is made up mostly of her letters, and it is entirely introspective, brooding on the particular hardship of being a single, impoverished woman, who nevertheless rejects a conventional life.

In *Chéri* (1920) and its sequel, *La Fin de Chéri* (*The Last of Chéri*, 1926), she traces the story of a young man's love for a woman who is 50 years old and their gradual mutual decline. Chéri, like many of Colette's men, is idle, essentially adolescent, immature and weak. He wears pearls and silk pyjamas and is kept by Lea, his rich older lover, who is increasingly certain that he will come to despise her ageing body and leave her for somebody younger. In the end it is she who makes their liaison impossible, choosing to grow old alone, rather than have Chéri observe her. Temporary companionship is judged to be not worth the loss of self-respect that his inevitable leaving will bring.

Duo (1934) is an unsentimental study of a marriage destroyed – and a man also destroyed – by the violence of jealousy.

Colette has been criticized for being sentimental, and it is true that as a person she may have been, but her analysis of her characters is instinctively sharp. As one critic has observed, she brings 'instinctive (not intellectual) female wisdom to the novel'. Her language is rich and pleasurably sensual, undercutting the bleak lives and emotional deprivation she describes. She clearly adores both the natural world and the bodies of all who inhabit it. In spite of the pain physical relationships cause, she celebrates and affirms the idea of love – between any combination of the sexes.

Pioneers

The twin problems for women writers at this time were how to describe how they thought, rather than what they actually did – 'Women think flowingly,' noted Dorothy Richardson – and how to interest the reading public in the lives of women who were, inevitably, restricted and poor because unless they had a man to support them (or a room of their own, bought with family money), that was how life was.

DOROTHY RICHARDSON (1873–1957)

The disintegration of her family fortune was the beginning of Richardson's life among a small group of women who were working in London at a time when 'the world for women was a prison, not a universe'. Her lifelong project was a series of 13 novels, entitled *Pilgrimage*, of which the first volume, *Painted Roofs*, appeared in 1915. She used a stream-of-consciousness technique to blend people, scenes and events in the life of her heroine, Miriam Henderson.

Richardson meshes autobiography and fiction throughout *Pilgrimage*, weaving the first and third person into a spacious, reflective narrative. She did not want her characters to be fixed but, rather, 'subjects in progress', constantly becoming themselves. Virginia Woolf identified in Richardson's work the first example of 'the feminine sentence', by which she meant the expression of a particularly fluid way of thinking, revealed through the heroine's consciousness as she engages with life. Space, movement and memories are intermingled to produce a 'story' that has no beginning, middle or end yet is a coherent history of a life. 'I want to produce a feminine equivalent of the current masculine realism,' Richardson wrote. Her impressionistic style was much admired by other feminist writers of her day, including May Sinclair, Storm Jameson and Rebecca West.

ANAÏS NIN (1903–77)

Although she was born in Paris, Anaïs Nin spent her childhood travelling with her father, a Cuban painter, and when he left his family for another woman in 1914 she and her mother emigrated to the United States. Nin spent the rest of her life writing a diary, which is, in a sense, one long plea for her father to come back. She described her journal as 'the only steadfast friend I have, the only one which makes life bearable'. She found it difficult to separate living from writing about it, but that itself was partly her subject; 'I relive my life in terms of a dream ... an endless story.'

Her novels – of which *House of Incest* (1936) is a typical example – are in much the same style as her journals. The 'house' of this book's title is the narrator's thoughts, through which she wanders in a trance-like state, using the idea of incest as an image for her own inertia and imprisonment.

Nin lived in Paris from 1923, where she was involved with Henry and June Miller, and she started a publishing house, which printed her own books among others. She saw the psychoanalyst Otto Rank, and later practised analysis herself. Although rather turgid, self-obsessed reading, Nin's *Diary* (published in seven volumes, 1966–83) was extremely influential, beginning a trend (which reached its height in the 1970s) for women to publish their innermost thoughts and to feel that those thoughts constituted a body of literary work, just as fiction itself does.

JEAN RHYS (1894–1979)

Born into the minority white community of Dominica, Jean Rhys (the pen-name of Ella Gwendolen Rees Williams) travelled to England when she was 17 years old and began a life of roaming poverty, working in music-halls, writing sporadically and living in Paris and London. Her books are bleak, semi-autobiographical accounts of exiled young women – 'perpetually moving to another place which was perpetually the same' – unloved, underfed, too alone to feel properly lonely, too bewildered by life to relate to anything much, except light and shadows, heat and cold. Deserted by the men they meet, Rhys's heroines often end up selling the gifts those men have given them in order to feed themselves or to pay for illegal abortions.

What is intriguing in her writing is the mixture of vulnerability and toughness in her central characters. *Good Morning, Midnight* (1939), for example, follows Sasha Jensen through two aimless weeks in Paris – a cheap hotel, cheap drinks and a man who steals her money – yet she never relinquishes her hold on herself – or us, for that matter. Rhys's heroines know life holds nothing for them, yet they joke and talk to themselves and keep on living – drinking, dancing and falling into

in her diary that she felt relief. 'I was jealous of her writing,' she said, and she was right to be. Katherine Mansfield's short stories perfect the art of responding to what G.K. Chesterton called the 'tremendous trifles' of life. There are no plots to speak of in her three volumes of stories, and there are no bold depictions of people at dramatic moments of their lives. Instead, there are the 'moments of being' that Virginia Woolf strove to describe – when the surface of life is rippled slightly, and some perception of the deeper causes of happiness and grief hovers for a second.

Mansfield's stories often centre on the lives of isolated women, who are not, in fact, physically alone –

Left: Katherine Mansfield; a severe profile, which belies the sparkle and sensitivity of her stories. She became increasingly drawn-looking as consumption claimed her health and eventually her life, aged 35.

Right: 1920s café life provided an often gloomy escape from the squalor and loneliness of the bedsit existence lived by many independent heroines of the literature of this era.

disastrous love. Her writing is flat but strangely moving. Nothing develops in any of her novels except the levels of misery her young women endure, but they are compulsive reading.

KATHERINE MANSFIELD (1888–1923)

When she heard that Katherine Mansfield had died of consumption at the age of 34, Virginia Woolf admitted

they have families, husbands, sisters – but they share with many fictional women of this era the sense that 'when you are by yourself and you think about life, it is always sad'. Mansfield's own life and her writing were increasingly restricted by the tuberculosis she contracted – perhaps from Lawrence or vice versa – when she and her husband, John Middleton Murry, shared a house in Cornwall with D.H. Lawrence and Frieda.

'When he has gone ... I cry in the way that hurts right down, that hurts your heart and your stomach. Who is this crying? The same one who laughed on the landing, kissed him and was happy. This is me, this is myself.'
JEAN RHYS, *Good Morning, Midnight* (1939)

ne second sex

The tremendous political and social changes that occurred in the 1930s and 1940s led women away from their traditional domestic role and into the world of work and ideas, which had so far been a solidly male arena. Women were now concerned not so much with finding expression for unexpressed ways of thinking as with developing new identities through writing.

Above: Simone de Beauvoir, as famous for her lifelong relationship with Jean-Paul Sartre as she is for her commitment to the emancipation of women.

Top right: Doris Lessing's *The Golden Notebook* (1962) perhaps did more than any other single novel of its time to accelerate and popularize the burgeoning women's movement.

SIMONE DE BEAUVOIR (1908–86)

Born in Paris to bourgeois parents, Simone de Beauvoir read philosophy at the Sorbonne, where she met Jean-Paul Sartre and where she was a professor (1941–43). She began to write about the possibilities of human choice and freedom, reflecting the preoccupations of the existentialist movement. Her first novel, *L'Invitée* (*She Came to Stay*, 1943) was not successful, but her feminist essay *Le Deuxième sexe* (*The Second Sex*, 1953) was enormously influential. Here she was concerned to examine the ways in which being a woman is perceived by the (male) world and how a woman experiences it. 'On ne naît pas femme: on le devient' ('One is not born a woman: one becomes a woman'), she famously decided. Although she wrote several more novels, including *Les Mandarins* (1954), which won the Prix Goncourt, she is most famous for her study of the female condition – and female conditioning – and for her four volumes of autobiography, which chart her own upbringing and the shape of intellectual life in France from the 1930s onwards. She was concerned to demonstrate the ways in which women internalize negative assumptions about themselves as they grow up. She identified woman as 'the other' in our culture: the woman is not male and therefore is not fully human as far as men are concerned. Some critics have suggested, however, that in dedicating her life (and her penultimate work) to Jean-Paul Sartre she was herself prey to assumptions of the superiority of male intelligence.

SYLVIA PLATH (1932–63)

Born in Boston, Massachusetts, Plath won a scholarship to Smith College in 1953 and the prize of working on a magazine in New York the same year. She wrote about the deep depression and breakdown that followed this period of her life in her only novel, *The Bell Jar* (1963). Esther Greenwood, the book's heroine, experiments with the possibilities available to graduate women in the late 1960s: she works in publishing and as a secretary, and she tries to involve herself with the type of men she is expected to date and to get on with her frustrated, controlling mother. She finds herself in a psychiatric hospital, having failed to make sense of what Germaine Greer was later to identify as 'the conflict between desire and conditioning'.

Plath is better known as a poet than as a writer of fiction. Her elegant, sparse poetry expresses everywhere the violent contradictions implicit in being both a domesticated, child-bearing woman and a fiercely intelligent – if unstable – person. 'The blood-jet is poetry,' she wrote, 'There is no stopping it.'

JANET FRAME (b.1924)

One of New Zealand's greatest writers, Janet Frame shared Sylvia Plath's obsession with the connection between writing and madness. She spent several years as a patient in psychiatric hospitals, and she wrote about her experiences in these institutions in three volumes of autobiography, *To the Island* (1983), *An Angel at My Table* (1984) and *The Envoy from Mirror City* (1985), which were later filmed as the highly acclaimed *An Angel at My Table*.

For Frame, like many of her female contemporaries, the idea of the impossibility of the existence of any objective truth is central. Her style is self-consciously childlike and non-realistic, allowing her to examine the way 'reality' is created in fiction.

MARGUERITE DURAS (1914–96)

Born in Indochina, Duras moved to Paris to study when she was 19 years old. Her novels focus on women whose obsession with a person or an incident leads them to experience themselves in a different, more intense way. Her fiction is concerned with the connection between sexual desire and the activity of writing itself. She writes in a sparse, limpid prose, which relies more on atmosphere than on character or plot to absorb the reader in its erotic reality. From the late 1950s she wrote screenplays, as well as fiction, the most famous of which was *Hiroshima mon amour*, which was filmed by Alain Resnais in 1959.

DORIS LESSING (b.1919)

Like Simone de Beauvoir, Lessing was concerned to involve questions about women's writing and sexual relations with politics and their history with ideas of possible narrative structures. Born in Iran, she spent the early part of her life in South Africa where she became involved in communism and black politics after the break-up of her first marriage. She re-married in 1945, but left for Britain in 1950, taking with her her youngest child and the manuscript of her first novel, *The Grass is Singing* (1950). The story of a white farmer's wife and her black houseboy, who is charged with his employer's murder, the novel explores the connection between violence and eroticism, between how an event is perceived by the (male) world and how the subject experiences it.

Her later works are often concerned with madness, a breakdown that inevitably occurs when the boundaries between different sorts of experience seem to prevent any emotional coherence for her female protagonists. 'The point is,' says Anna Wulf at the beginning of *The Golden Notebook* (1962), 'everything is cracking up.' But this fragmentation is a necessary part of becoming 'free women' for many of Lessing's heroines.

> And hadn't Buddy said, as if to revenge himself for my digging out the car and his having to stand by, "I wonder who you'll marry now, Esther." ...
> 'And of course I didn't know who would marry me now that I'd been where I had been. I didn't know at all.

SYLVIA PLATH, *The Bell Jar* (1963)

Surfacing

During the 1970s women writers continued to explore different voices, often returning to the more traditional genres of science fiction, fairy tales and fables to raise issues about how their relationships with themselves and the world are impinged upon by destructive social and political forces. The burgeoning women's movement brought with it an increasing confidence and a new critical interest in feminist writing, which ensured that the readership remained alert and curious.

MARGARET ATWOOD (b.1939)

Margaret Atwood, who was born in Ottawa, is now Canada's most prolific and important writer, and her influence on current women's writing has been enormous. She writes both poetry and fiction and has developed a method of using humour creatively to criticize the society she depicts. Her novels are generally constructed around a central metaphor. The heroine of her first novel, *The Edible Woman* (1969), for example, so resents being manipulated by consumerism and male ideas of perfection that she decides to stop eating. In a tale that is both funny and terrifying, we watch her change from a passive object to a subject in control of her own story, albeit a starving one. In *Bodily Harm* (1981) a woman journeys to the Caribbean after having a mastectomy and finds herself in the middle of a political coup. She is imprisoned and starts to re-evaluate her own 'harmed' body in the context of other people's larger suffering and tolerance of pain. Other works include *The Handmaid's Tale* (1986), about a woman forced to become a child-bearing mistress to powerful males, and *Lady Oracle* (1976), in which a woman changes her identity to become a writer of romances. Her books are driven by a palpable feminist anger, but they are often funny, with odd moments of tenderness and affection for her characters and the world.

JEANETTE WINTERSON (b.1959)

Born in Lancashire, Jeanette Winterson lived with an adoptive family of Evangelical Christians. She used this claustrophobic experience as the basis for her first

novel, *Oranges Are Not the Only Fruit* (1985), which was so successful that she said she need never work again. The book succeeds largely because of its first-person voice, which combines comedy with bewilderment and fear as the young heroine is involved in her parents' 'great struggle between good and evil'. Winterson's central character rebels by entering into a lesbian relationship, which allows her to explore larger issues

of religious obsession, sex, love and exile. Since this novel, Winterson's popularity and critical acclaim have diminished somewhat. She started writing more 'experimental' novels in which there is an unfortunate tendency to be rather pompous and abstract.

FAY WELDON (b.1933)

Born in Worcester, Fay Weldon worked as a copywriter in a London advertising agency before writing her first novel, *The Fat Woman's Joke* (1967). This book,

typically, was concerned with analysing the pressures on woman to conform to a particular physical type. 'It was obvious ... that it was Ruth's body that was at fault,' she tells us. Weldon always has her tongue in her cheek, but her relentless irony can verge on bitterness as she surveys male-female relationships and women's competitive attitude to each other. She is consistently interested in the biological aspects of womanhood and often moves into Gothic scenarios in order to explore this or sets her fictions in another, imaginary world. In *The Life and Loves of a She-Devil* (1983), for instance, a woman quite literally becomes her husband's body. 'I like to control nature and make things beautiful,' she says. Weldon also likes to point out how ugly our natures are.

ANGELA CARTER (1940–92)

Born in Eastbourne, Sussex, and first published in 1965, Angela Carter was fascinated by the distinctions between biological 'sex' and socially constructed 'gender'. 'I wanted to say some quite specific things about the cultural production of female identity,' she said of her novel, *The Passion of New Eve* (1977). This work, like many of hers, links science and myth in a brilliant manipulation of genres, including science fiction, biblical myth and popular romance. Another key issue in her work is the relationship between aggression and eroticism. In *The Magic Toyshop* (1967) a 15-year-old girl is forced to partake in amateur dramatics by a vicious uncle whose wife is mute. The work is edgy and dark. Sexual fantasy is always lurking – a sinister force – in Carter's work.

ERICA JONG (b.1942)

Born in New York to a family of Jewish artists and intellectuals, Jong shot to fame in 1973 with the publication of *Fear of Flying*, which has since sold more copies than the Bible. Although somewhat hollow, the book had enormous influence in the United States because of the way it deals with female desire and eroticism. Its premise is that both women and men want the same thing from sex – the famous 'zipless f**k', with no emotional involvement or guilt on either side. But there is an undercurrent of dissatisfaction with being female throughout, which undercuts the exuberant, raunchy tone. Isadora Wing (the narrator) never does feel free and is always vaguely aware of a lack of fulfilment. She realizes that woman will never achieve contentment by simply imitating male roles. Erica Jong has published two books of poetry and several further novels, but *Fear of Flying* is her bestselling book, and she is not now regarded as a serious talent.

> Women do not favour heroines who are tough and hard. Instead they have to be tough and soft. This leads to linguistic difficulties. Last time we looked, monosyllables were male, still dominant but sinking fast.

MARGARET ATWOOD, *Women's Novels*

8 Depression and after

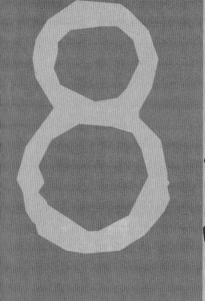

Wigan Labour Exchange, 1939. The spectre of unemployment continued to haunt European life and literature right up until the outbreak of the Second World War.

In 1929 the New York Stock Exchange crashed, triggering the worst worldwide economic slump in history. Shares fell to 20 per cent of their value; world trade halved; tens of thousands of firms folded; and in every advanced Western country millions of ordinary people became unemployed. This economic disaster coincided with a sharpening of the political division between left and right. Writers everywhere were politically engaged as never before nor since. The majority were on the left, and many writers and intellectuals from Europe and the United States supported the Republican cause in the Spanish·Civil War (1936–39), some even fighting as volunteers in the International Brigades.

British poets of the 1930s

W.H. AUDEN (1907–73)

Once described as 'the Picasso of modern poetry', Wystan Hugh Auden was a controversial, outspoken and ceaselessly experimental writer, who gave his name to a generation of British poets who were increasingly disillusioned with post-war politics and society. His first collection of verse was hand-printed for him while he was still at Oxford, where he also met Christopher Isherwood, with whom he formed a life-long friendship. Offered a year abroad by his parents, he chose to go to Berlin, rather than to Paris, and he fell in love with its language, poetry, cabaret, songs and plays, especially those by Brecht (see page 70). His early work is often obscure, fusing Old English poetry, public school stories and the ideas of Karl Marx and Sigmund Freud into uneven poems, pulled between the subjective impulse of poetry as personal therapy and the desire for it to have social and political implications. He later famously described this period of his work as being 'dishonest or bad-mannered or boring'.

His second phase found him a hero of the left, warning against totalitarianism in the collection *Look, Stranger!* (1936), in which his verse is more open and accessible. He visited Iceland with Louis MacNeice, and China with Isherwood, writing essays about these experiences, as well as the long poem, 'Spain' (1937), about the civil war, where he was (briefly) an ambulance driver. In 1939 he moved to America with Isherwood, and at this time decisive changes occurred in his religious perspective, as he moved nearer to the commitment to Christianity that informs his later long poems. In 1948 he met Chester Kallman, with whom he lived alternately in New York City and Kirchstetten, Austria, over the next 20 years. They collaborated on plays, while Auden wrote four more volumes of poetry as well as editing – among the books he edited was *The Oxford Book of Light Verse* (1938). When Kallman died

Auden moved back to Oxford, where he was an honorary fellow at Christ Church College. He has now come to seem more of an intimate poet – as well as a faultless craftsman – than he was in his lifetime, partly due to changing attitudes towards homosexuality, about which he never openly wrote. His *Collected Shorter Poems* were published in 1966, and his *Collected Longer Poems* in 1968.

LOUIS MACNEICE (1907–63)

Unlike his friend Auden, Louis MacNeice never wanted to change the world, merely to describe it. His characteristic mood is of a slightly detached, wryly observant and witty but lyrical commentator. Conrad Aitken typically admired him for his 'sheer readability, for speed, lightness and easy intellectual range', but felt (also typically, among critics) that the poetry had 'little residual magic'. The magic of MacNeice lies, in fact, in his sense of rhythm and his ear for the patterns of colloquial speech, which he used journalistically to create poems of intensely communicated exuberance. 'Each event implies the world,' he wrote. 'I give you the incidental things which pass.' It is the particulars of lived experience that concern MacNeice, but these fleeting events are always connected to public life, so that *Autumn Journal* (1938) – one of his best known works – interleaves a love-affair with the political events leading up to the outbreak of the Second World War.

His father was a clergyman in the Church of Ireland – Louis was born in Carrickfergus – and his mother died early, leaving him feeling isolated, a feeling that permeates the sardonic humour and Celtic energy of his work. His first collection, *Blind Fireworks* (1929), was followed by more than a dozen other volumes, including the posthumously published *Collected Poems* (1966) and *The Burning Perch* (1963). He died of pneumonia, contracted while recording a radio programme in a damp cave.

'September has come and I wake
  And I think with joy how whatever, now or in future,
    the system
Nothing whatever can take
  The people away.'

LOUIS MACNEICE, *Autumn Journal* (1938)

Political novels

During the 1930s and after, many writers in the West began to express their sympathies with Marxism. An opposition to fascism, coupled with the experience of economic hardship during the Depression, led them to turn a blind eye to the realities of life under communism. In the Soviet Union itself, voices of dissent were quickly silenced, and it fell to a handful of writers to protest against what later came to be seen as the ruthless exploitation of political power.

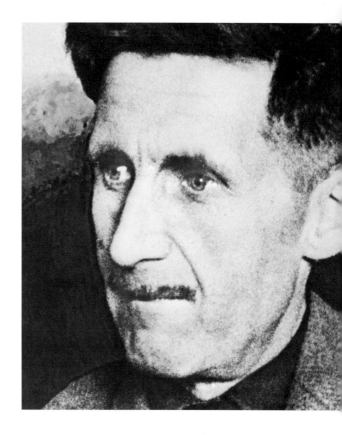

GEORGE ORWELL (1903–50)

George Orwell, the pen-name of Eric Arthur Blair, was born in Bengal, the son of a British official in the Indian civil service. He was educated at Eton and then went to Burma as a superintendent in the Imperial Police. His experiences there left him with a revulsion for the values of the British ruling class. He resigned his commission and for several years shared the life of the unemployed and destitute working class. *Down and Out in Paris and London* (1933) recalls this period in a wonderfully vivid, semi-fictional account of washing dishes in hotels and restaurants and other poorly paid work.

From thinking of himself as an anarchist, Orwell moved to the political left. His position was broadly one of democratic socialism, but he rejected all party labels, and much of his work is sharply critical of existing socialist movements. He was opposed, he said, to every form of 'man's dominion over man'.

Orwell's writing includes novels, essays, a large body of journalism and the overtly political works *The Road to Wigan Pier* (1937) and *Homage to Catalonia* (1938). In the latter, he describes his experiences in the Spanish Civil War, in which, while fighting on the Republican side against Franco's fascists, he developed a passionate mistrust of, and hatred for, communism. His best known novels, *Animal Farm* (1945) and *Nineteen Eighty-four* (1949), are directed against the evils of totalitarianism as embodied in the Stalinist Soviet Union. *Animal Farm* is a satire on the Russian Revolution and its consequences. It takes the form of a fable in which farm animals revolt against their masters and set up their own rule, with the pigs as their leaders. Before long, the pigs become tyrants themselves, adopting the slogan: 'All animals are equal but some animals are more equal than others.'

Nineteen Eighty-four is a vision of a nightmarish, all-powerful police state set in the future. Orwell intended this more as a warning of the dangers of totalitarian government than as a prophecy. In its depiction of the way the state uses propaganda to establish absolute control over the lives and minds of its citizens – particularly through the techniques of newspeak and doublethink – the book is as topical as ever. The hero, Winston Smith, is arrested by the thought police, but he is guilty only of harbouring unorthodox beliefs and of having a love affair.

Left: As esteemed for his personal integrity as for his writing, George Orwell turned his back on his upper-class upbringing to castigate political and moral cant through his fiction and journalism.

Right: An illustration for Mikhail Bulgakov's satirical novel *The Master and Margarita*, showing the magician cat rescuing a dissident writer from the clutches of the KGB – by making him vanish into thin air.

ARTHUR KOESTLER (1905–83)

Koestler's work is often bracketed with that of George Orwell, who became his friend when he settled in England. Unlike Orwell, he wrote from first-hand experience of Soviet Russia, having spent a year in the country after joining the Communist Party in 1932. Koestler was born in Budapest, Hungary, was educated in Vienna and wrote his first books in German. Imprisoned, under sentence of death, by the fascists during the Spanish Civil War and then again by the French when the German army entered Paris, he escaped to England in 1941.

Koestler's novel *Darkness at Noon* (1940), which was written after his break with the party, was one of the earliest revelations of the true nature of communism under Stalin, and it remains one of the most powerful indictments of totalitarian rule as well as being a thoroughly convincing study of the psychology of extreme political idealism. The book tells the story of an old-guard Bolshevik, N.S. Rubashov, who is arrested in one of Stalin's many purges. Rubashov is held in complete isolation in prison, interrogated, sent to trial and, finally, executed.

WRITING UNDER STALIN

No books even mildly critical of the state ideology were published in the Soviet Union from the start of Stalin's rule to the limited 'thaw' that followed his death in 1953. The most gifted writers of this period expressed their dissent indirectly through satires and fables. Yevgeny Zamyatin (1884–1937) circulated his novel *We* (1920) in manuscript form and was later forced into exile. This brilliantly executed anti-utopian satire is the forerunner of Aldous Huxley's *Brave New World* (although Huxley always denied he had been influenced by it) and Orwell's *Nineteen Eighty-four*. Many critics consider it superior to both these novels.

The greatest work by Mikhail Bulgakov (1891–1940), *The Master and Margarita*, was not printed in Russia until 1967 and then only in a censored form. The novel is a dazzlingly witty and at the same time profound allegory on the theme of government suppression of literature. Its central character is the Devil, who arrives in contemporary Moscow and proceeds to expose the corruption of the Soviet cultural elite, while also becoming involved with a novelist who has been sent to a psychiatric hospital.

The proletarian novel

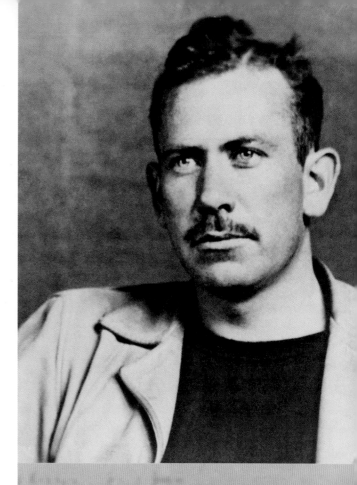

Despite the Marxist overtones of the word 'proletarian', the best writers of fiction about the working classes and working-class life have not been political activists. In fact, quality literature disappeared in the Soviet Union once the Russian Revolution had established 'the dictatorship of the proletariat'; novels in the 'socialist realism' school were little more than propagandist tracts. Only in the United States, the heartland of capitalism, did a genuine proletarian fiction emerge. These authors showed their sympathies for the conditions of working people without being politically dogmatic.

Above: John Steinbeck, whose novel *The Grapes of Wrath* conveyed the suffering and tragedy of working people during the Great Depression more vividly than any other contemporary fiction.

Below left: The cover of Steinbeck's novel, *Of Mice and Men*, the compassionate tale of two migrant farm workers, one a giant of great strength and little intelligence.

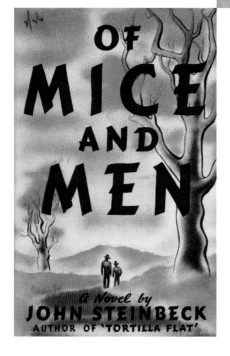

JOHN STEINBECK (1902–68)

Steinbeck was born in California and studied marine biology at Standford University but did not take a degree. A series of jobs working on the land followed, which supplied the background for many of his novels and short stories. *Tortilla Flat* (1935), the book that brought him to prominence, is a realistic and sympathetic portrait of the lives of poor Mexican Americans living on the outskirts of Monterey. *Of Mice and Men* (1937) tells the tragic story of Lennie, a simpleminded, itinerant farmhand of enormous strength, who is both protected and exploited by his weaker, more intelligent friend.

Steinbeck's most famous novel, *The Grapes of Wrath* (1939), describes the Joad family's migration

from Oklahoma to California in search of work. Their story mirrors the plight of thousands of families – 'Oakies' – who were driven from the dust bowl that Oklahoma had become in the early to mid-1930s. With its epic sweep and compelling narrative, the book seemed to sum up the bitterness of the decade of the Great Depression, and it did much to arouse public sympathy for the sufferings of migratory farm workers. It is simultaneously realistic and lyrical, interspersed with passages of brilliant impressionistic writing and commentaries that give the Joad family's story a wider scope. Steinbeck was awarded the Nobel prize in 1961, largely on the strength of *The Grapes of Wrath*.

His later books, which include *Cannery Row* (1945) and *East of Eden* (1952), are less impressive. *East of Eden*, which was made into a successful film in 1955, is a family saga about the conflict between generations, but it is flawed by melodrama and sentimentality.

UPTON SINCLAIR (1878–1968)

Upton Sinclair's best known and probably finest novel, *The Jungle* (1906), was written well before the Depression, but it stands as a prototype for the protest novel, intended to open people's eyes to corruption in American corporate and political life. The book's exposé of the brutal conditions in the Chicago meat-packing industry was dramatically successful, and public reaction was so strong that an investigation into the Chicago stockyards was set up by the US government and soon afterwards led to reform in food legislation. Sinclair, branded a 'muckraker' by President Theodore Roosevelt, used the profits from the book to establish Helicon Hall, an early experiment in co-operative living, which ended in a disastrous fire.

Sinclair was a man of prodigious energy, with more than 100 books to his name. While he was still under the age of 20 he wrote more than two million words a year for juvenile pulp fiction, and he continued to produce mainly polemical and socialist novels up to the Second World War. Two of the most readable are *King Coal* (1917), which documents the treatment of striking Colorado miners, and *Oil!* (1927), another work exposing corruption, this time during President Harding's administration. In 1940 he wrote *World's End*, the first in an immensely popular series of novels with an international setting and centring on Lanny Budd, the illegitimate son of a munitions manufacturer.

JAMES T. FARRELL (1904–79)

The Studs Lonigan trilogy, which made James Thomas Farrell's reputation, is one of the period's bleakest depictions of city life during the Depression. Although never fashionable in literary circles, the trilogy – *Young Lonigan: A Boyhood in Chicago Streets* (1932), *The Young Manhood of Studs Lonigan* (1934) and *Judgement Day* (1935) – has been described as 'the most powerful work of naturalism in a post-naturalistic era'. The books trace the dissolution of Studs Lonigan, a young Irish Catholic brought up in Chicago's south side. His toughness and sexual prowess at first bring Studs success in the world of street gangs and petty crime (the books were ahead of their time in their treatment of sexual brutality and gang violence), but in *Judgement Day* he becomes unemployed, is rejected by his girl and dies a drunkard at the age of 29.

Farrell was sympathetic to Marxism, and his intention was to portray Studs 'not only as a character for imaginative fiction but also as a social manifestation'. Studs is shown as fundamentally decent, but stifled by an unremittingly harsh and squalid urban environment. Farrell's commitment to Marxist determinism mellowed somewhat in a later sequence of novels based on Danny O'Neill, one of the marginal characters in the Studs Lonigan trilogy. Now the hero is no longer entirely the victim of his social circumstances and succeeds in making a life for himself away from Chicago.

ERSKINE CALDWELL (1903–87)

Like Farrell, Erskine Caldwell has not received the critical attention he deserves. His best known books, *Tobacco Road* (1932) and *God's Little Acre* (1933), relate tragi-comic, sometimes grotesque, stories of the rural poor in the American South. He writes about people whose lives are shaped by economic and social deprivation – the impoverished sharecroppers, tenant farmers, backwoodsmen and mill-hands – whom he depicts with an equal measure of humour and sympathy as well as a sharp ear for dialect. Sex and violence are the most prominent features of the lives of his characters, and both books ran into censorship trouble but became bestsellers with a worldwide readership.

Caldwell was born and grew up in Georgia, the son of a peripatetic Presbyterian minister. The characters in his fiction are drawn from first-hand experience, gained while accompanying his father on his missions.

Dramatic realism

The major dramatists of the period immediately after the First World War made a conscious artistic decision to abandon the elegant dialogue, unrealistic sets and improbable plot mechanics of their predecessors. Instead, they confronted the political and the personal in the language of real people in real situations. Their exploration of large issues was firmly based in the domestic and the mundane – as can be seen in O'Casey's *The Plough and the Stars* – but this does not prevent the best works of dramatic realism from having a rough, poetic grandeur, which makes them still worth seeing and reading.

EUGENE O'NEILL (1888–1953)

O'Neill came from a fraught, bohemian New York family – his father was a well-known romantic actor, his mother was a drug addict, and his brother was an alcoholic – and this would provide material for the plays that he began to write after various unsuccessful attempts at starting a life of his own. He went to Princeton University for a year, tried writing poetry, gold mining, marriage (which was kept secret and later dissolved), the navy (he travelled to South America, South Africa and England), became ill with tuberculosis, became a journalist and, finally, in 1916, joined the experimental theatre group, the Provincetown Players, which staged his early works.

In a sense he had two careers as a playwright. He wrote at least eight strong plays before 1931, then nothing until 1946 (although he received the Nobel prize in 1936). His first full-length play, *Beyond the Horizon* (1920), is a naturalistic study of two brothers, both of whom make wrong choices and are ultimately defeated by fatal mistakes caused by their sexual drives. This, typically, used an uncompromising realism to present what amounts to a dramatic case study of failed lives. O'Neill's characters are inevitably losers, drifting but driven – by their own self-loathing, self-deception or inarticulate guilt – to make fatally wrong life-choices, which in turn damage the lives of those they love or will not let themselves be loved by. His most powerful early

play is *Mourning Becomes Electra* (1931), an intense family drama, based on the *Oresteia* of Aeschylus.

His later, supreme achievements are *The Iceman Cometh* (1946) and *Long Day's Journey into Night* (1956). The second of these is an autobiographical family tragedy. Each character is flawed by self-delusion, a theme also developed in *The Iceman Cometh*, in which the assorted down-beats of the cast drink all day at

Harry Hope's bar, talking about the pipe-dreams they have been discussing for years. Hickey, a travelling salesman, attempts to energize them into reality, but it is revealed that he has, in fact, killed his wife, which effectively frees the others to continue their self-destructive self-delusion.

CLIFFORD ODETS (1906–63)

Odets wrote the main body of his work before he was 30 years old, and he wrote a confident, forward-looking preface to a collection of his six best known plays on his 30th birthday: 'We are living in a time when new art works should shoot bullets.' Eight years before he had been a founder member of the Group Theatre in

Below left: Playwright Eugene O'Neill. The turbulent and often tragic lives of his characters reflect his own private turmoil and self-destructiveness fuelled by a family history of alcoholism.

Right: One of the foremost Irish dramatists of the 20th century, Sean O'Casey's plays take Irish Nationalism as their subject but have a universal appeal.

Philadelphia (his home town), which followed the naturalistic methods of the Moscow Art Theatre, and he made his reputation when the theatre produced his short play *Waiting For Lefty* in 1935. The play opens with Harry Fatt, a crooked union leader, trying to persuade a group of taxi-drivers not to go on strike – 'You're so wrong I ain't laughing,' he tells them as the curtain goes up – and ends with the chant: 'Strike, Strike, Strike!'.

Odet saw his plays as describing 'a struggle for life against petty conditions', a life stripped of dignity. His drama was intensely provocative – a call for change – as exemplified in the title of *Awake And Sing!* (1935), which is taken from the Book of Isaiah 26:19; 'Awake and sing, ye who dwell in the dust.' A family of embittered Jewish New Yorkers are divided into those who move painfully forwards and those who cannot. Odet's language is ungrammatical, funny and vibrant. His is a realism tinged with humour and infused with an affirmatory warmth for mankind, despite its acute analysis of the injustices that stunt it.

SEAN O'CASEY (1880–1964)

O'Casey brought his gift for searing realism to the Irish stage at a particular historical moment and for a specific Nationalist purpose. He was educated, according to his excellent six-volume autobiography, on the streets of Dublin, which he roamed from the age of 14, before getting a job labouring on the Great Northern Railway of Ireland. When he was a teenager he began publishing articles, broadsheets and songs under the name P. O'Cathasaigh, and he came to the attention of Lady Gregory, who encouraged him to write.

His first play was rejected by the Abbey Theatre, Dublin, but *The Shadow of a Gunman* was performed to great acclaim in 1923. *Juno and the Paycock* followed a year later, and in 1926 *The Plough and the Stars* provoked Nationalist riots. The subject of all three plays was the danger of Irish patriotism, presented in the context of tenement life, pubs and family squabbles. Tragi-comedies, they show how false bravado and heroic posturing can result in casual death and anguished disillusionment. Noble rhetoric is set against the chaos and helplessness of lives ruined by violence. *The Plough and the Stars* ends with two blustering soldiers in the Nationalist army pouring tea, while a woman their comrades have mistakenly shot is dying, untended. The noise of the storming of the Post Office is vaguely noticed. The soldiers mindlessly sing a Republican anthem, '(joining in the chorus, as they sip their tea)'.

'Ralph: ... We don't want life printed on dollar bills, Mom!
Bessie: So go out and change the world if you don't like it.
Ralph: I will! And why! 'Cause life's different in my head. Gimme
the earth in two hands. I'm strong ... and it's no time to die.'
CLIFFORD ODETS, *Awake And Sing!* (1935)

9 New movements in the 50s and 60s

Albert Camus, Algerian-born novelist, essayist and playwright, whose writing explored the implications of the absurd nature of the human condition, and influenced a generation of French intellectuals and writers.

The mood of the 1950s was very different from that of the 1920s. After the Second World War both Europe and America were entering a period of unprecedented prosperity, which led to increased leisure and a climate of experimentation, which focused more on ideas and philosophies than on new literary forms. This was also the era of the Cold War, and literature from both sides of the Iron Curtain continued to reflect ideological divisions between the two world powers.

Existentialism

The main feature of existentialism in so far as it affected the literature of this period was its emphasis on individual freedom and its rejection of the idea that there is a common humanity – or human nature, in fact – determining a person's character or role in life. Both Sartre and Camus used their fiction to explore notions of the hero as a universal character, 'thrown into the world' and confronting the absurd situation of being in sole charge of his personal destiny, with nothing but his own 'authenticity' to guide him.

For many young people, existentialism was as much a lifestyle as a philosophy. The black polo-neck that was their uniform is worn here by Juliette Greco, the popular singer who became an iconic figure for the movement.

JEAN-PAUL SARTRE (1905–80)

Philosopher, novelist, playwright, literary critic and political activist, Jean-Paul Sartre was the most influential thinker of the second half of this century. His ideas dominated France for more than 30 years, and his death prompted some 25,000 people to throng into the streets of Paris. His autobiography, *Les Mots* (*Words*, 1963) explains how, as an undersized child with a squint, he made few friends and retreated to his mother's sixth-floor apartment – 'on the height where dreams dwell' – to write. He studied philosophy and psychology at the prestigious École Normale Supérieure (where he met his life-long companion, Simone de Beauvoir), then taught between 1929 and 1939, when he was drafted into the war. He was taken prisoner in 1940, but released a year later, when he became active in the Resistance. At this time he was working on his major thesis of existentialism, *L'Être et le néant* (*Being and Nothingness*, 1943). A novel, *La Nausée* (*Nausea*, 1938) had already described

the dread at the heart of his philosophy, following its angst-ridden hero, Roquentin, around Paris as he struggles to separate himself from the inert world of existing 'things' and become a self-determining person.

His three-novel sequence *Les Chemins de la liberté* (*The Roads to Freedom*) – *L'Âge de raison* (*The Age of Reason*, 1945), *Le Sursis* (*The Reprieve*, 1945) and *La Mort dans l'âme* (*Iron in the Soul*, 1949) – was another attempt to fictionalize his ideas by describing the effect of the war on a group of Parisians. 'A writer must attempt to show man where he is,' Sartre said, but the novel proved less satisfactory for this purpose than drama. He wrote seven plays after 1943, of which *Huis clos* (*No Exit*, 1944) is typically pessimistic. A lesbian, a cowardly man and an infanticide girl find themselves trapped in a drawing room in hell. They each love one of the others, but none of their loves is mutual. 'Hell is other people,' is the conclusion they reach.

ALBERT CAMUS (1913–60)

Camus was born in Mondovi, Algeria, and brought up in a working-class district of Algiers with his widowed mother, his grandmother and a paralysed uncle. His first published works were collections of essays (1937 and 1938), which contain lyrical meditations on the beauty of his homeland and contrast the fragile life of humans with the enduring physical world, a theme that was to become central to his fiction. After studying philosophy at the University of Algeria, he worked as a journalist and began work on *L'Étranger* (*The Outsider*), his first novel, which was published in 1942. This work, which describes a man who shoots an Arab and is condemned to death – as much for insisting that it was 'because of the sun' – as for the murder itself, became the cornerstone of 'alienated' fiction. In the same year his enormously influential essay *Le Mythe de Sisyphe* (*The Myth of Sisyphus*) was published.

His second novel, *La Peste* (*The Plague*, 1947), developed his concept of the 'absurd' predicament of man into a philosophy of moral rebellion whereby individual, anti-social, direct action can lead to personal freedom. A collection of short stories followed, continuing his themes of individual estrangement, the problem of evil and the pressing awareness of death. *L'Exil et le royaume* (*Exile and the Kingdom*, 1957), a collection of short stories, assured his position as spokesperson of his generation. He was awarded the Nobel prize in 1957.

The French 'New Novel'

The emergence of the *nouveau roman* in France was a specifically literary reaction to the idea of personal freedom that these writers felt existentialism demanded. It was also an expression of a rather severe philosophy that held that there was no longer any place for individuality in the modern world. 'The novel of characters,' Alain Robbe-Grillet announced, 'belongs entirely in the past. It describes a period that marked the apogee of the individual.' Perhaps we can take the fact that character is still alive and well in the modern novel as an indication that Robbe-Grillet was being unduly pessimistic.

NATHALIE SARRAUTE (b.1902)

Sarraute was born in Russia but went to Europe when she was just two years old, when her parents divorced. She settled in Paris in 1910 and after studying at the Sorbonne went to Oxford University in 1922–23. She practised as a lawyer for 12 years before she began to write. Her first novel, *Portrait d'un inconnu* (*Portrait of a Man Unknown*), was published in 1948 with a preface by Jean-Paul Sartre, in which he gave a name to the genre of literature being produced by French writers who were working at this time. Sarraute, Sartre decided, had written an example of the *nouveau roman* ('new novel') – the 'anti-novel', in fact. Her books – together with those by Claude Simon (b.1913), Alain Robbe-Grillet (see below), Michel Butor (b.1926) and Marguerite Duras (see page 77) – systematically reject the traditional frameworks of fiction: chronology, plot, character and an identifiable authorial voice. Instead of setting out to describe what things are, or appear to be, these writers seek to show what they *feel* like. The reader is presented with events that are unexplained or unfinished or serially repeated in such a way that it is never clear exactly what has occurred at any point.

Sarraute draws her subjects from sensations of people and events and from what she calls the 'writing adventures' to which these sensations give rise. In her first book, *Tropismes* (*Tropisms*, 1939), which was a collection of sketches on bourgeois life, she introduced the idea of 'tropisms', a term used in botany that, crudely translated into literary technique, implies trying to make a book move and grow as imperceptibly as a plant does. The continual emotional movement of a book must be as subtle as the changes in nature are and as lacking in personal motivation as a flower is when it opens. This makes for difficult, intense and slow-moving reading, especially when sentences themselves are interrupted by what Sarraute calls 'sub-conversations', in which images are transformed falteringly into words, which go on to form different unrelated images as the writing moves on. This is 'scientific writing' at its most introverted and abstract, and few readers have the concentration (or desire) to read Sarraute's work as closely as its writing demands.

ALAIN ROBBE-GRILLET (b.1922)

Having trained as a statistician and agronomist, Robbe-Grillet wanted to write novels 'for his time', which would give their attention to 'the ties that exist between objects, gestures and situations, avoiding all psychological and ideological "commentary" on the actions of the characters'. Unlike the fiction of Nathalie Sarraute, Robbe-Grillet's work is jammed with solid objects. These objects are unconnected to mankind but observed with clinical precision, and their function is to underline the simply absurd fact that the world is where we are: we cannot escape it but neither should we expect any emotional nourishment from it.

His first novel, *Les Gommes* (*The Erasers*, 1953), is typically ingenious. A detective called Wallace kills the man (his father), whose murder he has been sent to

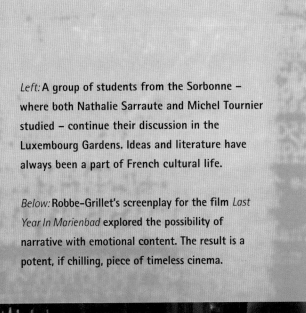

Left: A group of students from the Sorbonne – where both Nathalie Sarraute and Michel Tournier studied – continue their discussion in the Luxembourg Gardens. Ideas and literature have always been a part of French cultural life.

Below: Robbe-Grillet's screenplay for the film *Last Year In Marienbad* explored the possibility of narrative with emotional content. The result is a potent, if chilling, piece of timeless cinema.

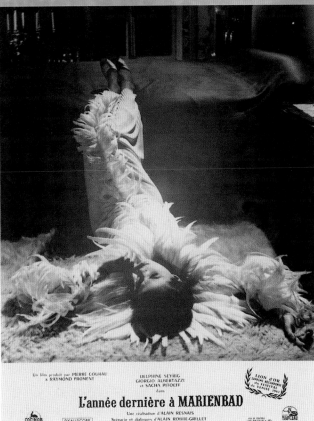

important than its surroundings – indeed it may not be an affair at all.

Robbe-Grillet's screenplays are as well-known and as arid as his novels. *L'Année dernière à Marienbad* (*Last Year at Marienbad*, 1961) was a minor cult in its day. Nothing happens (very beautifully), except that something that one person thinks happened last year in Marienbad happens in exactly the same way again – if it does, in fact, happen, which is never made clear.

MICHEL TOURNIER (b.1924)

Like Nathalie Sarraute, Tournier studied law at the Sorbonne, but an academic career was denied him when he failed the examination that would have allowed him to teach. Between 1949 and 1954 he wrote and produced for French radio and television, but it was while he was chief editor of the publishing firm Plon that his literary reputation was established with the novel *Vendredi, ou les limbes du Pacifique* (*Friday, or the Other Island*, 1967), which won the Grand Prix de Roman that year. The literary audience was by now tired of the abstractions of the *nouveau roman*, so this re-telling of the Robinson Crusoe story, in which Crusoe and Friday reverse roles, and Robinson chooses to stay on his island, rather than return to the brutal civilization of his potential rescuers, achieved immediate popularity.

Three years later *Le Roi des Aulnes* (*The Ogre* or *The Erl King*, 1970) won the prestigious Prix Goncourt. This story blends various mythical tales, but makes the monstrous and naive character of its title a French prisoner in Nazi Germany, who sacrifices his life for a little Jewish boy. In 1980 *The Four Wise Men* moved definitively away from contemporary French fiction, weaving realistic with fantastical elements to rework the Christian legend of the three kings who visit Bethlehem, including a fourth king who exists in Russian mythology. In Tournier's account this king is an inveterate sweet-eater and is distracted from visiting Jesus by an absurd quest for a recipe he yearns for.

At this point Tournier was considered France's leading novelist, but his career has since declined, perhaps because of a tendency his work has to 'know everything before it starts out on its journey', as at least one reviewer has noted.

investigate. 'The book has everything except feeling,' one critic said, and the same might be said of all his work. *Le Voyeur* (*The Voyeur*, 1955) tells of a young girl who is murdered for no reason by a passing stranger. *La Jalousie* (*Jealousy*, 1957) describes a man who spies on his wife and her supposed lover through a shutter, but it is constructed through obsessive repetitive detailing of objects, so that the 'affair' becomes less

The Beats

The 'Beats' were a cluster of young writers who centred in and around Columbia University, New York, in the 1950s. At their core were Allen Ginsberg, Jack Kerouac and William Burroughs, while others – Ken Kesey, Robert Creeley, Lawrence Ferlinghetti, Gary Snyder and Charles Olson – came from further afield. The word 'beat' – as in exhausted – was used by jazz musicians and hustlers, but Ginsberg's set (and it was he who systematically 'promoted' the group) adopted the term for its 'beatific' implications as well. These writers were anti-establishment, but celebratory in their condemnation of traditional America. They sought to liberate literature from academic precocity and bring it 'back to the streets'. Theirs was a literature of immediacy, created through heightened sensory awareness, induced through drugs, jazz, sex or the discipline of Zen Buddhism.

Above: Jack Kerouac, shortly after the publication of *On the Road*. This relaxed portrait gives little hint of the ravaging effects that drink and paranoia were to have on him in later years.

Below left: The Café Bizarre in New York was one of many Beat haunts. Jazz, poetry, conversation, alcohol and drugs flowed freely through the night.

JACK KEROUAC (1922–69)

Kerouac was born in Lowell, Massachusetts, into a French-Canadian immigrant family. He was encouraged to write by Ginsberg and Burroughs, but had reservations about their wild behaviour and criminal associations, as well as being bored by what he called 'their tedious intellectualness'.

A first novel, *The Town and the City* (1950), met with little critical acclaim. Disheartened, he travelled America with fellow-Beat Neal Cassady (whom he described as 'a true brother'), then recorded their vagabond adventures, typing on one continuous roll of paper – like a road itself, he noted – in a three-week writing spree. The resulting novel, *On the Road* (1957), was a long way from its final draft; but after six years of rejections, it was massaged into shape by the editor and critic Malcolm Cowley, and quickly came to represent the Beat generation. It records the physical and spiritual journey of Sal Paradise, Carlo Marx and Dean Moriarty (all trying to out-race their own potential breakdowns) in 'spontaneous prose', based on Kerouac's philosophy, 'first thought, best thought'. With its mixture of tough rebelliousness, poetic sentimentality and violent energy, its appeal to the uneasy young of America was powerful and immediate.

Kerouac published several more autobiographical novels, including *The Dharma Bums* (1958) and *The Subterraneans* (1958), but, unlike Ginsberg, he was not a natural 'personality' and retreated soon after *On the Road* was published to live with his mother in Orlando ('Always go back to my mother. Always,' he wearily wrote to a friend.) Demoralized by harsh criticism from his literary peers – Truman Capote referred to him as a 'glorified typist' – and overwhelmed by the shallow glamour of his popular appeal, he drank more and more and wrote increasingly badly structured, self-indulgent novels, of which *Satori in Paris* (1966) is typical.

ALLEN GINSBERG (1926–97)

Until his death Ginsberg remained the most prominent and revered member of the Beat generation – mentor to numerous counter-culture activists and political agitators, latterly preaching Buddhism and ecology to the Western world.

Born in New Jersey to Russian-Jewish immigrants, Ginsberg attended Columbia University, where he met Burroughs, Kerouac and Neal Cassady (the model for Kerouac's restless iconoclast, Dean Moriarty), and was initiated into petty crime and drugs. Discouraged by his excursions into delinquency, he then dabbled – briefly – with a conservative lifestyle. According to Ginsberg's biographer, Barry Miles, the great appeal of breaking rules for Ginsberg was that an unconventional lifestyle implied 'the acceptance and approval of madness'. This gave him a context in which to come to terms with his mother's illness (she suffered a series of nervous breakdowns) and his confused feelings about his homosexuality. He moved to San Francisco in 1954 and began to express himself freely as a poet, borrowing from Walt Whitman, but experimenting with Kerouac's 'spontaneous prose'. He unofficially inaugurated the

Beat movement with his first book, the prophetic and incantatory *Howl and Other Poems* (1956). An obscenity trial followed, making Ginsberg a national symbol of sexual and political defiance. Thereafter he was frequently arrested for his involvement in anti-war, drug legalization and nuclear disarmament movements. The publication of *Kaddish and Other Poems, 1958–1960* (1961), a long, moving, elegy in memory of his mother, was the culmination of his early work and gave powerful impetus to the movement. His last notable book of prose, *Straighthert's Delight*, was published in 1980.

WILLIAM BURROUGHS (1914–97)

Without Burroughs the late 20th-century novel would be unrecognizable. His experimental techniques in prose, which involved Dada-esque 'cut-ups', collaging his own writing with random chunks of other published work, and a unique and irreverent mixing of myriad literary styles, had a great influence on younger writers.

Born to a Southern bourgeois family, Burroughs later moved to New York City, where he met Ginsberg and Kerouac, whom he impressed with his erudite style and sardonic humour. He took on the role of teacher, encouraging them to write, but did not see himself as primarily a writer. Instead, the search for authentic experience drew him to a criminal existence. He married fellow addict and member of the Columbia group, Joan Vollmer, with whom he had a son. They travelled to Mexico, where drugs were easily available. In Mexico City, Burroughs wrote *Junkie* (1953), the first in a series of novels recounting the perils and ecstasies of addiction. In 1951 he accidentally shot and killed his wife, an action that focused his literary vocation: 'I had no choice but to write my way out,' he explained.

After settling in Tangier, Burroughs enlisted Kerouac to type the manuscript that eventually became *Naked Lunch* (1959), a vivid satire of a drug-centred life, preoccupied with homosexuality and police persecution. Three further novels made up the 'Nova Mob' quartet, dealing with his account of addiction in a post-apocalyptic world: *The Soft Machine* (1961), *The Ticket that Exploded* (1962) and *Nova Express* (1964). Other important works include *Cities of the Red Night* (1980), *Queer* (1984) and *Mind Wars* (1980).

> ❛ Goddam it, feeling is what I like in art, not craftiness and the hiding of feelings. ❜
> JACK KEROUAC

In opposition

In the post-war era a new generation of writers around the globe suffered censorship, incarceration and exile, not only for the political and social criticism their writing expressed but often also for active participation in politics, particularly in support of civil and human rights. In South Africa Alan Paton exposed the racism of apartheid in *Cry, the Beloved Country* (1948). Group 47, which included Heinrich Böll and Günter Grass, forced a complacent Germany to face its Nazi past. The horror of Stalin's *gulags* was finally exposed in Solzhenitsyn's work. In the United States some writers responded to the seeming absurdity of the early decades of the Cold War, while others, such as James Baldwin, were active in the struggle for black civil rights.

ALEXANDER SOLZHENITSYN (b.1918)

Born into a family of Cossack intellectuals, Alexander Solzhenitsyn attended the University of Rostov-on-Don and graduated in mathematics. He fought in the Second Word War but was arrested for writing a letter that criticized Stalin. He was imprisoned for eight years, then exiled for three more. Rehabilitated in 1956, he settled in central Russia, where he became a teacher and began to write.

The early 1960s saw a relaxation of government restraints, as Stalin's policies began to be relaxed. Solzhenitsyn submitted his short novel, *One Day in the Life of Ivan Denisovich* (1962), a harrowing account of life in a labour camp. Its simple prose, vivid dialogue and uncompromising frankness brought him instant recognition, creating a political furore in the Soviet Union and abroad.

After Khrushchev's fall from power in 1964, Solzhenitsyn met with increasing criticism and suffered overt harassment when he openly opposed repressive government policies. The two novels he wrote in the late 1960s, *Cancer Ward (1968)* and *The First Circle* (1969), were published abroad to great acclaim. In his own country, however, they were banned and found a readership only as *samizdat* literature, printed in secret and circulated illegally. Both these semi-autobiographical novels are in the tradition of 19th-century critical realism. *The First Circle* recounts his experiences in the Soviet prison system; *Cancer Ward* is based on the time he spent in hospital as a cancer patient. Although they can be read simply at a realistic level, the symbolism of the books by which the plight of individuals comes to stand for the condition of an entire nation gives them a profound resonance.

In 1970 he won the Nobel prize for literature. Following the Paris publication in 1973 of the beginning of his epic work, *The Gulag Archipelago*, which effectively documented a system that destroyed millions of lives, Solzhenitsyn was arrested and tried for treason. He was exiled, and lived in Switzerland and, later, the United States. The late 1980s brought renewed access to his work, and his citizenship was restored in 1990. He returned to Russia in 1994.

GÜNTER GRASS (b.1927)

From the publication of his extraordinary first novel *Die Blechtrommel* (*The Tin Drum*) in 1965, Grass has been the literary spokesman for a generation that came

Above: **One of the most significant forces in post-war German fiction, Günter Grass has been concerned to chart the repercussions of his country's traumatic past.**

Left: **A poster for the film** *One Day in the Life of Ivan Denisovich,* **Solzhenitsyn's gruelling short novel about life in one of Stalin's labour camps.**

Katz und Maus (*Cat and Mouse*, 1961) and *Hundejahre* (*Dog Years*, 1963) complete the Danzig trilogy, which *The Tin Drum* began.

Grass is a linguistically exuberant, highly inventive writer, with a style sometimes described as baroque. Although he insists that the artist should be serious in life, he is equally insistent that art should be playful. His work is always relaxed and humorous but at the same time deeply committed.

HEINRICH BÖLL (1917–1985)

A Christian and a pacifist, Heinrich Böll wrote ironic novels of German life during and after the Second World War that are all to some extent reflections on the necessity of personal responsibility in the forging of a national morality. But the starting point of his books is practical – using a human situation to explore what people actually feel and what they can feasibly do. He served for six years in the German army, and his first stories – *Der Zug War Pünktlich* (*The Train was on Time*, 1949) and *Wo Warst Du, Adam?* (*And Where Were You, Adam?* 1951) – centre on the grimness and despair of soldiers' lives and on his own experience of suffering 'the frightful fate of being a soldier and having to wish that the war might be lost'. His first novel, *Das Brot der Frühen Jahre* (*The Bread of our Early Years*, 1957), dwelt on the uneasy reality experienced by a mechanic.

In 1959 came his most complex work, *Billard um Halb Zehn* (*Billiards at Half Past Nine*), which uses flashback and interior monologue to follow a family of architects through a single day. In its compassionate understanding of the concerns that both divide and connect two generations, it becomes more than an examination of a particular family, and is ultimately a rich and wryly affectionate comment on Germany itself.

Böll's work – which includes stories, novels, plays and essays – has been translated into at least 17 languages. He was awarded the Nobel prize in 1972.

of age in the Nazi era, and in 1999 he became the first German to be awarded the Nobel prize since his fellow Group 47 member, Heinrich Böll in 1972. He worked as a ghost speech-writer for Willy Brandt, German Chancellor between 1969 and 1974.

The Tin Drum tells of a boy who resolves not to grow up as a protest against the cruelty of German history and who refuses to communicate except by banging his drum. It is a richly textured, historically exact examination of the period 1925–55, narrated by a dwarf, whose fantastical voice perfectly counterparts Grass's historical accuracy to create a fictionalized account of both his personal childhood in the Polish-German town of Danzig and the effect of Nazification on ordinary people. In this, as in all of his subsequent novels, Grass challenged the complacency of post-war Germany. The moral fervour that underlined his anarchic fantasy earned him the role of 'conscience of his generation'.

'For a country to have a great writer ... is like having another government. That's why no regime has ever loved great writers, only minor ones.'

ALEXANDER SOLZHENITSYN

Cult fiction

In the 1950s and 1960s young people were influenced and excited by a handful of books that are now widely available but at the time were ignored by the large publishing companies. Each of these books in some way imagines an escape from a society seen as conformist and stultifying – whether through drugs, sexual experimentation, individual rebellion or alternative ways of living.

One of the first fictional heroes to attract a cult following in the 1950s was J.P. Donleavy's irresponsible Sebastian Dangerfield, the protagonist of *The Ginger Man* (1955). Donleavy (b.1926) was an American who became an Irish citizen and wrote the book after studying at Trinity College, Dublin. Dangerfield, too, is ostensibly a student at Trinity, but he is wholly given over to the pursuit of pleasure, particularly sexual pleasure. The book's success owed much to the bawdy comedy Donleavy extracts from his hero's generally unscrupulous adventures, as he lies, drinks, sponges and seduces his way through Dublin.

Ken Kesey's intention in *One Flew Over the Cuckoo's Nest* (1962) was more subversive. He uses the repressive politics of a Californian mental hospital to express his opposition to mainstream society. Its hero, Randle McMurphy, is incarcerated in a psychiatric ward, not for insanity but because of his anarchic behaviour. By the end of the book, the system has reduced Randle from a state of feisty defiance to one of complete helplessness. The novel's cult status was reinforced when it was made into a film in 1975. Kesey's quest for an alternative lifestyle (assisted by drugs) is described in Tom Wolfe's *The Electric Kool-Aid Acid Test* (1968), which follows Kesey and his Merry Pranksters on a trip around America in a bus painted with Day-Glo colours.

In *Fear and Loathing in Las Vegas* (1971), Hunter Thompson (b.1937) takes just as critical a stance as Kesey – the book has the ironic subtitle *A Savage Journey to the Heart of the American Dream*. Most readers are more struck by its hilarious account of the hallucinations that ensue when the two main characters indulge their insatiable appetite for illegal drugs. Journalist Rowell Duke and his 200 pound Samoan lawyer travel to Las Vegas to cover a motorbike race in the desert. Reality becomes increasingly bizarre as their quest for the ultimate high eventually makes them too paranoid to leave their hotel room.

The hippie influence

Richard Brautigan (1935–84) represented the gentler side of the 1960s sub-culture in America. His is a West Coast world of hippie communes and the retreat to a dream of rural innocence. His novel *Trout Fishing in America* (1967) takes us through parks and forests on a search for the perfect fishing spot. *In Watermelon Sugar* (1968) tells of an idyllic commune where sensuality is unrestrained and the highest fulfilment is through personal relationships. Brautigan writes beautifully crafted prose and poetry, which is often whimsical – 'By now I was so relaxed you could have rented me out as a field of daisies.' – but it is never cloying. Typical of his philosophy is his remark that 'it is never too late to have a happy childhood'.

The cult popularity of the German-born American Charles Bukowski (1920–94) rests more on his fictional

persona and his depiction of urban low-life than on any single book. His writing began to be noticed in the mid-1950s when magazines published his combative and deliberately unworked poetry. He was vaguely connected to the Beat movement but was too individualistic to ally himself with any specific group. Among his most admired works are the novel *The Days Run Away Like Wild Horses Over the Hills* (1969), followed by *Post Office* (1971) and *Ham on Rye* (1982). Bukowski's fiction is mainly based on himself: his troubles with women, his gambling, his drinking and the brutality of a down-and-out existence in Los Angeles. His easy, conversational style and affectionate humour have grown on the reading public to such an extent that by the time of his death in 1994 he was the most widely read contemporary American author.

In John Fowles's *Magus* (1966) a young man takes a teaching post on a Greek island and becomes involved with a mysterious Greek millionaire (the magus of the title) and his circle. The book has the same kind of appeal as Hermann Hesse's *Steppenwolf*, another cult novel in the 1960s although written more than 30 years earlier. Fowles's book suggests the possibility of a secret, more magical world that coexists with mundane reality but is open only to the chosen few. Fowles's later fiction had a wider readership, particularly his semi-historical novel *The French Lieutenant's Woman* (1969).

Above: Jack Nicholson's portrayal of Ken Kesey's subversive hero Randle McMurphy helped to make *One Flew Over the Cuckoo's Nest* a cult classic.

Significant others

Other books in this category include *Last Exit to Brooklyn* (1964) by Hugh Selby Jr, which was prosecuted for obscenity in Britain, although Selby's writing is perhaps too grimly realistic to inspire any substantial following. The book is a collection of short stories about homosexuals and transvestites in Brooklyn. *A Confederacy of Dunces* (1980) was written by John Kennedy Toole (1937–69) in the early 1960s and would undoubtedly have been the cult success it became later if the author had found a publisher. Its hero, Ignatius J. Reilly, is an obese eccentric, living in New Orleans, who single-handedly wages war on all aspects of the modern world. The title comes from Jonathan Swift who said: 'When a true genius appears in the world ... the dunces are all in confederacy against him.' Toole committed suicide in 1969, partly out of desperation at the lack of interest in the book.

chapter 10

Post-war fiction

International fiction in any historical period will always be as varied and various as the people who write it. In so far as there is anything general to observe about post-war trends, it is that writing returned to its long-established narrative roots. The fervour of experimentation that had produced the masterpieces of modernism subsided, and writers were once more absorbed with people as social beings rather than with probing individual consciousness.

Below: Vanessa Redgrave as the strong-willed café proprietor, destroyed by her passion for a manipulative hunchback who transforms the town she runs, in the film version of Carson McCullers' *Ballad of the Sad Café*.

Right: The young Truman Capote in his New York apartment. Capote's early fame gave him a taste for the pleasures of high society that in the end proved fatal to his career as a serious writer.

Fact-based fiction

NORMAN MAILER (b.1923)

Norman Kingsley Mailer is known as much for his public persona as for his substantial achievements as a writer. He has been married five times, has stood for mayor of New York, has engaged in public brawls and stabbed his wife at a party while in a semi-psychotic state. On top of this, he has consistently presented himself at centre-stage in his non-fiction works, even giving a collection of essays and short stories the apparently grandiose title *Advertisments for Myself* (1959). These and other acts have contributed to a reputation for egotism and boastfulness that has blinded many critics to his true value. It would be fairer to say that Mailer's self-dramatizations are integral to his writing: they have acted as a spur to his creative energies, often with startling results.

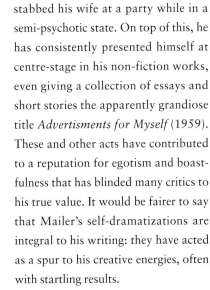

His best works are 'factions', in which the author relates actual events using the techniques of fiction. *Armies of the Night: the Novel as History, History as a Novel* (1968) is a first-person account of a march on the Pentagon against the Vietnam War. Among many passages of astonishing virtuosity, the description of his encounters with the poet Robert Lowell (see page 150) stands out. He succeeds in portraying himself and Lowell with an imaginative richness and complexity that has rarely been matched – in and out of fiction. *The Executioner's Song: a True Life Novel* (1979) is another work pitched between fact and fiction in which Mailer reconstructs the life of the murderer Gary Gilmore.

Mailer's novels are more uneven in their quality and have had a mixed reception. His first, *The Naked and the Dead* (1948), considered one of the finest novels to come out of the Second World War, made him an overnight celebrity. The books that followed took a very different turn. Two of the most notable are *An American Dream* (1965), about a man who murders his wife and afterwards feels 'touched by magic', and *Ancient Evenings* (1983), set in the Egypt of the pharaohs. The latter has been praised as 'a marvelous anatomy of humbuggery and bumbuggery' and as 'one of the great works of contemporary mythopoesis', but it is more commonly dismissed as a bad novel. Similarly, after the publication of the 'existential murder mystery' *Tough Guys Don't Dance* (1984), one reviewer said he wrote 'like an angel, fallen but flaming', while another castigated his 'pulp style'. Mailer's preoccupations are distinct and not to everyone's taste.

TRUMAN CAPOTE (1924–84)

Truman Capote claimed to have invented what he called the 'documentary novel' when he wrote *In Cold Blood* (1966). The book relates the slaughter of a respectable farming family in Kansas by two roaming psychopaths. Capote did intensive research on the story and grew close to the two murderers before their executions. Dismissed by some as superior journalism, it is nevertheless both chilling and fascinating. Like Mailer, Capote deploys his skills as a novelist to give the account an authenticity lacking in even the best journalism.

This was in sharp contrast to his early novels, which were dreamlike in their Gothic intensity. *The Grass Harp* (1951) is about an 11-year-old orphan, driven by the world to live in a tree-house where he creates his personal community. In *Breakfast at Tiffany's* (1958) Capote turned to New York with the light-hearted tale of a high-class call-girl. A film (1961) of the book was made, with Audrey Hepburn as Holly Golightly.

Capote became increasingly drawn to the world of the rich and famous, turning himself into a kind of court jester to New York high society, and effectively gave up writing serious fiction after *In Cold Blood*.

> 'Ultimately a hero is a man who would argue with the gods, and awakens devils to contest his vision.'
> NORMAN MAILER, *The Presidential Papers* (1963)

Jewish-American writing

Jewish writers were a particularly invigorating force in post-war American literature, although not all of them fall neatly into a specifically 'Jewish-American' category: Salinger, Heller and Mailer are notable exceptions. Bellow, Malamud and Roth, however, make the experience and spirit of contemporary Jewish life central to their work.

SAUL BELLOW (b.1915)

The award of the Nobel prize to Saul Bellow in 1976 confirmed his status as the foremost living American writer. Outstanding for his range, the richness of his language and the depth of his concerns, Bellow has been described as the most intellectual of American novelists. In many ways, however, his books are anti-intellectual. His heroes are often Jewish intellectuals – academics of one kind or another – but their high cultural references usually serve as a background to their personal issues. Bellow's characters typically suffer from a surfeit of feeling, referring wistfully to the giants of European thought and modernism as someone else might discuss sporting heroes or as an expression of their search for a sage-like figure who will offer a solution to their private turmoil.

In one of his finest novels, *Herzog* (1964), the protagonist is a neurotic, middle-aged professor who has been driven to the brink of a nervous breakdown by his wife's adultery. He writes a stream of unsent letters to famous people in a comic and moving attempt to understand his unhappiness and to try to explain, as he puts it: 'The story of my life – how I rose from humble beginnings to complete disaster.'

One of Bellow's great strengths is his style. It is an odd blend of elegance and colloquialism – what a critic has called 'a mingling of high-flown intellectual bravado with racy-tough street Jewishness'. Even at their most agitated, the heroes of his novels are exhilaratingly vivid, vigorous and witty in their endless conversations with themselves and others. In *Humboldt's Gift* (1975) a playwright and academic reminisces about his friend Von Humboldt Fleischer, a brilliant but unfulfilled and anguished poet who died in poverty. Like *Herzog*, the novel is both comic and serious, displaying a remarkable sympathy and insight into the psychology of its characters.

The style adopted in *Herzog* and *Humboldt's Gift* is the most successful of Bellow's range of different fictional modes. An earlier novel, *The Adventures of Augie March* (1953), has a euphoric, boisterous tone, which seems less natural to the author (although the book is one of which many other writers could be proud). It is a rambling, picaresque story that follows the progress of a Chicago Jew from childhood to maturity as a black-marketeer.

All Bellow's works have a larger dimension, a subtle cultural analysis concerned with the decline of the self in

Above: Alan Bates and Dirk Bogarde in the film of Bernard Malamud's *The Fixer*, a harrowing study of anti-Semitism in pre-Revolutionary Russia.

Left: Saul Bellow showing in his person the blend of elegance, flair and pessimistic scepticism that characterizes much of his writing.

modern urban society, in which, he says, 'the individual struggles with dehumanization for the possession of his soul'. More recent novels, such as *The Dean's December* (1982) and *More Die of Heartbreak* (1987), reflect Bellow's increased pessimism about contemporary Western civilization.

BERNARD MALAMUD (1914–86)

Like Saul Bellow, the novelist and short-story writer Bernard Malamud was the son of Russian-Jewish immigrants. He was born in Brooklyn, the setting for many of his finest stories. His first novel, *The Natural* (1952), is a comic masterpiece, which both celebrates and parodies the idea of a baseball player as the American hero. It was followed by a more serious work, *The Assistant* (1957), in which he deals directly with the experience of Jewish immigrants and the tensions between them and other New York ethnic groups. It is the story of a small-time, gentile crook who robs a poor Jewish shopkeeper, then out of pity goes to work for him. In the end, he marries the shopkeeper's daughter and when her father dies takes over the store. 'Every man is a Jew though he may not know it,' the author remarked, and the novel's wider theme is the idea of goodness and redemption. His best known novel, *The Fixer* (1966), set in tsarist Russia, describes the ordeal of Yakov Blok, an innocent Jewish workman accused of the ritual murder of a Christian child.

Malamud was also greatly esteemed for his short stories. Some of these belong to the world of *The Assistant*, charting the lives of characters, such as Jewish peddlers, charlatan rabbis, frozen-food salesmen and assistant bookkeepers, in a manner devoid of sentimentality and wholly convincing. Others, such as 'The Magic Barrel' and 'The Jew Bird', take the form of sparkling Jewish fables.

PHILIP ROTH (b.1933)

The son of second-generation American Jews, Philip Roth focused on the painful concerns of sexuality and family love in Jewish middle-class society in his early work. His first published work, *Goodbye Columbus* (1959), a novella and five stories, brought instant fame for its clear-eyed portrayal of a young man under pressure from his utterly materialistic family. It was followed by the novels *Letting Go* (1962), *When She Was Good* (1967) and *Portnoy's Complaint* (1969), which made him a great commercial success while outraging the Jewish community, which felt it traded unfairly on comic stereotypes of Jewishness. The book is an extremely funny account of a Jewish boy's attempt to escape the influence of his domineering mother. His 'complaint' is an excessive indulgence in masturbation.

In subsequent novels, Roth has turned to the situation of the artist in contemporary America, his principal themes being the debilitating effects of fame, and the guilt attendant on artistic self-expression. The Zuckerman trilogy – *The Ghost Writer* (1979), *Zuckerman Unbound* (1981) and *The Anatomy Lesson* (1983) – is about a Jewish-American author, Nathaniel Zuckerman, who writes a scandalous bestseller. Here Roth plays with various different narrative modes, the purpose of which is partly to keep the reader guessing how much his fictional novelist has in common with the real author.

Into the 1960s

Post-war fiction in America found many new voices to challenge the cultural changes of its time. This was a period of growing material prosperity, increasing aspirations and, more specifically, a relaxation in attitudes towards sex. Nabokov uses a sexual obsession to expose the hollowness of consumerism, whereas Updike celebrates infidelity to mourn the spiritual void of the American dream. Even Joseph Heller's renowned novel *Catch-22* is as much a satire on contemporary society as it is a critique of patriotism and war.

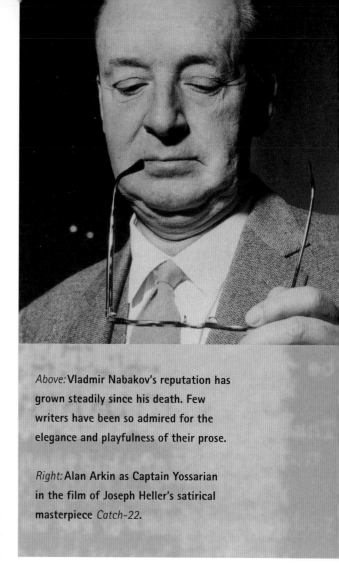

Above: Vladmir Nabakov's reputation has grown steadily since his death. Few writers have been so admired for the elegance and playfulness of their prose.

Right: Alan Arkin as Captain Yossarian in the film of Joseph Heller's satirical masterpiece *Catch-22*.

VLADMIR NABOKOV (1899–1977)

The author of the ground-breaking *Lolita* (1955) was born into an old aristocratic Russian family. He was educated at Trinity College, Cambridge, and lived in Germany, France and America, before retiring to live in a Swiss hotel. His first novel, the explicitly autobiographical *Mashenka* (*Mary*, 1926), described his family estate and first love, both of which recur in his elegant autobiography, *Speak, Memory* (1967).

His early novels sold badly, and Nabokov lived by teaching until the tremendous success of *Lolita*, which shares many of the artistic concerns of his earlier work but had the sensationalist appeal of the 'nymphet', Lolita, at its centre. The book is narrated by Humbert Humbert, who develops an obsessive passion for the 12-year-old daughter of his widowed landlady, Charlotte Haze. He marries the mother to be near the daughter and finds himself single again when Charlotte is killed by a car. Humbert's own car then becomes the intimate backdrop to his illicit relationship with Lolita, whom he drives all over America in an effort to keep her distracted from his sexual impositions.

The idea of examining love through the twisted filter of perverse lust outraged the reading public, but Nabokov's primary aim was to analyse suburban American culture. The novel is written with the linguistic virtuosity and playfulness for which Nabokov is supremely admired.

JOHN UPDIKE (b.1932)

After completing his education at Harvard, John Hoyer Updike worked for *The New Yorker* and, like many of his fellow writers there, made white American suburban life the subject of his fiction. His first major success was *Bech: A Book* in 1970, to which he characteristically wrote a sequel ten years later. Bech (a writer who can do everything well except write) is a typically intelligent, sensitive, articulate but anxious Updike hero.

With *On the Farm* (1965) Updike took firm control of the material that would go on to provide his staple ever since: the family, romance, unhappy marriage and mild domestic strife. Adult sexual partnerships preoccupy him and come under enormous strain in his work, since he sees erotic fulfilment as a necessary substitute for religious experience in the contemporary Western world.

Couples (1968) is a perfect exposition of Updike's standpoint, being an anatomy of both a marriage and the religious crisis endured by its womanizing hero, Piet Hannema. This, with the Rabbit tetralogy – *Rabbit Run* (1960), *Rabbit Redux* (1971), *Rabbit is Rich* (1981) and *Rabbit at Rest* (1990) – is his most significant work of long fiction. His many short stories share the same concerns and have the same easy, reassuring, conversational tone. What attracts readers to Updike is his ability to invest domestic detail with a particular poetry, an almost elegiac affection.

CARSON MCCULLERS (1917–67)

A series of paralytic strokes left Carson McCullers confined to a wheelchair from the age of 30. This experience may have intensified her tendency to focus on the physically infirm or grotesque to illuminate the impact of

abnormality on individuals or the community in which they live. *The Heart is a Lonely Hunter* (1940) is structured around a deaf-mute, whose lonely existence in a run-down hotel is exacerbated when he is deprived of his closest friend by other guests who dislike their mutual need.

In the title story of the collection entitled *The Ballad of the Sad Café* (1951) a village is disrupted when a hunchback arrives one night and ingratiates himself with the richest woman there. McCullers's depiction of the emotional isolation of enforced outcasts is moving but never sentimental. Her best full-length work is *The Member of the Wedding* (1946), in which a young girl is desperate to join her older brother's life with his bride. 'They will be the we of me,' she says.

J.D. SALINGER (b.1919)

The novelist and short-story writer Jerome David Salinger is best known for his only novel, *The Catcher in the Rye* (1951). This story of Holden Caulfield's expulsion from an expensive private school and subsequent wanderings in New York has become a modern classic. What endears Holden to generations of readers is Salinger's perfect rendering of his particular voice – wise-cracking, bewildered, knowing but naive, affectionate yet disenchanted. Holden finds everything 'phoney', except a nun he meets in a café and his sister, Phoebe, who is the only person he feels close to. He gets drunk, meets a girl for a date, talks in all-night cafés, reflects on his schoolfriends and life in general. At the close of the book he is in a psychiatric hospital.

Salinger's later fiction – which includes *Franny and Zooey* (1961) and *Raise High the Roofbeam, Carpenter* (1963) – tended toward the sentimental and cute. He has published nothing since 1963 and now lives in complete seclusion.

JOSEPH HELLER (1923–99)

As a young bombardier in the US air force, Joseph Heller served in the Mediterranean in the Second World War, and he used the experience to create one of the greatest comic and satirical novels of post-war American fiction, *Catch-22* (1961). It is set in an American air base on an imaginary Mediterranean island, Pinosa, during the Italian campaign of 1943–44. Captain John Yossarian, the book's hero, and his fellow aviators are victimized by superior officers, who are either fools or rascals. Determined to fly no more missions, Yossarian pretends to be insane. The 'catch' of the title refers to the twisted bureaucratic logic that thwarts him: if he really is mad he can be grounded, but if he asks to be grounded he cannot be mad.

Heller's later fiction never matched the brilliantly quirky humour, satirical bite and characterization of this first book. *Something Happened* (1974) is noteworthy as a rare instance of a novel dealing with a subject more familiar to readers than to authors – office politics in a large corporation.

> I was damn near bawling, I felt so damn happy if you want to know the truth. I don't know why. It was just that she looked so damn nice ... God I wish you could've been there.
>
> J.D. SALINGER, *The Catcher in the Rye* (1951)

The short story in America

The United States has provided fertile ground for the short story, largely because of the plethora of magazines that provide an outlet for them. Of these, *The New Yorker* in particular has a distinguished history of publishing the early works of many of the USA's leading writers. While the form of the short story is no longer restricted by the need for a conclusion with a 'twist' in the tail, its traditional virtues of telling dialogue and depiction of character and atmosphere are clearly apparent in work as different as John Cheever's stories of wealthy suburbanites and Raymond Carver's observations of life on the fringes of society.

JOHN CHEEVER (1912–82)

John Cheever's first published story, which was based on his expulsion from the Thayer Academy in Massachusetts, was written when he was 17 years old. In 1979, 60 stories later, he wrote of his collected work: 'Here is the last of that generation of chain smokers who woke the world in the morning with their coughing, who used to get stoned at cocktail parties and perform obsolete dance steps ... sail for Europe on ships, who were truly nostalgic for love and happiness.'

His work is shot through with a tremendous sense of the passing of traditional morality and a longing for an emotional and social coherence that is everywhere on the brink of disintegration. He worked from what he called 'the interrupted event', and the events his prose disrupts are those of middle-class American suburbanites. Self-satisfied couples throng his world – dancing in country clubs, basking on manicured lawns or drinking highballs anywhere they can, unaware of the desolation lurking beneath the surface of their interminable socializing, which Cheever's narrators make painfully plain, often despite themselves. 'I always have the feeling that if I look at the cove it will reveal something to me,' the man on the verge of breakdown in 'A Vision of the World' confides. But nothing is revealed in Cheever except an increasingly haywire sense of emptiness. His prose has been described as 'lapidary in precision'. It is also sensuous and extremely visual, with a languorous elegance to it that intensifies the slow collapse of the society he describes.

FLANNERY O'CONNOR (1925–64)

Born in Savannah, Georgia, Flannery O'Connor spent most of her life in the South, living with her mother, raising peacocks and pheasants for pleasure and writing strange, intense tales of small-town or rural Southern eccentrics as she battled with the inherited disease, lupus, that eventually claimed her life. Her voice and sensibility are startlingly her own, although rooted in the tradition of 'Southern Gothic', associated with, among others, Carson McCullers, whose 'grotesque' characters are less bizarrely funny than O'Connor's and whose vision is less God-obsessed. When a New York publisher criticized a 'sense of aloneness' in her first novel, the remarkable *Wise Blood* (1952), she wrote back that her value as a writer came 'precisely from the

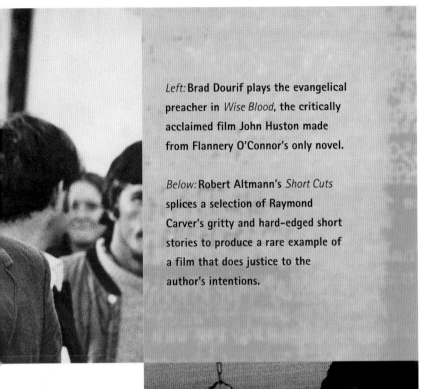

Left: Brad Dourif plays the evangelical preacher in *Wise Blood,* the critically acclaimed film John Huston made from Flannery O'Connor's only novel.

Below: Robert Altmann's *Short Cuts* splices a selection of Raymond Carver's gritty and hard-edged short stories to produce a rare example of a film that does justice to the author's intentions.

his books. Her sensibility is robustly shrewd, understanding the nastiness of her fellows, but also deeply compassionate about their emotional helplessness. She writes stark, intense and vivid prose, which has, as Elizabeth Bishop observed, 'more real poetry than a dozen book of poems' in any one of her tremendously compelling stories.

RAYMOND CARVER (1938–88)

The son of a sawmill worker, Raymond Carver married almost as soon as he had finished high school, and he supported his wife (the writer Tess Gallagher) and two children by working as an attendant at a gas station, as a janitor and as a delivery boy. In 1958 he took a creative writing course and started writing short stories in his own distinctive 'dirty-realist' style. Like John Cheever, he is concerned to describe a society in moral and emotional jeopardy, but Carver's characters seem to begin their stories at the point where Cheever leaves his: going crazy.

His first success came with the collection *Will You Please be Quiet, Please?* (1976), whose title anticipates the restless desperation of its stories' narrators, who are inevitably near breaking-point in their search for a peace of mind that always eludes them. In this and subsequent collections, Carver's people are the working poor of the Pacific Northwest, who are crushed by broken marriages, financial problems and failed careers but who are unable to articulate or even wholly notice the depths of their anguish. They are observed in a sparse, hard-edged prose, which plays consistently on the tensions between authorial control and the randomness of the events in the lives he describes.

In spite of critical and popular success, Carver developed a drink problem and spent the 1970s battling with alcoholism, which he overcame by the time *What We Talk About When We Talk About Love* was published in 1981. A literary award in 1983 allowed him to concentrate on his writing full time, and he produced two more collections – *Cathedral* (1984) and *Fires: Essays, Stories, Poems* (1983) – before dying of lung cancer at the age of only 50.

peculiarity or aloneness of the experience I write from'.

She was a Catholic who was desperately unhappy about the contemporary Church, and her stories have at their centre a violent sense of the spiritual deprivation of the world she observed. In 'Good Country People', for example, a man selling bibles from a suitcase makes off with the wooden leg of a girl who has just bought one of

African-American writing

Race is fundamental to the American experience, yet as a fictional theme it had been approached almost exclusively by white writers. In the 1920s the members of the 'Harlem renaissance' had found new and vigorous forms of expression in poetry and drama, but after the Second World War a new generation of African-American writers found its voice in novels that demanded attention, both for their power and for their subtle command of the fictional form.

RICHARD WRIGHT (1908–60)

The first major black American writer to emerge in the 20th century, Richard Nathaniel Wright remains one of the most influential, as much for his vehement non-fiction as for his compelling, often nihilistic fiction. His grandparents were slaves, and his father disappeared when he was five years old, leaving him to be brought up by a repressive evangelical mother. His first book, *Uncle Tom's Children* (1938), staked out the violent territory of racial injustice that his future career would relentlessly highlight. This collection of stories, all but one of which ends with the death of the central character, is based on the previously unformulated question of how a black man can live in a country that denies his humanity.

A bestselling novel, *Native Son*, followed in 1940. Bigger Thomas, its hero, is a black man who reluctantly becomes involved with the Communist Party through his white employer's daughter. He inadvertently kills this woman, then his own girlfriend as he flees the crime. He is captured, tried and executed, having rejected communism and Christianity and taken on the whole of Chicago in his remorseless self-assertion. His triumph is, in fact, to celebrate his murderous self: he has no choice, Wright implies, but to be what society made him. The book was filmed in Argentina in 1950, with Wright playing Bigger.

In 1946 Wright moved to Paris, where he wrote his second sensational novel, *The Outsider* (1953). His autobiography *Black Boy* (1945) is a dazzling critique of racism in America, which is also the subject of his collections of potent essays, of which *Black Power* (1954), *The Color Curtain* (1956) and *White Man, Listen!* (1957) are among the best.

RALPH ELLISON (1914–94)

'The remarkable mythologizing author of ... the great American Negro novel', as Ralph Waldo Ellison's obituary read, was born in Oklahoma City and studied music in Alabama before arriving in New York, where he remained as interested in jazz as in literature. He met the poet and Negro cultural leader Langston Hughes (1902–67) and Richard Wright (see above) who encouraged him to write, which he did after a stint in the merchant marine.

Invisible Man (1952) is the one novel Ellison finished. Hailed as 'the first Negro novel to transcend its genre', it led Philip Larkin inadvertently to insult Ellison by describing him as 'a writer who happens to be an American Negro'.

Invisible Man is narrated by a nameless man, who is 'invisible' because (as he is black) no one sees him. But the novel goes far beyond this schematic explanation to describe a whole world through the eyes of one man. 'All life seen from the hole of invisibility is absurd,' we are warned. The novel moves its hero from a Southern college (from which he is expelled), through the black liberal 'Brotherhood' in New York (which exploits and disillusions him while he is holed-up in a Harlem basement), to his job in a paint factory and on to a final, chaotic race riot. The writing is blisteringly vivid, surreal and stubbornly moving. 'Why should I be the one to dream this nightmare?' the narrator asks. 'Why do I write, torturing myself to put it down?' Critics have drawn comparisons with Kafka and with Joyce, and certainly Ellison's vision is equal to theirs in its breadth and universality. 'There's a possibility that even an invisible man has a socially responsible role to play,' the close of the novel points out. 'Who knows but that ... I speak for you?'

Above: Freedom Riders outside their bus, which had been attacked by whites in 1961. Civil rights issues dominated African-American writers throughout the 60s.

Left: James Baldwin's novels about the twin predicaments of being black and homosexual in 50s America were a significant force in changing race attitudes.

JAMES BALDWIN (1924–87)

James Baldwin was born in Harlem, New York. 'My mother was given to the exasperating and mysterious habit of having babies,' he explains in some autobiographical notes. 'I took them over with one hand and held a book in the other.' He was plotting novels from the time he started to read but took almost ten years to complete his first, *Go Tell It on the Mountain* (1953). This draws on his experience of being a preacher between the ages of 14 and 17, as does his first play, *The Amen Corner*, written two years later, but not performed until 1965.

Baldwin was a homosexual, and he wrote movingly of the pull between hetero- and homosexual love in his second work, which was written in Paris, where he settled to write and work in 1948. *Giovanni's Room* (1956) is a desperately tender novel, which describes a man torn between his feelings for his fiancée, Marie, and his love for the stunning but vulnerable Giovanni.

Baldwin explores his notion that for a black man a male/female relationship intensifies the hate between black and white, whereas a homosexual bond soothes racial tensions.

Sexual and racial issues are paired again in his last major work, *Another Country* (1962), a searingly lyrical account of lost love, and youth.

In addition to fiction, Baldwin wrote at length on racial politics. *The New Yorker* gave itself over to an article of his on the civil rights struggle in November 1963, which later became a bestseller in book form as *The Fire Next Time* (1963). His analyses of the ills of his 'morally bankrupt and desperately dishonest countrymen' are self-effacing, cool and extremely potent. 'The American Negro really is part of this country, and on the day we face this fact ... we will become a nation,' he wrote. With typical wryness, he noted: 'I do not like people who are earnest about anything. I don't like people who like me because I'm a Negro.'

Englishmen abroad

While the outstanding post-war British novelists form a group disparate in social background and intellectual interests, their novels do show some thematic similarities. The exotic – often the colonial or post-colonial – regularly forms the backdrop to action where a drama of mythic or existential significance is played out. Sometimes, as in the case of Burgess and Greene, this drama can have a darkly comic aspect. With writers such as Lowry and Golding the examination of the human condition presents us with a bleaker view of man and his prospects.

MALCOM LOWRY (1909–57)

Malcom Lowry started work on his great novel *Under the Volcano* in 1937. When it was published ten years later, it went largely unnoticed by the public, and it was only after Lowry's death that the book was widely recognized as one of the most powerful novels of its time.

Under the Volcano is set in a small Mexican town on the Day of the Dead, the last day in the life of Geoffrey Firmin, British ex-consul and helpless alcoholic. His ex-wife and half-brother arrive but are powerless to prevent his self-destructive drinking. Firmin yearns for a return to a pure and innocent life yet feels himself fatally committed to death. The Spanish epigraph to the book draws a parallel between this doomed life and the myth of the Fall of Man: 'Do you like this garden which is yours? We evict those who destroy it.'

With enormous skill, Lowry interweaves Firmin's alcoholic musings and memories with the events of the day. His narrative technique draws on Joyce and Faulkner and is also distinctly cinematic in its splicing together of past and present. The Mexican landscape and the volcano of the title loom throughout, becoming intensely menacing as the day passes.

Between leaving school and attending Cambridge University, Lowry went to sea, working as a deck-hand for a year and a half, and he based his first novel, *Ultramarine* (1933), on these experiences. After a wandering and drink-ridden existence in Paris, New York and Mexico, he settled in Canada, where he lived in a squatter's shack near Vancouver. He died in England.

WILLIAM GOLDING (1911–93)

'Man produces evil as a bee produces honey,' wrote William Golding. His first, most famous novel, *Lord of the Flies* (1954), which was written when he was 40 years old after a career as a schoolteacher, works through the implications of this belief with the story of a group of schoolboys stranded on a Pacific island. Their attempts to organize themselves as civilized beings gradually collapse, and they revert to a savagery that culminates in the sacrificial killing of one of the boys.

Golding's novels are primarily allegorical and are concerned with fundamental questions of good and evil, with the possibility of spiritual redemption in a godless age. The subject of *Pincher Martin* (1956) is the guilt-filled reflections of a naval officer fighting for his life after being torpedoed. In *Darkness Visible* (1979), a novel 'about England', the hero is a social misfit who was horribly burned in the London Blitz. Events in *Rites of Passage* (1980) take place on a ship sailing to Australia, a separate world inhabited by 'men who live too close to each other and too close thereby to all that is monstrous under the sun and moon'. Golding was awarded the Nobel prize in 1983.

GRAHAM GREENE (1904–91)

One of the most widely read British writers of the century, Graham Greene was one of the few to bridge the gap between serious and popular fiction (see also page 136). His output includes thrillers, comedies and sophisticated adventure stories, which he called 'entertainments' – like

Left: A scene from the film of *Lord of the Flies*. William Golding's novel of schoolboys on a desert island brilliantly demonstrates his conception of the barbarism lying beneath the veneer of civilization.

Right: Malcolm McDowell as the teenage gang leader (with a liking for classical music) in the film of *A Clockwork Orange*. The film's controversial treatment of violence gave Burgess a public profile he came to regret.

The Third Man (1950) and *Our Man in Havana* (1958) – and weightier books, such as *The End of the Affair* (1951) and *A Burnt-Out Case* (1961).

Greene was a convert to Roman Catholicism, and much of his serious fiction is driven by the themes of moral failure and guilt. In *The Heart of the Matter* (1948) the colonial official, Scobie, commits adultery and kills himself out of compassion for the women involved. *The Quiet American* (1955), which is set in Vietnam and deals with political responsibility, is remarkably prescient about the issues that spawned the Vietnam War 12 years later. Greene's novels are distinguished by their technical proficiency, crisp narrative pace and sheer readability.

ANTHONY BURGESS (1917–93)

Burgess wrote his first novel, *Time for a Tiger* (1956), after being told that he had only a year to live. He survived to produce a body of work that is exceptional for its range and versatility. It spans more than 20 novels, many books on literature and linguistics, television

scripts, children's stories, countless reviews for the quality press and two volumes of autobiography. A gifted amateur musician, he also found time to compose a number of orchestral works.

A Clockwork Orange (1962; film 1971) made his reputation as a writer of great verbal virtuosity and satirical power. Set in the near future, it is about an incurably violent leader of a gang of delinquents and the unsuccessful attempts by the authorities to rehabilitate him. The novel is striking for the teenage street-talk, which Burgess invented by combining slang terms from English, Russian and several other languages.

His other novels include *Honey for the Bears* (1963), *Nothing Like the Sun* (1964), which has been hailed as the only successful work of fiction based on Shakespeare's life, and *Enderby Outside* (1968), one of a comic series about a middle-aged poet. His most ambitious novel, *Earthly Powers* (1980), takes on the history of the 20th century as seen by an 81-year-old homosexual writer, whose life story mixes real and fictional characters.

Post-war Britain

The ironic observation of individuals as they make their way in society has been a preoccupation of the novel form since it began. In the work of these post-war British novelists, each operating from a different social perspective, the comedy ranges from the bitterly satirical to the gently compassionate. Whatever their tone, these writers highlight in vigorous form the changes that are taking place – or that they feel should take place – in British society.

ANGRY YOUNG MEN

The label 'angry young men' was applied, mainly by journalists, to a group of playwrights and novelists in the 1950s – principally, John Osborne (see page 124), Kingsley Amis (1922–95), Alan Sillitoe (b.1928) and John Braine (1922–86) – who had little in common except a general disenchantment with post-war Britain.

Sillitoe's *Saturday Night and Sunday Morning* (1958) and Braine's *Room at Top* (1957) are novels about working-class life in the provinces. Both writers are sometimes known as a 'man of one book': each of them continued to write fiction, more or less around the same subjects, without ever repeating the success of their first novels.

Kingsley Amis is often hailed as a central figure in this group, but his first and most popular novel, *Lucky Jim* (1954), now reads more as a romantic comedy than as an expression of dissent. It remains an extremely funny book and, in many people's view, is still his best work. The central character, Jim Dixon – referred to at the time as an 'anti-hero' – is a truculent and irreverent university lecturer from a lower-middle-class background, who is opposed to all forms of pretension and phoniness.

Over the next 40 years Amis's mild radicalism turned into a cantankerous hostility to contemporary life and manners. His special gift was a very acute ear for the distinctive idioms and speech patterns of certain social types, particularly those of whom he was contemptuous. In later works, such as *Jake's Thing* (1978), a study of middle-aged impotence, and *Stanley and the Women* (1984), he registers the speech of his satirical targets with an almost phonetic accuracy. Amis's novel

The Old Devils (1986) won Britain's Booker prize for its sardonic account of a group of retired people kept vigorous by malice and spite.

ANTHONY POWELL (1905–2000)

Like many English writers of his generation, Anthony Powell had been hugely impressed by Proust's *À la recherche du temps perdu*, and his 12-novel *roman fleuve*, *A Dance to the Music of Time* (1951–75), pays a kind of homage to Proust in its scope and intricate pattern. The only thing the two authors really have in common, however, is their feeling for the quirkiness and variety of human behaviour, which shows itself in an exceptional gift for creating characters.

As in Proust's work, Powell's characters sometimes reappear in quite different walks of life or contexts – always distinct, often comic, at times tragic in their misfortunes. The most unforgettable is the comic monster Kenneth Widmerpool, who starts as a grotesque figure of fun in the narrator's schooldays and ends as a senior politician. This wonderfully vivid novel sequence paints a unique picture of English life in upper-class and

Above: Angus Wilson's fiction moved from the satirical cameos of his early stories to a broader canvas that earned him comparisons with Dickens.

Left: Most famous for his first novel, *Lucky Jim*, in his later fiction Kingsley Amis drew an increasingly acerbic portrait of middle-class English society.

Green. He married into the English aristocracy and worked for a time in publishing. The five comic novels he wrote before *A Dance to the Music of Time* are among the finest of the period. The first, *Afternoon Men* (1931), is perhaps the best, with its brilliant evocation of young bohemian London. Despite Powell's reputation for being a pre-modernist writer, the book shows the influence of Hemingway in its use of laconic dialogue, which he adapts to great comic effect.

ANGUS WILSON (1913–91)

Beneath its surface of acidly comic observation and social satire, Angus Wilson's fiction presents a serious and thoughtful analysis of post-war Britain. Until 1955 he worked at the British Museum, where he was deputy superintendent of the Reading Room. His career as a writer began with *The Wrong Set* (1949) and *Such Darling Dodos* (1950). These are collections of short stories, which portray with a sharp and sometimes malicious accuracy a variety of types representative of the English middle classes.

Wilson's first novel, *Hemlock and After* (1952), is about a novelist and married man who succumbs in middle age to the homosexual and sadistic impulses he has previously repressed. A prominent theme is the relation between public and private life, which is explored through the clash between the character's high-minded liberalism and his personal behaviour. Wilson's long and panoramic novel *Anglo-Saxon Attitudes* (1956) takes the investigation into British hypocrisy and self-deception further, with the story of academic fraud perpetrated during an archaeological dig.

These novels, in which Wilson adapted the framework of 19th-century fiction, are crowded with vividly drawn characters somewhat reminiscent of Dickens. Critics have frequently noted his brilliant powers of mimicry. He is particularly effective at registering the intricacies of English middle-class social manners – for example, in describing embarrassment or capturing the speech of bores and fraudulent experts. Among his later works are *The Old Men at the Zoo* (1961), a satire set in the near future, and *As If by Magic* (1973), whose central figure is a scientist who has discovered a 'miracle rice', which he hopes will solve the problems of the Third World.

artistic circles from the 1930s to the 1960s. Modern academic criticism tends to dismiss the role of character in fiction, which may explain why Powell's work has been consistently underrated.

Powell was educated at Eton, where his schoolfellows included the writers George Orwell and Henry

Feminine perspectives

Before writing by women became 'women's writing', some specifically female concerns – the family, personal relationships and, of course, the social limitations of not being male – were explored in British fiction. While Ivy Compton-Burnett mapped family malice, Iris Murdoch plumbed the vicissitudes of personal relationships. Muriel Spark's social comedies, despite their sparkle, were incisive commentaries on the unsatisfactory state of being female in the world at large.

IVY COMPTON-BURNETT (1884–1969)

Ivy Compton-Burnett was born in London and educated privately before attending London University. She published a novel, *Dolores*, in 1911, but it was not until *Pastors and Masters* (1925) that she found the setting and formula that suited her particularly 'bitter and severe' intelligence. The 18 novels that followed have a very distinct, rather eerie tone, which is rooted in her belief that 'nothing is so corrupting as power' and in her decision to examine this notion in the confines of Edwardian domestic settings. The families she writes of live in large and gloomy, often dilapidated houses, full of children, servants and dependent relations. Each family is inevitably ruled by a tyrannical parent or grandparent and completely isolated from the outside world, which leads to an intense rate of domestic crime – adultery, incest, child abuse, fraud and murder all feature persistently.

Her novels are made up almost entirely of dialogue, which is rarely commented upon or judged by the author, so that the power struggles she describes are disturbingly abstract, self-referential affairs. 'Appearances are not held to be a clue to the truth,' says one of her characters, 'But we seem to have no other.'

Left: Muriel Spark's novel *The Prime of Miss Jean Brodie* is a chilling portrait of a controlling schoolteacher, here played in the film version by Maggie Smith.

Right: The combination of passionate and volatile relationships with intellectual seriousness in Iris Murdoch's fiction made her one of the most popular 'highbrow' English novelists of the century.

Compton-Burnett's life was effectively destroyed by the First World War, after which she suffered from a prolonged physical and mental breakdown. Her later novels are increasingly preoccupied with the well-ordered surface of social life being disrupted by family envy, spite and mutual hatred. *A House and its Head* (1935), *A Family and a Fortune* (1939) and *Manservant and Maidservant* (1947) are among the most outstanding of these.

IRIS MURDOCH (1919–99)

Born in Dublin, of Anglo-Irish parents, Iris Murdoch completed her education at Somerville College, Oxford. She then worked for a while as a civil servant, before becoming a philosophy lecturer at Oxford and London, and was respected as much as a philosopher as a prolific writer of fiction.

Her first novel, *Under the Net* (1954), which has, typically, a male narrator, was an immediate success and more completely successful perhaps than anything else she wrote, although she went on to complete some 25 more novels. Her characters are always professional people, usually involved in convoluted sexual relationships and much given to ponderous conversational abstraction. Her philosophical preoccupations – the

nature of good and evil, the religious life, the sacred and the taboo, the nature of sexuality – are always overtly present in her fiction, which has led one critic to comment that 'the results are as mediocre as the philosophy'. Certainly her characters are at the mercy of her ideas about them, which leads to an often stilted result. 'Oh Barb, you were so wonderful, I worship you,' is a not uncharacteristic piece of Murdochian dialogue. But her books are compelling reading, because of – rather than in spite of – their freedom from 'realistic' constraints. Her characters' emotions are violent, intense and without seemingly reasonable cause, and they elicit equally violent responses from the rest of the cast, with inevitably drastic consequences – sudden death often features in her dénouements.

The Bell (1958), *A Word Child* (1975), *The Sea, the Sea* (1978), which won the Booker prize, and *The Philosopher's Pupil* (1983) are undoubtedly among her strongest works.

MURIEL SPARK (b.1918)

Spark began her literary career as an editor and biographer, working for the poetry society and editing the *Poetry Review* between 1947 and 1949. After winning the *Observer* short story competition in 1951, she turned to fiction and wrote *The Comforters* (1957), the first of her mostly short, elegant and sophisticated works, whose malicious wit has been compared to Evelyn Waugh. *Memento Mori* followed in 1959. This is a dark tale of the deviousness of a group of old, slightly bohemian Londoners.

Her books adapted neatly for radio, which helped her growing reputation, which was consolidated when *The Prime of Miss Jean Brodie* (1961) was made into a film (1969), starring Maggie Smith. Spark drew on her Edinburgh upbringing to write a disturbing portrait of a repressed schoolmistress and her drive to manipulate her favourite girls, 'the crème de la crème'. Other works include *The Girls of Slender Means* (1963), a tragi-comedy set in a Kensington hostel, *The Driver's Seat* (1970), about a woman with a death wish, and *A Far Cry from Kensington* (1988), about a plump woman who becomes a secretary in a publishing house, where she finally triumphs by writing a novel herself.

Her writing is elegant and intelligently perceptive as well as often very funny. In the 1970s she settled in Italy, where her novel *The Take Over* (1976) is set.

The novel in Europe

Continental Europe was more deeply scarred by the Second World War than either Britain or the United States. The experience of the holocaust was felt there more profoundly and personally, while both the post-war prosperity in the West and totalitarianism in the East presented novelists with their own challenges. Western responses range from the intensely personal and moving memoir fiction of Primo Levi to the sardonic, sometimes cruel, gaze of Moravia. In Eastern Europe Milan Kundera's playful yet serious novels attempted to make sense at a personal level for those trapped in an absurd political system.

MILAN KUNDERA (b.1926)

Poet, novelist, playwright and short-story writer, Kundera was born in Brno, Czechoslovakia, and became one of the first members of his literary generation to react against the limiting and dreary realism of the Stalinist regime. His favourite subjects are really sex and the erotic imagination, but he uses this preoccupation as a context in which to raise political ideas. He sees the human desire for utopia as the root of its ills, and his novels chart the emptiness of East European life under communism and point out that meaningful choice in the contemporary world is effectively exhausted.

His first international success was *Zert* (*The Joke*, 1969), which led to his enforced emigration to France and the banning of his work in Czechoslovakia. The joke of the book is, typically, on everyone in it. The hero, Thomas, has been sentenced to hard labour because he criticized Trotsky. Once free, he decides to seduce his informer's wife as a way of revenging himself. But the man is indifferent to his wife's adultery (he is already having an affair himself). Thomas is indifferent to the wife. She is heartbroken by his cavalier seduction and tries to kill herself but takes an overdose of laxatives by mistake. Kundera's characters exist to illustrate his thoughts, and his elegant prose – with its frequent surreally tinged images – reinforces the detachment behind his thinking. His stance is always ironic, as his titles

often imply: *The Book of Laughter and Forgetting* (1979), *Life is Elsewhere* (1974), *Laughable Loves* (1974) and *The Unbearable Lightness of Being* (1984).

PRIMO LEVI (1919–87)

In 1986 the chemist and writer Primo Levi explained: 'Having spent more than 30 years sewing together long molecules presumably useful to my neighbour ... I might have learned something about sewing together words or ideas, or about the general and specific properties of my colleague, man.' Levi's scientific training saved him, both spiritually and practically, when he was arrested by the SS in 1943 and taken by train to Auschwitz with 650 other Jews. His memoir of his two years there, *Si questo è un uomo* (*If This is a Man*, 1959), earned him his status as 'one of the most valuable writers of our time'. Together with its sequel, *La tregua* (*The Ceasefire* or *The Truce*, 1963), the book constitutes one of the most distinguished, intelligent and compassionate works of holocaust literature, bringing Levi's relentlessly inquisitive mind to bear on humanity under barbaric conditions. His memoir is never brooding or angry, but rather a mingling of science and poetry to represent man's reflex resistance to evil.

He was spared the gas chambers by being drafted to work in the Auschwitz laboratories and wrote later, in *Il sistemo periodico* (*The Periodic Table*, 1984), of his

eerie correspondence after the war with a chemist, who turned out to have been one of his captors there. This collection of autobiographical stories again achieves an epic quality by synthesizing science – each chapter of the book describes a chemical element and parallels it with human tendencies – with quietly profound analysis of his fellow man. Levi also wrote poetry and a novel, *La chiave a stella* (*The Wrench*, 1978). He committed suicide in 1987.

ALBERTO MORAVIA (1907–90)

The journalist, short-story writer and novelist Alberto Moravia is a major figure in 20th-century literature, well known for his fictional portrayals of social alienation and loveless sexuality. Moravia, the pen-name of Alberto Pincherle, was born in Rome and contracted tuberculosis when he was eight years old. He subsequently spent many years in bed and in sanatoriums, experiences that clearly informed his view of the world as a bewildering, lonely place, as well as allowing him time to study French, German and English writers. His first novel, *Gli indifferenti* (*The Time of Indifference* or *The Indifferent Ones*, 1929), is a damningly realistic portrait of a middle-class mother and the moral corruption involved as she brings up two children in a fascist regime, in which people exploit each other sexually, without wanting to but somehow needing to.

La romana (*The Woman of Rome*, 1947) examines the life of a prostitute in the Italian capital city. Moravia exhibits here a characteristic fascination with sexual detail, as well as his pervasive love of womankind (his short stories are claimed by some Italian women to show a remarkable understanding of female sexuality). Emotional aridity is everywhere in Moravia's fiction, and it is combined with an overwhelming sense of the frustration to which sexual intercourse gives rise, no matter how much his characters want it to function as an embracing escape.

His stark language, narrative skill and meaty dialogue have made his books ideal material for films – *Il conformista* (*The Conformist*, 1951), for example, was made into a powerful piece of cinema by Bernardo Bertolucci in 1970.

Moravia's one-time wife (they divorced), the equally anti-bourgeois Elsa Morante (1916–85), is also a highly regarded novelist. Her best known work, *La Storia* (*History*, 1974), has been called 'one of the most remarkable works to have come out of Italy since the Second World War'. Set in Rome between 1941 and 1947, it tells of the arduous life of a simple, half-Jewish, primary school teacher and her son, the result of her rape by a German soldier. Her writing weaves realistic detail with a texture of lyrical unreality to produce an intense yet delicate prose.

Latin American fiction

Like currencies, works of fiction often have different values outside their own countries. Some great English-language writers are ignored abroad, while minor figures are read avidly. Latin American writers are particularly under-exposed. Carpentier's work has been available in translation for many years, but Onetti and Arguedas are hardly known, despite being highly celebrated in their own language. As more Latin American literature is translated, there will presumably be further reassessment.

JUAN CARLOS ONETTI (1909–94)

Only two of Juan Carlos Onetti's novels have been translated into English, but critics and fellow authors alike regard him, nevertheless, as one of the most important writers of the century. For one critic, he is the 'greatest novelist of the urban, the dirty, the soiled and the unhappy'.

Born in Uruguay, Onetti was educated in Buenos Aires, where he lived and worked for many years as a journalist, before returning to Montevideo as director of the city's municipal libraries. The setting for Onetti's fiction is the imaginary city of Santa Maria, a fusion of Buenos Aires and Montevideo. His protagonists are often isolated individuals, who stoically accept the way things are, even though their dreams of fulfilment invariably end in disillusionment and frustration. A character in one of his short stories notes: 'Every morning I register the fact that I'm still alive without feeling either bitterness or gratitude.'

In *El Astillero* (*The Shipyard*, 1961), the anti-hero Larsen, who is described as 'dirty, calm and hardened', discovers that the city's shipyard has no ships, no work and no employees, apart from two men who make a living from the sale of scrap. Larsen's earlier career as a pimp is part of the tangled plot of *Bodysnatcher* (1964), in which a town councillor enlists his aid in setting up Santa Maria's first brothel.

Onetti's use of narrative and interior monologue and his blending of reality with the characters' fantasies and inner experience reveal the influence of William Faulkner, but his style has its own very different flavour. His view of modern urban existence is usually branded as nihilistic and bitter, yet there is an affirmative note underlying his writing, and a warmth and restrained optimism that led one critic to remark that 'there radiates from his work the glow of a love of life'.

JOSÉ MARIA ARGUEDAS (1911–69)

The Peruvian novelist and short-story writer José Maria Arguedas is another Latin American writer who has not had the attention he deserves. The son of a white travelling judge and a Quechuan Indian, he grew up in Indian communities and later trained as an anthropologist. This background provided the inspiration and material for his fiction, which is a unique attempt to portray South America's indigenous people from their own perspective: 'To discover the universe in the Quechua language whose sounds are charged with the natural language of things.' He wrote his novels in a Spanish that tries to distil the essence of Quechua by incorporating its words and expressions, especially in dialogue.

Arguedas's greatest novel, *Los rio profundos* (*Deep Rivers*, 1958), deals with the conflict in an adolescent caught between his sympathy for the Indians who brought him up and a Catholic education aimed at severing his roots. Through this autobiographical story, he succeeds brilliantly in evoking the Quechuan mind and way of life, a culture he depicts as in many ways superior to modern civilization.

It was followed by *El Sexto* (*The Sixth One*, 1961), a grim and laconic account of prison life based on his experience of imprisonment during the Benevides dictatorship. In *Todas las sangres* (*All the Races* or *Everyone's Blood*, 1964) the Indians reclaim their land

Although he spent much of his life in Europe, Alejo Carpentier represented South American fiction for most English-readers until the continent's 'magical realist' writers appeared in translation.

but are then crushed by the police and white landowners. Arguedas committed suicide before finishing his last novel, *El zorro de arriba y el zorro de abajo* (*The Fox from Above and the Fox from Below*, 1971). Written on the advice of a psychiatrist who was treating him, it is an intensely harrowing record of the course of his depression up to his final day.

ALEJO CARPENTIER (1904–80)

The French-Cuban writer Carpentier was, in the opinion of Arguedas, 'a European who happens to speak Spanish'. It is easy to see why Arguedas was dismissive. Carpentier was a highly cosmopolitan figure, who studied music in Paris and later became the cultural attaché at the Cuban embassy there. His most acclaimed novel, *Los pasos perdidos* (*The Lost Steps*, 1953), tries to define the nature of Latin American society as a fruitful exchange between primitive and civilized cultures, but comes down ultimately in favour of modernity.

The contrast between Arguedas and Carpentier could not be greater. Whereas Arguedas imagines the experience of his country's native people from within, Carpentier pictures them as exotic and strange – and does so in a lush and ornate prose. The hero of the book is a musician who travels up the river Orinoco in search of primitive musical instruments. In a remote region of the Amazon jungle he meets a group of idealists who are trying to build a utopian community based on the rejection of all things modern. Although tempted to remain with the idealists, he finds that he cannot go backwards in time and returns to civilization to carry on 'Adam's task of naming things'.

The international experience

The Nobel prize committee is sometimes eccentric in its choices – most people are puzzled to learn that Bertrand Russell and Sir Winston Churchill won the prize for literature. The three Nobel laureates discussed here, however, are both significant and deserving writers, and although their work is rooted in distinct national and ethnic backgrounds, its appeal is universal.

Above: Nadine Gordimer's lifelong commitment to charting life in South Africa under apartheid led her to win the Nobel prize for literature in 1991.

Left: Among its many strengths and riches, Isaac Bashevis Singer's fiction has an inestimable value as a portrait of the lost world of European Jews before the holocaust.

ISAAC BASHEVIS SINGER (1904–91)

Singer wrote in Yiddish and supervised the English translations of his novels and short stories – *Gimpel the Fool* (1957), for example, was translated by Saul Bellow. 'Nothing fits a ghost story better than a dying language,' he said. Spirits, demons and dybuks from Jewish folklore often appear in his characters' daily lives, but his remark has a far greater significance. Singer writes of a world that no longer exists, the vanished world of East European Jewry before the holocaust, and it is a world he recreates with incomparable richness and vitality.

He came from a family of Hasidic rabbis in Poland and spent some years in Warsaw, before moving to the United States in 1935, where he settled in New York.

Singer's work gives a vivid and multi-dimensional portrait of Jewish life over different periods of Polish history. *Satan in Goray* (1955), which takes place in the 17th century, tells the story of the turmoil caused by a false messiah. His wide-ranging family chronicles – the novels *The Family Moskat* (1950), *The Manor* (1967) and *The Estate* (1969) – describe traditional ways of life in close-knit Jewish villages and the changes they

undergo in the modern era. He also writes about Jewish life in America after the war, predominantly in short stories. His is a world of superstitious peasants, wise rabbis, fools, whores, penitents, fanatics and ordinary people, whose lives are transformed by their own passions or by events – rabbinical students who reject their religion to become intellectuals in Warsaw café society, successful businessmen who throw away everything for love or intense sexual desire, Jewish emigrants meeting each other again years later in New York.

Singer's stories frequently contain occult and supernatural elements. In one of them, for example, a vain married woman from Krashnik is consumed by erotic fantasies, finally entering the mirror in her boudoir after a demon seduces her.

Singer writes in a simple, uncluttered prose, which is striking for its naturalness and warmth of feeling. He was awarded the Nobel prize in 1978.

PATRICK WHITE (1912–90)

One of the most original literary voices of the century, Patrick White has been justifiably compared to both Tolstoy and Dostoevsky in his scope and clarity of vision. His early childhood was spent on a sheep station in Australia, but at the age of 13 he was sent to boarding school in Cheltenham, England, where he was deeply unhappy. He returned to Australia after the Second World War.

White's writing is taut with a visionary intensity, even when he is dealing with the most mundane events. *The Tree of Man* (1955), for example, is the story of a New South Wales farmer and his unfulfilled wife, Amy. White describes their day-to-day existence in such a way that they achieve a kind of majesty. Their human dignity is heightened by the immense Australian landscape, which shapes their lives as much as their own aspirations do. *The Vivisector* (1970) is the life story of a painter, Hurtle Duffield, seer and diagnostician of a society he despises and cannot engage with, except by effectively dissecting it in his art. His embittered eye analyses relentlessly. Unable to love – or to receive affection – his passion goes into his painting. When the young Kathy Volkov enters Duffield's life her unconscious self-love mirrors Duffield's emotional barrenness to devastating effect.

White was a homosexual, and he shared his adult life with Manoly Lascaris, to whom he pays tribute in his autobiography *Flaws in the Glass* (1981). His later work – particularly his novel *The Twyborn Affair* (1979) – concerns itself with notions of sexual identity and transsexuality. These themes occur most potently in the novella *A Woman's Hand*, a chilling study of two couples, which charts the subtle and complex cruelty of one person's seemingly benign influence on another. White received the Nobel prize in 1973.

NADINE GORDIMER (b.1923)

Born in South Africa, Nadine Gordimer was an outspoken opponent of apartheid, and much of her work deals with the way the insupportable political situation in her native country intrudes into the emotional lives of her characters. Her fiction is driven by the tensions between personal isolation and the commitment to social justice, between the anguish of living (and loving) within a system one cannot change but is loathe to leave.

Gordimer started writing when she was nine years old, and her first short story was published when she was aged only 15. *The Soft Voice of the Serpent*, a collection of stories, was published in 1952, and this was followed by a novel, *The Lying Days* (1953). Both exhibit her characteristic lucid, unsentimental control of highly charged material. *A Guest of Honour* (1970) began her exploration of how a rigid political system can potentiate (and then destroy) extreme interpersonal passion. This theme had appeared in *Occasion for Loving* (1963), which charts an affair between a bohemian young white woman and a volatile black communist. *My Son's Story* (1990) again takes love in an impossible society as its subject.

Gordimer's most admired novel is probably *July's People* (1981), in which a white family is forced into hiding in the native village of their black servant, July. They slowly become 'his' people, unable to talk, think or relate to each other, in the role-reversals they unwittingly choose for themselves. She was awarded the Nobel prize in 1991.

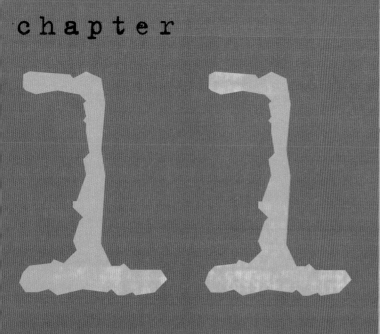

Post-war theatre

Below: **A production of Samuel Beckett's** *Waiting for Godot*. **Often regarded as inaccessibly avant garde, the play can be enjoyed at many levels, particularly in its borrowing of the techniques of music hall and popular stage.**

Right: **Samuel Beckett. Perhaps the last great modernist writer of the century, Beckett expresses his bleak vision of life and humanity in prose of exceptional purity and power.**

Theatre since the Second World War has been characterized by a belief that 'realism' alone cannot adequately represent the drama of modern life. The seeming lack of cause and effect in the wider world is translated into an unconnectedness between the people on stage and the events in which they participate, most notably in what has come to be know as the 'theatre of the absurd'. Here, the motivation of characters is mysterious, if not unknowable, yet out of such unpromising material many plays of great dramatic impact, not to mention humour, have been written.

Samuel Beckett (1906-89)

A NOBEL IRISHMAN

Of all the great writers of the 20th century, Samuel Beckett stands out as the one whose work has been most insistently consistent in its central theme: the paring down of language in a work of art to produce something meaningful out of the fact that there is no meaning in life and yet it must be lived. 'Where I am, I don't know, in the silence you don't know, you must go on, I can't go on, I'll go on,' says the narrator of *Malone Dies*. To 'go on', you must engage with other people, which means you must speak, even though there is nothing to say.

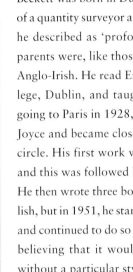

Beckett was born in Dublin. The second son of a quantity surveyor and of a mother whom he described as 'profoundly religious', his parents were, like those of Yeats and Shaw, Anglo-Irish. He read English at Trinity College, Dublin, and taught in Belfast before going to Paris in 1928, where he met James Joyce and became closely involved with his circle. His first work was a study of Joyce, and this was followed by a book on Proust. He then wrote three books of fiction in English, but in 1951, he started to write in French and continued to do so for the next 20 years, believing that it would be easier to write without a particular style in a language that had been acquired than in one effortlessly learned as a child. The trilogy *Molloy* (1951), *Malone meurt* (*Malone Dies*, 1951) and *L'Innommable* (*The Unnamable*, 1953) are all desolate, obsessional, interior monologues, lightened with flashes of black humour and word-play.

These works of fiction were not widely read, but Beckett's first play, *En attendant Godot* (*Waiting for Godot*, 1953), made an enormous impact when it was performed in Paris and quickly established his international reputation as a playwright associated with what became known as the 'theatre of the absurd'.

Like all Beckett's subsequent drama, *Waiting for Godot* is both terminally desolate, yet funny, tender and strangely exhilarating. Two tramps – Vladimir and Estragon – are waiting for someone called Godot, who will, they believe, somehow change their lives. Their relationship is typical of Beckett's characters, in that they are in turn reluctantly affectionate and bitterly dependent on each other. They pass their time wishing they could be alone yet in terrible fear of solitude. They banter, often very humorously. They complain of physical pain and deprivation. They fall over, take their hats and boots on and off, eat carrots, reminisce, reflect and contemplate suicide. Someone called Pozzo arrives, leading his servant, Lucky, on a rope, and this passes the time for them. A boy arrives twice, with a message from Godot, who cannot come today but will come tomorrow. Neither the tramps nor the audience quite believe this, but Vladimir and Estragon have no choice but to wait until he arrives.

In a sense, it is not the action of Beckett's plays that concerns us but rather the lack of anything happening and the fact that nothing really happens except that words are exchanged. But the words in Beckett do not connect the characters to each other. Rather they deliberately draw attention to the fact that no one communicates anything. The plays have been described as being like poetry, and certainly Beckett's later work moves further and further away from any conventional sense of drama.

Krapp's Last Tape (1959) features an old man listening to his own voice, recorded when he was a young man. *Breath* (1969) is simply five seconds of silence, between two baby's cries. His last work *Not I* (1973), took his strategy of a lyrical but inarticulate anguish as far as it could possibly go: a disembodied mouth is illuminated on stage to utter a brief fragmentary monologue. Samuel Beckett was awarded the Nobel prize in 1969.

'Ah yes, so little to say, so little to do, and the fear so great, certain days, of finding oneself ... left, with hours still to run ... That is the danger.'

SAMUEL BECKETT, *Happy Days* (1961)

The theatre of the absurd

The term 'absurdism' is applied to a number of dramatists who were working in Europe during the 1950s. They shared particular attitudes towards the predicament of mankind in the universe and developed a new style of drama to convey feelings of anger, purposelessness and despair. The notion of life as futile was the implicit subject of Albert Camus's influential *The Myth of Sisyphus* (1942; see page 89), in which the hero is forever rolling a stone up a hill. These playwrights were radical in the way that both the content and the form of their work were shaped by notions of life as an irrational, absurd predicament.

EUGÈNE IONESCO (1912–94)

What astonished Ionesco, he said, was 'the fact that we do not understand each other' yet 'there is a degree of communication between people. They talk to each other. They understand each other. That's what's so astounding.'

Eugène Ionesco was born in Romania and was brought up speaking both French and Romanian. He lived alternately in France and Romania, before settling in Paris in 1940. He was supposed to write a thesis on the subject of sin and death in French literature, but instead he started to teach himself English from a phrase book and was struck by the way words and phrases seem deeply absurd when they are taken out of context. He began writing a play, *La Cantatrice chauve* (*The Bald Prima Donna*, 1950), using language the way a manual does, to point out how futile communication can be. In the play, Mr and Mrs Brown are visited by another couple who discover, quite by chance, that they are, in fact, married. His next play, *Les Chaises* (*The Chairs*, 1952), features an old couple who are convinced that an audience is about to arrive on the stage. More and more chairs are carried on, so that the stage is crowded with them, but no one arrives to sit down.

His best known play, *Rhinocéros* (*Rhinoceros*, 1958), depicts a world in which everbody but one person become rhinoceroses. Ionesco said later that he was concerned with the rise of fascism here, but he is not primarily a political writer. Rather, he constructs plays in which there is no coherence – of character, memory, plot or time. 'I have the feeling that the world could start running haywire, like a machine,' he said. His plays resonate with that feeling and are hilarious but terrifying experiences.

JEAN GENET (1910–86)

Identified with Antonin Artaud's ritualistic theatre of cruelty as much as with the absurdists, Jean Genet is a complete original, who made his solitary way through French literary life as iconoclastically as he lived his life of extremes. He was abandoned by his mother to a society for foundlings and branded as a thief by his foster parents. His first work was a novel, *Notre-Dame des fleurs* (*Our Lady of the Flowers*, 1944), which was written in pencil on brown paper while he was in prison, where he also wrote an autobiography, *Le Journal du voleur* (*Thief's Journal*, 1949).

His subject matter was often disgusting and disgust itself, but the beauty of his prose undercuts his studiedly 'nasty' content. His first play, *Les Bonnes* (*The Maids*, 1947), was a drama of two sisters who plot to kill their mistress. The mood is one of ritual, dream and fantasy,

in which realities are replaced by 'absurd' reflections, which come to seem as real as the concrete world they mirror. *Le Balcon* (*The Balcony*, 1956) is set in a brothel, where false dignitaries act out their erotic fantasies as a revolution goes on outside. The atmosphere is claustrophobic, and the shifts from fantasy to reality are as disturbing, if not more so, as those in *The Maids*.

HAROLD PINTER (b.1930)

Pinter wrote his first play, *The Room*, in 1957, since when he has produced a body of work so distinct that the word 'Pinteresque' is now part of contemporary culture. Like Beckett's, his world is comic yet menacing, with characters who are amusing but frighteningly helpless. Harmless actions are drenched in vague horror, domestic settings are eerily threatening, conversation is empty, and silences are uncomfortably acute.

His best known work is probably *The Caretaker*, which was first staged at the Arts Theatre, London, in 1960. The scene is, typically, a cluttered room, where nothing works or has any function. Its inhabitant, Aston (who is obsessed throughout with putting up a shed), has picked up a vagrant called Davies who has no fixed history or identity. He is obsessed with getting down to Sidcup to get his 'papers', without which he feels trapped and impotent. A third man, Mick, comes and goes, in disturbingly differing moods. Non sequiturs, silences and exaggerated gestures are mixed with naturalistic moments in this work, as in all Pinter's plays, to intensify the sense of unease.

Pinter has written screenplays, including *The Servant* (1963), *The Go-Between* (1969), *The French Lieutenant's Woman* (1982), as well as short plays for radio broadcast (see also page 130). There is a prodigious and international Pinter critical industry but little consensus about his work, except for the acknowledgement that he is indisputably at the forefront of contemporary drama.

I'd have to get down to Sidcup ... they want my references. That's where they are see. Trouble is, getting there. That's my problem. The weather's dead against it.
HAROLD PINTER, *The Caretaker* (1960)

The British renaissance

The 1950s saw a resurgence of vitality in British theatre, which reflected widespread disillusion at the failure of expectations of a new, egalitarian society. Contemporary drama was backward looking and class bound, stuffed with drawing-rooms, small-talk and the pleasures of tennis. The 'angry young men' who now wrote plays in reaction to this – about working-class lives in the stifling austerities of post-war Britain – gave a voice to a generation of non-conformist rebel-heroes.

JOHN OSBORNE (1929–94)

'The birth of modern British theatre has an actual date, a genuine birthday,' wrote a critic in the *New York Post*, reviewing a 1980 revival of *Look Back in Anger*. That date was 1956, the year of the premiere at London's Royal Court Theatre of Osborne's ground-breaking drama of Jimmy Porter, the original angry young man, who rages against a world that has no 'good brave causes left'. 'If the big bang does come, and we all get killed off,' he shouts, 'it'll just be for the Brave-new-nothing-thank-you-very much. About as pointless and inglorious as stepping off a bus.' Jimmy's large statements are made in the cramped, seedy bed-sit he shares with his middle-class wife and their lodger. An ironing-board is centre-stage, and this was partly responsible for the term 'kitchen sink drama', which was applied to the work of Osborne and his successors.

Like many of his fellow playwrights, Osborne left school early. He was, in fact, expelled when he was 16 years old for slapping the headmaster. He wrote three plays before *Look Back in Anger* was produced and more than 20 afterwards. Central to his strength as a dramatist is the vigorous articulacy of his central characters, their casual insolence (perhaps learned in the pub Osborne's mother ran) and their restless awareness that they are out of their element. The early plays had a powerful sense of their own historical moment, but the complexity of their characters does not date. Jimmy Porter, for example, is not only an often tender, nostal-gic idealist, but also a cruel and morbid misfit in a group of reasonably well-disposed people.

Osborne's later works – including *The Entertainer* (1957), *Luther* (1961) and *Watch It Come Down* (1976) – became increasingly vituperative and never generated the critical excitement attached to *Look Back in Anger*.

Above: **With Jimmy Porter in** *Look Back in Anger,* **John Osborne created a character who spoke for the disillusionment and bitterness of a generation who saw post-war Britain as class-ridden and hidebound.**

Right: **The son of poor Jewish immigrant parents, Arnold Wesker is committed to the idea that social change could be brought about through art.**

ARNOLD WESKER (b.1932)

Arnold Wesker was born in Stepney, London, to Jewish immigrant parents, and he left school when he was 16 years old. He had a variety of jobs before writing his first play, which he started immediately after having seen *Look Back in Anger*. His second play, *The Kitchen* (1959), was produced at the Royal Court and was extremely influential in the way it integrated the rhythm of physical work into the drama of life behind the scenes in a restaurant.

In 1962 *Chips with Everything*, a study of class attitudes in the RAF during the period of national service, established his commercial reputation, but his trilogy of plays dealing with one family over a span of 23 years – the Wesker Trilogy – was his most substantial achievement. *Chicken Soup with Barley* (1958) began this drama about the impact of politics and social issues on the Kahn family, with its communist Jewish matriarch,

Sarah, her enfeebled husband, Harry, and their volatile son, Ronnie. This was followed by *Roots* (1959) and *I'm Talking about Jerusalem* (1960).

Wesker wanted his drama to 'teach'. 'I write ... for those to whom the phrase "form of expression" may mean nothing,' he said, but he is never didactic. The trilogy is concerned primarily with understanding the limitations of socialist ideas in a materialistic world.

His attempt to popularize theatre through trade union support – the Centre 42 project in 1960 – was a tribute to his belief that art could indeed change people's lives.

EDWARD BOND (b.1934)

A radical humanist whose plays challenge moral and political uncertainties, Edward Bond first alarmed London audiences in 1965 with *Saved*, which was banned by the Lord Chamberlain, who was, until 1968, responsible for granting licenses to theatres.

Bond was raised in north London by working-class parents, and he attended the local secondary modern school, where he saw a production of *Macbeth*, which gave him 'a sense of human dignity, of the value of human beings'. His works focus on the connections between politics and moral decisions and on the tensions between social organization and the quality of individual life. 'Art must be the equivalent of hooliganism on the streets. It has to be disruptive and questioning,' he has explained.

Saved, which includes a scene in which a baby is stoned to death, certainly outraged the public. Bond pointed out that, compared with the 'strategic' bombing of German towns, the murder of an infant in a London park is 'a negligible atrocity'. 'I write about violence as naturally as Jane Austen wrote about manners,' he has said, but he is not driven by pessimism but by a conviction that people have to learn morality for themselves now that religion no longer provides a viable behavioural guide.

Bond's later provocative works include *Early Morning* (1968), *Lear* (1971), a version of Shakespeare's play that emphasizes its physical brutality, *The Fool* (1975) and *Restoration* (1981).

American drama

In the United States, drama in a realist style dominated the commercial theatre. The emphasis continued to be psychological realism, an emotional honesty that was central to the expression of the play. Memory scenes, dream sequences, symbolic characters and non-realistic scenery were all used to suggest the interior world of the characters and the 'message' of the play. Unlike their counterparts in Europe, who were more concerned with ideas, American playwrights wholeheartedly adopted realism, influencing Stanislavsky and contributing to the development of the 'method' school of acting, which still dominates theatre and film.

TENNESSEE WILLIAMS (1911–83)

Tennessee Williams was born in Columbus, Mississippi, and graduated from the University of Iowa in 1938. His first play, *American Blues* (1939), won an award, but he continued to work in menial jobs and to write in his spare time until 1944 and the success of *The Glass Menagerie*. In 1947 he won a Pulitzer prize for *A Streetcar named Desire*, a play about the moral ruin of Blanche Dubois, a faded beauty, whose romantic yearnings and sexual frustrations are violated by the cruel Stanley Kowalski.

Williams wrote sensitively about human passion and perversion, and his tenderness towards his female characters underpins his work. His plays are set in the American South, and he used the location and local dialogue to create a decadent and erotic feeling in his characters. He went on producing work in the 1950s and 1960s and was awarded another Pulitzer prize for *Cat on a Hot Tin Roof* (1955), which became a film (1958), as did *The Night of the Iguana* (1962; film 1964), the story of a minister who finds God in a seedy Mexican hotel.

Suddenly Last Summer (1958; film 1959) and *Sweet Bird of Youth* (1959; film 1962) deal with lobotomy, cannibalism and venereal disease as Williams continued in a Gothic vein. His later plays were less successful, and ill-health and addiction to drugs caused a breakdown from which he recovered to write novels, essays, poetry and an autobiography. His work is widely translated and is performed around the world.

ARTHUR MILLER (b.1915)

Arthur Miller was born in New York and grew up in the aftermath of the Wall Street Crash, which ruined his father financially. He studied at the University of Michigan and won an award for his comedy *Honors at Dawn* (1936), before returning to New York to write for radio. He continued to write plays for the stage. *All My Sons* (1947) was followed by the powerful *Death of a Salesman* (1949), which won him a Pulitzer prize and the beginnings of a reputation as America's finest contemporary dramatist. The play deals with the story of Willy Loman and the effect his failed but driven career has on his wife and two sons, which results in the central tragic

> We're all of us sentenced to solitary confinement inside our own skins.
> TENNESSEE WILLIAMS

Left: Paul Muni as Willy Loman in a 1944 production of Arthur Miller's *Death of a Salesman*, the play that made him famous.

Above: Paul Newman and Elizabeth Taylor in Tennessee Williams' *Cat on a Hot Tin Roof*. The frustrations and anguish of a Southern family are the theme of this intense and steamy drama.

character struggling with self-knowledge and his own futile aspirations.

Miller's work is dominated by the themes of social injustice, personal responsibility and the struggle to ignore the false values of a capitalist world. *The Crucible* (1953) uses the Salem witchcraft trials as an allegory for Senator Joseph McCarthy's anti-communist 'witch hunt'. Other dramas include *A View from the Bridge* (1955), *After the Fall* (1964), about Soviet dissident writers, and a screenplay for the film *The Misfits* (1961), which starred his second wife, Marilyn Monroe.

EDWARD ALBEE (b.1928)

Edward Franklin Albee was born in Washington, D.C., and was adopted by the wealthy Reed A. Albee of the Keith-Albee chain of vaudeville and motion picture theatres. The play, *The Zoo Story* (1959), a study of schizophrenia, is firmly set in the theatre of the absurd. Lost or lonely children, real or imaginary, recur in a number of Albee's plays, notably *The American Dream* (1961) and *Who's Afraid of Virginia Woolf?* (1962).

His most successful play, later made into a film (1966), *Who's Afraid of Virginia Woolf?* exists, like Pinter's best work, on two levels: as a realistic examination of mutually destructive love and longing in a relationship (Martha drinks, flirts with other men and abuses her husband, George, who eventually retaliates by telling her that their imaginary child is dead), and as a wider critique of American middle-class values. Albee went on to win Pulitzer prizes for *A Delicate Balance* (1966) and *Seascape* (1975).

His later works include an adaptation of *Lolita*, *The Lady from Dubuque* (1980), *The Man Who Had Three Arms* (1982) and another Pulitzer prize-winner, *Three Tall Women* (1991). The last is a naturalistic play in which a woman has a conversation with her older and younger selves. It was based on Albee's stepmother and deals with rage, regret and the dissatisfactions of compromise. Critics have tried to categorize Albee variously as avant-garde, absurdist or post-modern, but his plays engage us with the searing realism of their emotional depth.

DAVID MAMET (b.1947)

Born in Chicago, David Mamet was the artist-in-residence at Goddard College, Vermont, throughout the 1970s. The greatest influences on his plays arose from the work he did at Sanford Meisner's Playhouse, where he developed the technique of using half-spoken thoughts and rapid mood changes to shape his dramas. His first plays, *Duck Variations* (1972) and *Sexual Perversity in Chicago* (1974), were produced in the fringe theatre of New York. New realism had arrived, and Mamet became closely associated with it. The early work was followed by *American Buffalo* (1975), *Edmond* (1982) and the Pulitzer prize-winning *Speed-the-Plow* (1988).

In 1983 came *Glengarry Glen Ross*, which manifests one of Mamet's most prominent themes: the interplay between strong male characters whose macho behaviour expresses itself in quiet but intense verbal battles. Pauses and silences underscore the rhythm of the play. Mamet has also written several screenplays, including those for *The Postman Always Rings Twice* (1981), *The Verdict* (1982), *The Untouchables* (1987) and *House of Games* (1987), which he also directed. *Glengarry Glen Ross* was adapted by him for the screen to critical acclaim in 1992.

New directions

Theatre has always been associated with the politics of dissent and the questioning of the *status quo*. For writers growing up during the political upheavals of 20th-century Europe, the experience of warfare on a global scale and the post-war polarization of Europe resulted in disillusion with, and a questioning of, traditional institutions and the authority of the state. Rigid state censorship behind the Iron Curtain forced writers such as Václav Havel (b.1936) to write satirically. In more liberal regimes, those on the left directed their creative anger towards America.

DARIO FO (b.1926)

Born in Lombardy, Italy, the son of a railroad worker, Dario Fo began his career by producing satirical revues in small theatres and cabarets. After spending three years in Rome, where he worked as a screenwriter, Fo founded his own theatre group with his wife, the actress Franca Rame, and wrote satirical dramas for television. His work was repeatedly censored, so in 1968 he started Nuova Scena, a theatre that was linked to the Communist Party and that performed in factories and workers' clubs. After disagreeing with the Party, Fo and Rame started another theatre group in Milan, Il Collettivo Teatrale la Comune.

Fo wrote more than 40 plays, some with Rame. His most popular are *Morte accidentale di un anarchico* (*Accidental Death of an Anarchist*, 1970), *Non si paya, no si paya* (*Can't Pay? Won't Pay!*, 1981) and *Mistero buffo* (*Mister Buffo*, 1969), which is based on the mystery plays but is so up to date in content that it changes with each audience.

In *Accidental Death of an Anarchist* an anarchist in police custody falls from a fourth-storey window. The people say state conspiracy; the judge says accident. The play develops into comical satire, with Freud, Bogart and Robert de Niro on display. Fo is heavily influenced by *commedia dell'arte* and the jesters of the Middle Ages. His main targets are capitalism, imperialism and corruption in the Italian government. He is widely performed outside Italy, and the comedies are adapted to reflect local political conditions. He was awarded the Nobel prize in 1997 for 'emulating the jesters of the Middle Ages in scourging authority and upholding the dignity of the downtrodden'.

PETER WEISS (1916–82)

Peter Ulrich Weiss was born near Berlin, the son of a Czech Jew and a Swiss mother. After the Nazis came to power in the early 1930s the family emigrated to Britain, where he studied photography. He then studied painting in Prague before settling with his parents in Sweden in 1939 and becoming a Swedish citizen. For almost 20 years he devoted himself to painting and film-making, beginning to write only in his middle age. His first novel, *The Shadow of the Coachman's Body*, took eight years to publish. An original and experimental piece of writing, it is a child's account of events in a remote house in an unclear fairy tale past. The atmosphere is menacing; the voice of the narrative is paranoid.

Weiss himself suffered severe feelings of alienation, as expressed in his two autobiographical writings *Abschied von den Eltern* (*The Leavetaking*, 1961) and *Fluchtpunkt* (*Vanishing Point*, 1962). He found a release in writing drama, describing the loneliness of writing a book as opposed to feeling 'alive' when his work reaches the stage. His most famous play, *The Persecution and Assassination of Jean-Paul Marat as Performed by the Inmates of the Asylum of Charenton under the Direction of the Marquis of Sade* (1965), usually known as *Marat/Sade*, is a unique mixture of the theatres of the absurd and cruelty and of Genet, Strindberg, Beckett and Brecht, whose political beliefs Weiss treated with dogged respect.

His earliest plays had less success, and the ones after *Marat/Sade* did not match its confidence. *Marat/Sade* is strongly influenced by the plays of Brecht. The action

Peter Weiss's play *The Persecution and Assassination of Marat*. Directed by Peter Brook, it was one of the most electrifying events on the London stage in the 1960s.

takes place in 1808, as Sade directs his play of the murder of Marat, while, in the background, the inmates of the asylum watch. The play dramatizes the tension in Weiss and in the world between imagination and action, individualism and socialism, and it creates an illusion of true dramatic action.

Weiss's later work, *Die Ermittlung* (*The Investigation*, 1965), was about the extermination camp at Auschwitz, and *Trotski im Exil* (*Trotsky in Exile*, 1970) expressed his Marxist outlook. Today the latter work seems old-fashioned and to oversimplify the arguments, reducing the character of Leon Trotsky to elevate the political ideology.

PETER HANDKE (b.1942)

Born in Griffen, Austria, the son of a bank clerk, Peter Handke studied law at Graz University, while writing for the avant-garde literary magazine *Manuskripte*. He began writing novels, plays, poetry and prose pieces with the specific aim of distancing himself from established literary forms. His first important drama was *Publikumsbeschimpfung* (*Offending the Audience*, 1966), which consists of four actors analysing the nature of theatre for an hour, after which they insult the audience, but praise its performance, turning the conventional theatrical experience on its head. This experiment was met with varying degrees of tolerance from the spectators. Several more plays in the same defiant spirit followed, but character development, plot structure and dialogue were significantly absent.

In 1968 his first full-length play, *Kaspar*, told of an orphan, Kaspar Hauser, who is discovered as a semi-mute savage, then destroyed by society's attempt to impose its language and values on him. Handke also wrote short stories, essays, radio drama and the successful thriller, *Die Angst des Tormanns beim Elfmeter* (*The Goalie's Anxiety at the Penalty Kick*, 1970).

The dominant theme in Handke's writing is that ordinary language, everyday reality and the rational order of things are constricting and life-denying, and result in collective chaos and madness. He collaborated with Wim Wenders on various films, most recently *Wings of Desire* (1987), which some critics considered self-indulgently ponderous.

Onto the screen

Before the arrival of film and, more importantly, television, the sole forum for drama was the stage. Only a minority went to the theatre, and not usually more than once a week. Drama is now available 24 hours a day through film, television and video. The impact of these new media on drama – and indeed, on literature in general – can scarcely be overestimated.

Writers have always been seduced by the screen and its potential to reach a wider audience for their work, but the first major writers to turn their hands to screenplays were novelists who were drawn to Hollywood in the 1930s and 1940s by the promise of high salaries. They were employed by the large studios as jobbing scriptwriters, always as part of a team, and they regarded their screen writing as hack work. In most cases, the contributions of figures as distinguished as F. Scott Fitzgerald, Christopher Isherwood, Aldous Huxley, Nathanael West and William Faulkner never saw the light of day (although the last shares the credits for the screenplay of *To Have and Have Not*). More recently, playwrights have begun to treat film and television as serious alternatives to the stage. Jean-Paul Sartre's screenplay for John Huston's film based on the life of Freud (1962) is an early example.

Today many playwrights and novelists, including Harold Pinter, Tom Stoppard, David Mamet, Ian McEwan and Peter Handke, regularly write adaptations and original screenplays. Pinter's scripts for the films of Joseph Losey, especially *The Servant* and *The Go-Between*, are notable for the way he adapts other people's novels to his own distinctive dramatic art. His screenplay of *À la recherche du temps perdu*, on the other hand, is a masterly feat of compression, in which he manages to translate Proust's massive work to the big screen without adulterating it and without imposing his authorial voice. The film was never made, but the script has been published and stands in its own right as first-rate dramatic literature.

The appeal, of course, in writing for the screen is that it commands an audience vastly greater than that for printed literature. Television now overwhelms all other media as the source of both entertainment and art. The novel and the stage play have long been unable to compete with this huge market, and as we enter the 21st century, it is not surprising that more and more writers are applying themselves exclusively to television drama.

TELEVISION DRAMA

Since the 1960s television had encouraged the dramatist to write for the small screen, albeit in the format of the single play. In Britain, the birthplace of the medium, the 1980s saw the birth of the independent Channel 4, where changes in funding and technique were responsible for a revolution in television drama. Scripts became screenplays, and the writer began to use the cinematic form. In the 1980s both Channel 4 and the BBC

commissioned writers to produce original work, which then found its way into the cinema, as the line between television drama and film drama became less clear.

ALAN BENNETT (b.1934)

Born in Leeds and educated at Oxford University, Alan Bennett made his name in the theatre in the 1960s. He scripted his first play, *A Day Out*, for television in 1972. In the 1980s he wrote five plays under the heading 'Objects of Affection', followed by a play, *An Englishman Abroad* (1983), about the spy and defector to Moscow, Guy Burgess, and *The Insurance Man* (1986), based on Kafka's life. These works, although complex in narrative and their use of flashback, were written in conventional film style.

His latest works, the *Talking Heads* series (1988 and 1998), hark back to early television dramas, in which actors had to perform 'live'. This straightforward approach resulted in a more theatrical kind of television, with a direct link between audience and actor. In each 'play', a character talks straight to camera about their life, which, as the beautifully crafted script reveals, is full of banal details and comic events but is, ultimately, tragic. Bennett has said that the inspiration for the characters came from an aunt in Leeds who used to

'tell everything' and that *Talking Heads* is a way of representing boredom. Bennett becomes almost Brechtian in his style, enabling the audience to observe closely the characters' behaviour as they comment in an extraordinary way on the everyday.

DENNIS POTTER (1935–94)

The son of a miner, Dennis Potter was born in the Forest of Dean and studied politics at Oxford University. He wrote his first play for television, *Vote, Vote, Vote for Nigel Barton* (1965), after failing to be elected to parliament. His work provoked strong reactions among the critics, and the BBC banned his play *Brimstone and Treacle* (1978) for 11 years for blasphemy.

A much later play for television, *Blackeyes* (1989), was also misinterpreted, perhaps with good reason, as it claimed to deal with the exploitation of the female form by portraying the naked female body throughout. His most autobiographical work, *The Singing Detective* (1986), was a huge success with audience and critics alike. Using television to its fullest capacity, the play includes actors playing multiple roles, cross-cutting, flashbacks, singing, dancing and social comment. The audience had to engage actively with the material in order to keep up with the story. Potter believed in the intelligence of the audience to sympathize with his central tragic character and his existential angst.

His finest plays abandon any attempt at naturalism. In *Blue Remembered Hills* (1979) schoolchildren are played by adults, and in *Pennies from Heaven* (1978) the characters suddenly sing songs, speak ironically or comment on the drama.

chapter

12 Genre fiction

Below: A poster for *2001: A Space Odyssey* (1968), the science fiction film made from Arthur C. Clarke's short story 'The Sentinel'. The film inaugurated a new popularity for the science fiction genre both on the page and on the screen.

It has always been the case that, with the notable exception of Charles Dickens, perhaps the last great writer to have a mass audience, most people's reading matter is by authors who are never mentioned in the history of literature. The gap between popular and highbrow literature has widened even further in the 20th century. In addition to the long-standing categories of bestselling romance and adventure stories, each of the more specialized genres of crime, science fiction, fantasy and horror now has its own substantial following. None of the authors here would be a candidate for the Nobel prize, but the best writing in genre fiction is compelling and often remarkably well written.

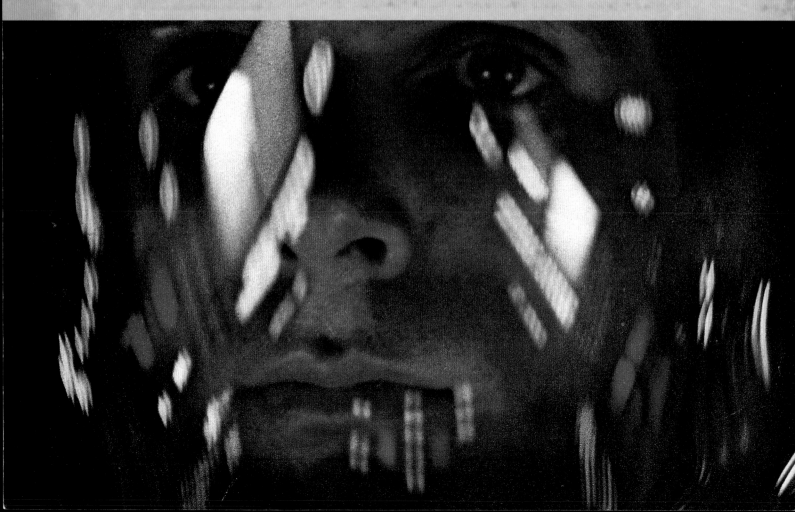

Science fiction and fantasy

SCIENCE FICTION

Novels such as *The Time Machine* (1895), *The War of the Worlds* (1898) and *The First Men in the Moon* (1901) by H.G. Wells anticipated many of the favourite themes of modern science fiction. The plots seemed implausible at the time, but a century later, technology has dramatically narrowed the gap between fact and fiction. Nevertheless, the main appeal of science fiction is still its capacity to create other worlds, quite unlike the one we inhabit.

Some of the finest works of science fiction this century were written by well-known authors who used the genre as a vehicle for ideas about the modern world. Novels such as George Orwell's *Nineteen Eighty-four*, Aldous Huxley's *Brave New World* and Anthony Burgess's *A Clockwork Orange* make predictions about the future on the basis of present-day trends and tendencies, although works like these are not generally seen as representative of the field.

Science fiction's status as one of the most widely read types of genre fiction dates from the 1950s, when a number of mainly American writers started to produce stories in a less highbrow vein, with books that are largely read for their escapism and entertainment value. The leading writers include Isaac Asimov (1920–92), Robert Heinlein (1907–88), Ursula Le Guin (b.1929), A.E. van Vogt (b.1912), Frank Herbert (1920–86) and, more recently, Gregory Benford and Greg Bear. Possibly the best examples of popular science fiction at its most engrossing are Asimov's 'Foundation' novels and the 'Dune' series by Frank Herbert. Both are about galactic empires, chronicling their rise and fall on an epic scale. Also notable are *Childhood's End* (1953) and *The City and the Stars* (1956) by the English writer Arthur C. Clarke (b.1917), although he is better known for his short story 'The Sentinel', which supplied the idea for the classic film *2001: A Space Odyssey* (1968).

FANTASY

The popularity of fantasy fiction is one of the great publishing phenomena of recent years. Almost one in every seven fiction books sold falls into the science fiction and fantasy category, and of these 70 per cent are fantasy. What is surprising about this is that most fantasy fiction follows more or less the same pattern. Fantasy sets itself

J.R.R. Tolkien, the scholarly and retiring Professor of Anglo-Saxon, who wrote in his spare time the century's greatest work of fantasy, *The Lord of the Rings*.

in a mythical past, in which sorcery replaces science, the hero is engaged in a battle between good and evil, and the most common plot is that of the 'quest', the search for a magic or sacred object that will enable the hero to defeat the forces of evil.

The greatest influence on modern fantasy fiction is the epic trilogy, *The Lord of the Rings* (1954–55) by J.R.R. Tolkien (1892–1973), which is probably the most successful fantasy work of all time, selling more than three million copies in nine languages. Tolkien was a professor of Anglo-Saxon and Middle English language at Oxford University. He started working on the trilogy while he was an undergraduate, and wrote *The Hobbit* (1937) as an introduction to it for his children. *The Lord of the Rings* creates its own richly detailed mythology of Middle Earth, involving a variety of different kingdoms, inhabited by a range of creatures (hobbits, dwarves, elves, wizards, humans and other species), all underpinned by a very compelling plot. It is a remarkable work of sustained, imaginative storytelling, and the many fantasy epics that have followed in its wake inevitably seem pale imitations. Two of the most noteworthy are Robert Holdstock's 'Mythago Wood' sequence and Stephen Donaldson's seven-volume 'Chronicles of Thomas Covenant'. In the past ten years, however, by far the most popular books in this field are Terry Pratchett's comic fantasy 'Discworld' series.

Science fiction: contemporary masters

In science fiction, as in other genre fiction, there is no substitute for literary skill. The best and most compelling works are invariably by writers who combine the gift of imagining different worlds from our own with the ability to write well. Apart from William Gibson – so far, the first and only major talent to have emerged from within science fiction – the writers described here are also accomplished at non-genre fiction.

PHILLIP K. DICK (1928–82)

Phillip Kendred Dick spent his most creative years in California when the drug-oriented counter-culture was at its peak. His novels reflect the concerns of this time as filtered through his own bizarre and quirky world-view. Some of his best fiction deals with paranoia and the blurring of the sense of reality induced by drugs. In *A Scanner Darkly* (1977) a police agent becomes addicted to the drug he is investigating and is then instructed to spy on himself. Other novels, such as *The Three Stigmata of Palmer Eldritch* (1965) and *Do Androids Dream of Electric Sheep?* (1968), which inspired the film *Blade Runner* (1982), explore the way ideas of illusion and reality can be insidiously subverted.

The philosophical depth of Dick's fiction partly accounts for the large cult following it has attracted in both America and Europe. His work is unlike anything else in the science fiction field, not least because of the economy and precision of his writing. It treats serious topics with exceptional wit and inventiveness.

WILLIAM GIBSON (b.1948)

A quarter of a century ago, the science fiction writer James Blish (1921–75) remarked that science fiction had so far produced no literary masterworks and that no such work could be expected of it in the future. With *Neuromancer* (1984) and *Count Zero* (1986), William Gibson went some way towards disproving the claim and in the process founded a kind of sub-genre within science fiction – the cyberpunk novel. Gibson is a genuinely original talent, whose vivid prose style owes more to mainstream literature than to his own genre. The cyberpunk novel posits a future dominated by multinational corporations where the Internet has evolved into the all-embracing virtual reality of 'cyberspace'.

In Gibson's novels the heroes are usually maverick figures, 'console cowboys', who are skilled at navigating cyberspace, breaking into corporate data banks and thwarting the corporate AIs (artificial intelligences). His main interest is not in the technology of the future (Gibson's fans were surprised to learn that he did not even own a computer until recently) but in its cultural and social landscape. This he depicts as a nightmarish (yet familiar) extension of today's consumerist pop culture. Ridley Scott's film *Blade Runner* (1982) gave a stunning visual expression of the cyberpunk world as one in which high-tech glamour coexists with old-world squalor in an endless urban 'sprawl'. Gibson saw the

film while he was writing *Neuromancer*, and he walked out after 30 minutes: 'It looked so much like the inside of my head.'

Dozens of cyberpunk novels have appeared following the success of *Neuromancer*, although none of them has come close to matching that book's imaginative depth. They are generally too formulaic in the way they copy the features of Gibson's fictional universe. Gibson's literary skills, particularly his brilliant use of language, have proved more difficult to emulate.

IAIN M. BANKS (b.1954)

Like William Gibson, the Scottish writer Iain Menzies Banks uses technology as a backdrop to his fiction rather than as the centre of interest. His novels contain many of the standard elements of science fiction: galactic civilizations spanning millions of planets, robots, spaceships 30 kilometres long, utopian societies and advanced alien or humanoid species. These serve primarily to enrich the texture of his imaginative worlds. Banks's AIs, for instance, are benign, god-like entities acting in the interests of mankind and are generally offstage. When we encounter them directly, however, as in *Excession* (1996), they are given all the qualities of human beings.

Banks alternates between writing science fiction and writing well-regarded mainstream novels (under the name Iain Banks), such as *Espedair Street* (1987) and *Complicity* (1993). In science fiction novels, like *Consider Phlebas* (1987) and *The State of the Art* (1989,

revised 1991), he brings many of the same literary strengths to bear. Written in a distinctive style that is in marked contrast to the neutral, lacklustre prose of most science fiction, they are well constructed, fertile in imagination and, above all, rattling good stories.

J.G. BALLARD (b.1930)

James Graham Ballard has described himself as a 'cosmonaut of inner space'. He believes that science fiction should turn away from its traditional subject matter – outer space, alien life forms and the like – and his novels have very little in common with standard science fiction works. Strongly influenced by surrealism, Ballard has always been more interested in images, visions and dreams than in plot or character.

Ballard's early novels and collections of short stories, which include *The Drowned World* (1962), *The Terminal Beach* (1964) and *Vermilion Sands* (1973), are set in a post-apocalyptic future where civilization has reached a point of terminal decay. They are powerfully atmospheric and full of striking images. *Crash* (1973), with its story of a band of car-crash fetishists, and *Concrete Island* (1974), set in the middle of a motorway, began a new phase in his writing. Ballard now concerned himself with the 20th century, interlocking the themes of sexuality, technology and violence.

Following the critical success of his autobiographical novel *Empire of the Sun* (1984), which was made into a film (1987), he left the 'landscapes of the mind' of his science fiction altogether.

Right: J.G. Ballard's novels broke new ground in their evocative and poetic use of language to explore inner space, and helped to close the gap between science fiction and mainstream literature.

Left: A scene from the seminal (and now classic) science fiction film *Blade Runner* based on Philip K. Dick's *Do Androids Dream of Electric Sheep?*

Spy fiction

Trust and betrayal, loyalty and duplicity, are the deep themes of the spy novel, a genre that epitomizes the 20th century's struggle between contending ideologies. In the spy novel stories of bravery or cowardice are played out against the cruel and impersonal forces pushing the world and the individual to the brink of disaster.

J. MORGAN

ERIC AMBLER (1909–98)

Eric Ambler studied engineering in London before he started to write fiction. Between 1936 and 1940 he produced six novels, which made his reputation, largely because of their success in capturing the queasily paranoid atmosphere of Europe on the brink of yet another war. At the centre of the murder, bribery and duplicity is Ambler's hero, an ordinary man caught up in events that place him in the greatest danger and require of him resources, both physical and moral, that he was hitherto unaware he possessed. In *Journey into Fear* (1940) Graham, a British engineer advising the Turkish navy, is plunged into a nightmare when he returns his hotel to find himself the victim of an attempted assassination. Nearly all the action of the tense plot is worked out on the ship that is taking Graham home but that also has onboard the man attempting to kill him and an entertaining cast of Central and East European drifters. Ambler's pre-war fiction broke the mould of the thriller, abandoning the story of the strong man fighting for empire or country for an unmistakable left-wing agenda, in which ordinary human beings are caught up in, and made aware of, the dangers of fascism – as, of course, is the reader.

GRAHAM GREENE (1904–91)

Throughout his career the English novelist Graham Greene (see page 108) wrote 'entertainments' – short novels in the form of the thriller, which did not have the same far-reaching ambition as his more serious fiction.

Despite the slightly disparaging label, they are nonetheless admirable achievements in their own right, demonstrating a mastery of plot, a superb gift for the depiction of atmosphere and location and an acute eye for the behaviour of flawed but redeemable human beings acting under extreme stress.

Greene's first popular success with an 'entertainment' was *Stamboul Train* (1932), which was set entirely on the Orient Express, and it was followed by *It's a Battlefield* (1934) and *A Gun For Sale* (1936). Later 'entertainments', such as *The Confidential Agent* (1939), move more towards the conventional spy thriller. In this book the agent, D., is sent to England to buy coal on behalf of the side he supports in the civil war in his homeland. In an atmosphere dripping with treachery and paranoia, he is pursued by both the British police and murderous rebel agents. Like most of Greene's entertainments, *The Confidential Agent* takes place in what has come to be known as 'Greeneland', a world of seedy pubs and hotels, sinister eccentrics, corrupt plutocrats and politicians, where even the hero is at odds with himself as he seeks safety and salvation.

Fleming's work is very much 'popular fiction'. Unlike the spy fiction of Ambler or Greene, it is not concerned with the complexities of character, motivation and loyalty. Instead, the free world is invariably threatened with disaster by an outlandish megalomaniac, such as the gold-hungry Auric Goldfinger in *Goldfinger* (1959) or the evil scientific genius Dr Julius No in *Dr No* (1958). Almost single-handedly Bond saves the world.

The two-dimensional nature of both heroes and villains in Fleming's books, combined with the straight-forward, tightly written plots, helped to make them a popular success and aided their transition into the film series that has made James Bond known throughout the world. So potent and lucrative is Bond's appeal that he lives on, long after Fleming's death, in new adventures by a variety of other writers.

JOHN LE CARRÉ (b.1931)

The macho glamour of James Bond is a world away from the fiction of John Le Carré, the pseudonym of David Cornwell. Le Carré worked for the British foreign service in the late 1950s, and his novels are steeped in the details of 'trade craft' – the everyday drudgery of real spying at the height of the Cold War. In his first popular success, *The Spy Who Came in from the Cold* (1963), the hero Lemas has to destroy an East German spy. It is a dirty and unheroic business from which nobody emerges with credit.

Le Carré's best known creation, George Smiley, who was introduced in *Call for the Dead* (1961), appeared in *Tinker, Tailor, Soldier, Spy* (1974), the first in a trilogy of books pitting Smiley against his Soviet counterpart, the master spy Karla. Smiley is the antithesis of the James Bond-style hero: donnish and middle-aged, his weapons are shrewdness and deceit rather than muscle and guns. The struggle between Smiley and Karla continued in *The Honourable Schoolboy* (1977) and concluded in *Smiley's People* (1980).

Le Carré overcame what was for many spy novelists a moment of crisis – the end of the Cold War. In novels such as *Our Game* (1995) and *Single and Single* (1999) he successfully transposed his themes of loyalty, betrayal and revenge into a new world order that is every bit as menacing as the one it replaced.

IAN FLEMING (1908–64)

No fictional spy has achieved the same kind of fame as James Bond, the British secret agent, 'licensed to kill', who first appeared in Ian Fleming's *Casino Royale* (1953). Bond himself is handsome, ruthless, suave, ultra-sophisticated and irresistible to women, and all the Bond books feature sex, snobbery and violence in a cocktail that the whole world has found irresistible.

The detective story

The detective is one of the great staples of 20th-century popular fiction, brilliantly solving mysterious crimes where the bungling police have drawn a blank or arrested the wrong person. Usually an amateur, but occasionally a policeman, the detective does not simply amaze us with his or her deductive powers but also reveals a dangerous or seamy underside to apparently safe and law-abiding worlds.

ARTHUR CONAN DOYLE (1859–1930)

Sir Arthur Conan Doyle's creation Sherlock Holmes first appeared in the story *A Study in Scarlet* in 1887. He is the archetype of the fictional detective, both brilliant and eccentric, as he uses his superior, almost super human, powers of observation and deduction to solve crimes that leave the comically bungling police baffled. Holmes, together with his slightly dim but good-hearted companion Dr Watson, enjoyed immediate and enormous success with the reading public – so much so that when Doyle tried to kill off Holmes, public clamour forced him to revive the sleuth. Between 1859 and 1927 Holmes starred in more than 50 short stories and in novels such as the classic *The Hound of the Baskervilles* (1902), with its mysterious setting on mist-shrouded Dartmoor, Holmes's brilliant use of deduction and disguise and the unexpected but entirely rational explanation for the strange events.

The figure of Holmes received even wider exposure with his appearances in both film and television versions from the 1930s on. As a result, even those who have not read Doyle's elegantly written and ingeniously plotted stories are familiar with the figure of the great detective of Baker Street, with his trademark deerstalker, magnifying glass and pipe.

AGATHA CHRISTIE (1891–1976)

Agatha Christie is the bestselling English-language author of the 20th century: more than 100 million copies of her books have been sold. This is largely because of the appeal of her two most famous detectives, Hercule Poirot and Miss Marple. The former made his debut in Christie's first book, *The Mysterious Affair at Styles* (1920), and went on to appear in more than 40 books, including *Murder on the Orient Express* (1934) and *Death on the Nile* (1937), both of which were made into successful films. Like Sherlock Holmes, Poirot is brilliant, using his 'little grey cells' to great

effect when lesser minds – usually those of the police or his assistant Hastings – have failed to find any significance. That he is an outsider – he is Belgian – in English society helps to highlight his sharpness and also provides opportunities for light comic relief, as does Poirot's tendency to pomposity.

Miss Marple, on the other hand, is a classic English spinster, whose outward conventionality masks a shrewd investigative brain – and one with a particular understanding of what monsters might be lurking in the gardens of a pretty English village.

Agatha Christie's enormous success owes much to her use of typically English settings – the country house,

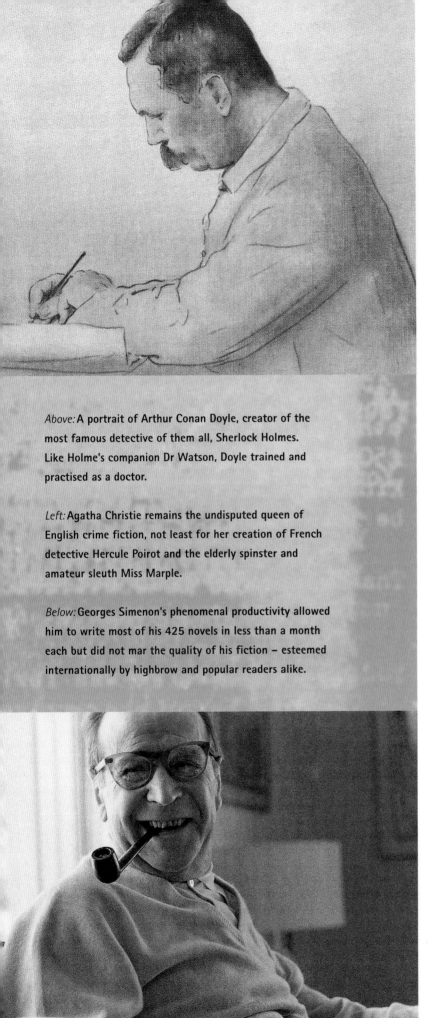

Above: A portrait of Arthur Conan Doyle, creator of the most famous detective of them all, Sherlock Holmes. Like Holme's companion Dr Watson, Doyle trained and practised as a doctor.

Left: Agatha Christie remains the undisputed queen of English crime fiction, not least for her creation of French detective Hercule Poirot and the elderly spinster and amateur sleuth Miss Marple.

Below: Georges Simenon's phenomenal productivity allowed him to write most of his 425 novels in less than a month each but did not mar the quality of his fiction – esteemed internationally by highbrow and popular readers alike.

the apparently idyllic village – but this would count for little if she had not had a gift for creating credible characters within plot structures that were always neat and sometimes brilliant, as in *The Murder of Roger Ackroyd* (1926), in which she was the first detective writer to use an unexpected plot device that astonished contemporary readers. To reveal it, however, would spoil any reader's pleasure in the book.

GEORGES SIMENON (1903–89)

Even Agatha Christie's output and sales are put in the shade by the record of Georges Simenon, who wrote more than 425 books, which have sold more than 600 million copies worldwide. Simenon, born in Francophone Belgium, wrote many psychological novels as well as short stories and autobiography, but it is on his detective Maigret that both his fame and his sales rest. Maigret appeared in the first novel to appear under Simenon's own name, *The Case of Peter the Lett* (1931), very much in the form he was to keep for more than 80 more novels: large, imperturbable, patient and puffing on his ever-present pipe.

Unlike Holmes or Poirot, Maigret does not rely on superhuman powers of deduction to solve a logical puzzle, and he is all the more credible because of this. Instead, he uses his psychological insight and his investigation into the whole background of a crime to tease out the truth. In many of his cases, patience, repeated questioning and the intolerable pressure of Maigret's presence and persistence combine to make a suspect crack. Simenon set his Maigret novels in a wide variety of settings, from Paris, both rich and poor, and throughout provincial France to novels where Maigret travels to London or New York to solve the crime. But no matter where Maigret must go, he remains resolutely himself, changing neither himself nor his methods.

Simenon used a spare style with a deliberately restricted vocabulary in order to make his books accessible to the widest possible audience, yet his work is as highly regarded by literary critics as it is by the public at large, both for its psychological acuity and for its superb evocation of place. Maigret himself remains one of the more credible of fictional detectives.

Private eyes

In the United States the detective story developed in a very different way from Britain, avoiding genteel or upper-crust settings and characters in favour of urban settings that were often seedy, where power and wealth were intimately connected to crime and corruption. At the centre of the American crime story is the lone figure of the private eye.

DASHIELL HAMMETT (1894–1961)

It is no exaggeration to say that Dashiell Hammett invented both the modern American detective and the modern American style of crime fiction that is known as 'hard-boiled' – a direct, earthy style, featuring vivid and often squalid locations, much slangy dialogue and wise-cracking, and liberal amounts of sex and violence.

Hammett himself had worked as a detective for the Pinkerton agency before he turned to writing in the late 1920s. His early stories appeared in pulp magazines, and he soon developed his characteristic style, influenced as much by the prose of Hemingway as by the subject matter of crime. His famous detective, Sam Spade, appeared in his most successful novel, *The Maltese Falcon* (1930) and was later memorably played by Humphrey Bogart in the film of the book (1941). Sam Spade sets the pattern for all subsequent American private eyes. Laconic and lonely, he is a tough man with a good heart, disillusioned by the corruption and duplicity he sees all around. As readers we are as interested in the character of the detective as we are in the 'whodunnit' elements of Hammett's books.

RAYMOND CHANDLER (1888–1959)

Raymond Chandler's fictional detective Philip Marlowe is the hero of seven novels, from *The Big Sleep* (1939) and *Farewell, My Lovely* (1940) to *Playback* (1958). Like Sam Spade, Marlowe is a loner, but he is a more sophisticated and complex character, a cool and reflective man, who likes to work out chess problems at home. Marlowe has a code of honour that makes him something of a modern knight-errant, and money is never the main reason for his taking on a case. Corruption is endemic in Bay City, the Californian city where Marlowe is based, from the police up to the rich who live in the big houses in the hills. Chandler's plots, frequently located at the point where greed and family dysfunction intersect, are often confused and hard to follow, but his writing is memorable for its strong characterization and striking combination of lyrical description and tough wisecracking.

There have been many film versions of Chandler's books, with Marlowe played convincingly by Humphrey Bogart in *The Big Sleep* (1946) and by Dick Powell in *Farewell, My Lovely* (1944).

ROSS MCDONALD (1915–83)

Lew Archer, the detective hero created by Ross McDonald in *The Moving Target* (1949) and sustained through a further 17 novels, is a direct descendant of Sam Spade and Philip Marlowe. Like them, he works on his own and lives alone in California. But McDonald's hero rapidly took an original turn. Archer is less of a tough

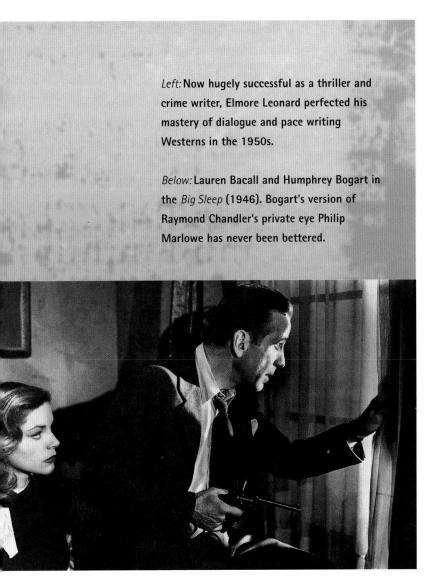

Left: Now hugely successful as a thriller and crime writer, Elmore Leonard perfected his mastery of dialogue and pace writing Westerns in the 1950s.

Below: Lauren Bacall and Humphrey Bogart in the *Big Sleep* (1946). Bogart's version of Raymond Chandler's private eye Philip Marlowe has never been bettered.

guy than are his predecessors, and the novels feature less action and conventional crime. Instead, they present a California that is full of dysfunctional families with missing children, absent fathers and flawed mothers. In this milieu Lew Archer plays the private eye as psychotherapist – as someone who listens seriously and asks the right questions in order to help clients make sense of their history.

The Underground Man (1971) is fairly typical, featuring as it does a 25-year-old murder, several abandoned wives and two runaway children. A weary Archer is reluctantly drawn into this tangle of frustrated loves and failed family relationships, ultimately guiding at least some of the characters to a form of redemption.

ELMORE LEONARD (b.1925)

Elmore Leonard's books are not strictly detective novels, since his main character is just as likely to be a minor criminal – as in *Stick* (1983) – as a law enforcement officer, and in *Out of Sight* (1996) the two main characters are a female US marshal and a male bank robber, whose love affair is the central theme of the book. Whatever side of the law the hero or heroine is on, they are inevitably faced with a situation where they must face down a set of villains by using their own ingenuity and courage.

Leonard's books are all richly researched – he employs a full-time researcher to gather background material – which results in extremely dense and credible settings. He has a gift for getting inside the minds of both heroes and villains, and an equal gift for memorable and telling dialogue, often resulting in passages of great comedy as well as excitement. His style appears effortless and almost artless, but it is finely achieved and reveals many brilliant touches. His brilliantly managed plots show evidence of the time he spent in the 1950s writing Westerns, many of which were filmed, including *Hombre* (1967) with Paul Newman and *Valdez is Coming* (1970) with Burt Lancaster. His crime stories have earned him large sales and a high critical reputation, and later film versions of his work, such as *Get Shorty* (1995) and *Jackie Brown* (1997) (from *Rum Punch*), have also been successful.

'Down these mean streets a man must go who is not himself mean, who is neither tarnished or afraid.'
RAYMOND CHANDLER, 'The Simple Art of Murder' (1944)

Horror fiction

Tales of terror have been a feature of the fictional landscape almost since the beginning of the modern novel. After several decades of neglect, the late 20th century has seen a resurgence in their popularity. There seems to be a deep human need to thrill to horrific dangers and mysterious events, and both fairy tales and novelists have long supplied stories that contain sufficient terror to make our hair stand on end.

The first sophisticated examples of this were the novels collectively know as 'Gothic', written in the late 18th and early 19th centuries. These sensational fictions established many of the situations and predicaments that recur in horror fiction to the present day: isolated castles and ruins; a hero or heroine endangered by mysterious and malevolent forces, often incarnated in an evil villain; dark family secrets; a pervading sense of unreality, leading the protagonist to question his or her own sanity; and scenes of inventive violence laced with eroticism.

BRAM STOKER (1847–1912)

All of the above features are present in *Dracula* by Bram Stoker. *Dracula* was first published in 1897, but a cheap edition in 1900 earned it a mass readership, while dozens of film versions have imprinted the figure of Count Dracula on the world's consciousness.

Stoker was born in Ireland and educated at Trinity College, Dublin, and he worked as a civil servant before becoming an assistant to the great Victorian actor Sir Henry Irving. It is perhaps not surprising that *Dracula* contains a great deal of melodrama and a number of theatrical effects – not unlike a lurid theatrical backdrop – in its descriptive passages. But there is much literary skill in the way Stoker merges the grisly story of blood-sucking vampires and their human victims with high suspense.

What makes *Dracula* so compelling is the way in which an unmistakable sexual element is mingled with the cruelty and, in particular, with the physical act of vampirism. The Count's first victim, after he has been shipped to England in his coffin, the hitherto pure and demure Lucy Westenra, is transformed by the Count's nocturnal attentions into a sensual predator. The other heroine, Mina Murray, spends much of the book after her encounter with the vampire wondering if his bite has rendered her 'unclean' and unworthy of her husband. Clearly, the vampiric act is a metaphor for the sexual act, and it is one that transforms women and troubles their menfolk. The unconscious message of the book, perhaps, is that female sexuality is too turbulent a force to be set free.

Of Stoker's many books, *Dracula* is the only one to have had any enduring reputation, but the vampire itself, after sleeping for some decades, had a successful reincarnation later in the century.

H.P. LOVECRAFT (1890–1937)

In his lifetime the work of the American writer Howard Phillips Lovecraft appeared mainly in pulp magazines, especially the US magazine *Weird Tales*, but in the decades following his death he has attained cult status, and now his stories and novels are nearly all in print.

As a cult writer Lovecraft is adored and reviled in equal measure. His admirers praise him for his unique capacity to create a macabre and unsettling atmosphere with minimum effort, as in the short story 'Dagon' (1917), which begins: 'I am writing this under an appreciable mental strain since by tonight I shall be no more.' In the few pages of story we are almost convinced that the narrator's vision after a shipwreck of an horrific fish-god has been enough to drive him to suicide.

Lovecraft's detractors, on the other hand, criticize his verbosity and what they see as the banal nature of his imagined worlds as presented in what he called the 'Cthulhu mythos'. This complex and complete mythological world, outlined in a number of works including 'The Call of Cthulhu' (1926), has been developed further by his disciples.

STEPHEN KING (b.1947)

Lovecraft set much of his macabre fiction in realistic New England settings, and the horror lurking behind the everyday is a key element in the fiction of Stephen King, who, in the last two decades of the 20th century,

Above: Shelley Duvall in a scene from Stanley Kubrick's film *The Shining*, one of the many film and TV productions based on Stephen King's chillers.

Left: More than anyone else, Stephen King has established horror fiction as a genre in its own right – and sales of his books dwarf those of all others in the field.

has almost single-handedly rescued horror fiction as a worthwhile popular fiction genre.

King's first book, *Carrie* (1974), sets the tone of nearly all his subsequent fiction in creating the most horrific situations out of the ordinary people, places and events of American life. Carrie, the persecuted teenage heroine of the novel, simply wants to have an ordinary life – date boys, attend the high school prom and so on – but her mother's puritanical religious fanaticism, the vicious cruelty of her fellow teenagers and Carrie's own growing discovery of her supernatural, telekinetic powers result in her exacting an horrific and destructive revenge. In what may or may not be a conscious reference to *Dracula*'s conflation of blood, sexuality and power, Carrie's apprehension of her powers occurs as she first menstruates.

Whatever King writes seems to appeal to the reading public's need to feel a frisson of horror, and all his books since his debut have been bestsellers, for in addition to his inventive imagination, King has a notably laconic, unfussy style that poses few problems for a mass reader-ship. His appeal has been extended by accomplished film and TV versions of his work, most notably *Carrie* (1976) and *The Shining* (1980).

ANNE RICE (b.1941)

'American Gothic' is a phrase that has often been used to describe Stephen King's fiction, but it is one that fits even better the author who provided the vampire with new life toward the end of the 20th century, Anne Rice. Her books take vampire mythology and bring it right up to date, most notably in *The Vampire Lestat* (1985), in which the eponymous hero wakes from his decades long vampire sleep and turns himself into one of the world's biggest rock music stars.

Rice's series of vampire novels began in 1976 with *Interview with the Vampire* (filmed 1994), in which Louis, the vampire, recounts his life story to a young reporter. Rice, as narrator, identifies with the vampire rather than with the victims. Her vampires suffer and doubt, trapped as they are in their immortality. She also makes explicit the eroticism of the vampire, drawing connections between sex and death in prose that some find sensuous and rich, but which others find turgid and repetitive.

Like Stephen King, however, Rice roots the extra-ordinary events of her fiction in the believable everyday world, giving her many fans a foot in the camps of both reality and the supernatural.

Bestsellers: adventure and faction

Popular fiction – in the sense of those books that sell the most copies – has rarely in the 20th century accorded with the critics' notions of what is good literature, but bestsellers cannot simply be dismissed as trash: they have a vigour and power of their own that are able to reach out around the world to hundreds of millions of people of different languages and cultures.

Bestselling fiction in the 20th century has sold on a scale that the more literary novelist can only dream about. The novels of Harold Robbins, for example, are thought to have had a total sale of well over 200 million copies, while the adventure novels of Alastair Maclean have sold only slightly fewer. Such figures are evidence of a profound cross-cultural appeal, based on the exploitation of universal human interests: love, sex, ambition and wealth. These figures also show how the world market for fiction has changed in the course of the 20th century. The introduction of mass education, first in the West and later elsewhere, necessarily led to much higher literacy rates. Literate people must have something to read, but not all literate people are sophisticated readers; indeed, not all sophisticated readers wish to read sophisticated literature all the time. Even literary critics need a rest.

Bestsellers, then, do not present any stylistic difficulties for the reader, nor do they attempt to experiment with form. They rely on boldly drawn, 'larger than life' characters, acting in taut plots that often have an element of suspense about them, and, perhaps most important of all, they offer the reader an intense dose of escapism – when we read a bestseller we flee from our dull, everyday life and enter the world of the captain of industry, the Mafia boss, the contract killer, the commando. And we can be sure that there will be lashings of danger, violence and, more often than not, sex to give us a vicarious thrill.

HAROLD ROBBINS (1916–97)

In many respects the American writer Harold Robbins is the emblematic bestseller of the century since his books combine all the elements mentioned above in a package the reading public has found irresistible. His novels take us inside the world of the elite, whether this is the international jetset – as in *The Pirate* (1979) – the motor industry – in *The Betsy* (1971) – or politics – in *The Carpetbaggers* (1961). Each one is the life story of an individual driven by intense ambition to achieve power. Strong evidence of the hero's will power is his insatiable sex drive, which leads to many sex scenes in each of Robbins's novels. Along the way there will be power struggles, treachery and violence (often exacted in revenge).

ALASTAIR MACLEAN (1922–87)

Alastair Maclean's adventure novels are a rather different kind of bestseller and one that found less favour in the more permissive atmosphere after 1960s. Like Robbins, Maclean makes us feel that he is giving us privileged 'insider information' about a hitherto secret world, but his books are nearly all set in a closed, exclusively male society, whether on a warship – as in his debut novel *HMS Ulysses* (1955) – or in a nuclear submarine – *Ice Station Zebra* (1963) – or in a commando squad – *The Guns of Navarone* (1957) and *Where Eagles Dare* (1967). There are action, tension, heroism and treachery aplenty, but there is no sex.

Left: In the 50s and 60s, British writer Alastair Maclean's adventure stories represented the more wholesome side of bestselling adventure stories with their tales of heroic action in a uniformly male world.

Right: The heady mix of wealth, power, ruthless ambition and sex has made Harold Robbins' books international bestsellers. Revenge is often a key element.

In the later 20th century bestselling writers in a similar mode, such as Wilbur Smith (b.1933), made sure the missing element was added to the mixture.

FACTION

Both Robbins and Maclean went to great lengths to make sure the factual elements of their books – the 'background' – were accurate. Neither, however, went quite so far as Arthur Hailey (b.1920) in supplying the reader with almost encyclopedic information. As a result, such novels have come to be known as 'faction' – a hybrid half-fact, half-fiction. Hailey would typically spend four years on each novel, only one of which was for writing; two were spent on planning and research, and one on 'production', the necessary business of advertising and promoting the finished product.

Hailey's books are typically set in a world of which we all have some limited experience but that he reveals in all its rich variety: *Hotel* (1965) takes us behind the scenes in a grand New Orleans hotel, *Airport* (1968) shows us what really goes on in the world of the airline business, while *Wheels* (1971) takes the lid off the motor industry.

The 'factional' has increasingly become a part of many different types of bestseller, particularly in adventures where military hardware or espionage techniques are crucial elements. The books of Tom Clancy (b.1947) exemplify this 'techno-thriller' genre. His first book, *The Hunt for Red October* (1984), makes much of the technology of the nuclear submarines on which it is for the most part set as well as giving the reader an 'insider's' view of high-level military and political decision-making.

In a series of thrillers through the 1980s and 1990s Clancy continued to marry action and tension with inside information and technological detail to such effect that he has become one of the biggest-selling authors of the late 20th century.

Other bestselling thriller writers rely on similar 'exclusives' or 'insider information' to add realism and fact to their improbable plots and sometimes wooden characters. The thrillers of Frederick Forsyth (b.1938), especially *The Day of the Jackal* (1971), in which a plot to assassinate President de Gaulle of France is foiled, combine meticulous research with a hint of the true story to gripping effect. Similarly, the legal background of John Grisham (b.1955) gives his books, such as *The Pelican Brief* (1992), a basis rooted in fact, which helps the reader to suspend disbelief at the twists and turns of the plot.

Bestsellers: saga and romance

Ruthless ambition, individual heroism and the technology of violence are the masculine staples of one kind of bestselling fiction, but there are other kinds of bestseller, generally – but not exclusively – written by women for women. While not lacking in narrative drive or tension, these novels concentrate more on the emotional lives and aspirations of individuals or of families, often in the form of the saga or romance.

MARGARET MITCHELL (1900–49)

Gone with the Wind (1936) is believed to be the only book ever to have outsold the Bible in a given month. It was the only novel of the American writer Margaret Mitchell, and was the publishing sensation of its age. An historical saga set during and just after the American Civil War, the Pulitzer prize-winning *Gone with the Wind* captivated its millions of readers with its memorably wilful and capricious central character, Scarlett O'Hara, and its huge sweep. Its popularity was reinforced by the film version (1939), starring Clark Gable and Vivien Leigh.

CATHERINE COOKSON (1906–98)

Gone with the Wind set the standard for a type of bestseller commonly known as the saga, in which the emotional, financial and marital fortunes of one family are charted, often over a number of generations. Such stories exploit themes of thwarted love and ambition or parent/child conflict, and they often contain a strong element of the 'rags to riches' motif, whereby the main character (normally a woman) rises from the humblest of beginnings to a position of wealth, status and power.

The more than 90 novels of the English writer Catherine Cookson were often produced as series in which one character or family would appear in a number of different books. The Mallen family saga, for example, begins with *The Mallen Streak* (1973) and continues with *The Mallen Girl* (1974) and *The Mallen Lot* (1974). Like many of Cookson's novels the saga is set in the vividly re-created northeast of England and depicts the affairs of the family against a background of the sins of the past. Cookson herself was born illegitimate and had a poor working-class childhood, themes that often recur in her writing. Her gift for plot, allied to a realistic depiction of the struggles of working-class women, earned her massive popularity – in Britain in 1988, for example, a third of all fiction borrowed from public libraries was by Catherine Cookson.

BARBARA TAYLOR BRADFORD (b.1933)

Often the saga uses an impoverished background merely as the humble beginnings out of which the heroine pulls herself through sheer force of will and ambition. In Barbara Taylor Bradford's *A Woman of Substance* (1979), for instance, the heroine, Emma Harte, overcomes her disadvantages to turn a small shop into the 'world's greatest department store'. Successful in business, she is thwarted in affairs of the heart. Twice unhappily married, the only man she loves is forbidden, and when treachery threatens to destroy her business empire she wreaks a terrible revenge.

Barbara Taylor Bradford's own personal story itself contains elements of the saga; she began working life as a secretary on a newspaper in the north of England, graduated to become a journalist, became a successful magazine editor and then achieved worldwide sales of over 60 million with her fiction. And, in common with many late 20th-century romantic sagas, a number of her books have been turned into TV mini-series.

DANIELLE STEEL

The novels of Danielle Steel do not follow quite such a straightforward rags-to-riches trajectory as those of

Barbara Taylor Bradford, but they do have many similarities, even in a book such as *Silent Honor* (1996), whose theme is the forcible internment of Japanese Americans in the Second World War. Families are torn apart and set against one another, feelings are stretched to breaking-point, lives are ruined and resurrected, and all is set against a sweeping and convincing historical background.

Although precise figures are hard to come by, it may well be that Danielle Steel is the top bestseller of the late 20th century. More than 300 million copies of her books are thought to be in print in 28 languages, and between 1982 and 1999 she was never once absent from the US annual bestselling fiction lists; in 1994 three separate novels by her featured there.

THE ROMANTIC NOVEL

The saga often contains at least some elements of the feminist agenda: women are presented as strong characters seeking to take control of their own destiny, often in a hostile male-dominated world. No such claims could be made for the pure romantic novel, where, after many twists of the plot, the heroine is eventually swept off her feet by the strong, handsome Mr Right to live a blissfully happy married life. Such novels sell in enormous numbers and are often bought by their devotees as much on the strength of an overall brandname – such as Harlequin in the United States or Mills & Boon in Britain – as for the individual author's qualities.

Perhaps the only well-known writer of such books is the British author Barbara Cartland (1901–2000). This prolific novelist's nearly 700 books have sold more than 700 million copies worldwide.

Although romantic novels are fundamentally about love and sexual relations, they remained demure and reticent until late in the 20th century, when readers began to demand a little more realism in the pure escapism. Thus was born the sub-genre of the 'bodice ripper', romantic novels that are more explicit about the physical side of love.

More explicit still, if not downright pornographic, are those novels described as 'sex and shopping'. The bestselling exponent of this genre is Jackie Collins (b.1939). Her books, such as *Hollywood Wives* (1977), are invariably set in a world of wealth and privilege, where sex and status are the only goals that supply the characters' self-fulfilment. The brandnames of luxury goods abound in this genre, as does strenuous and varied sex, all wrapped up in a plot involving power struggles and betrayal.

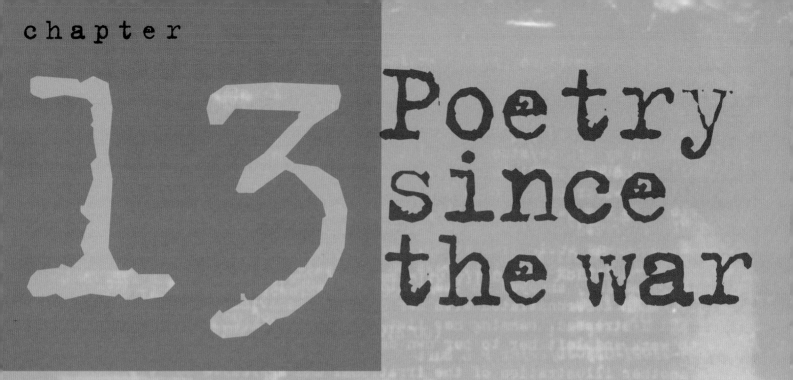

13 Poetry since the war

Below: **Richard Burton** in *Under Milk Wood.* This 'play for voices' was the most famous single work of the Welsh poet Dylan Thomas.

Right: **Wallace Stevens** spent his life working for an insurance company but produced some of the most dense poetic reflection of our time.

The years since the Second World War have produced a rich and varied body of poetry that, at its best, has engaged with the language that makes it possible. History, politics and personality have all played their parts, of course, and posed urgent questions, but increasingly the answers have been sought not in argument but in form. 'Some poems begin with words and others move towards them,' Dylan Thomas said. Whichever the approach, the poet's work has latterly been to involve the reader in the particular way he or she has chosen to write – given that there is no longer any one way for poetry to proceed.

Stevens and Moore

poem he completes. But there is always in his work the notion – which he took from the imagists in Britain – that the unfamiliar must be approached through the familiar. Nothing is too mundane to provide the basis for poetic construction. 'One may find intimations of immortality in an object on the mantelpiece,' he explained. Philosophical thought could come to be 'as real in the mind as the mantelpiece itself', if it began in concrete things. He experienced thought as 'radiant' and enjoyed poetry because it had the power to 'create a truth that cannot be arrived at by reason alone'.

His best known poem is 'The Man with the Blue Guitar' (1937), which uses the idea of a man playing a guitar to explore the work of the poet. 'Things as they are/Are changed upon the blue guitar', just as the world may seem to be changed by the poet's view of it. Stevens has been criticized for being too whimsical and unnecessarily wordy, but his work is always precise and elegant, woven together by repetitions and echoes, which make it compelling to read, despite the difficult ideas within it.

MARIANNE MOORE (1887–1972)

Born in Kirkwood, Missouri, Marianne Moore was brought up in her grandfather's home. He was a Presbyterian minister and clearly influenced her work, which has a strong moral concern. She took a course in typing in 1909 and taught stenography for ten years before moving to New York, where she worked as a secretary, eventually becoming editor of *The Dial*, which she transformed into an internationally successful journal. Her first collection of poetry, which was published without her knowledge in 1921, led Wallace Stevens to decide that she was 'a poet that matters'. T.S. Eliot, then at Faber, published her first book in Britain and wrote the introduction to it. He described her work as 'clear, learned, wise, witty, full of common sense'. Other critics have noted that her poems are like drawings, with a sophisticated conversational tone that describes a detailed situation.

She experimented with the form of her poetry, adopting a system (which Dylan Thomas later employed) of using the number of syllables in each line to give a poem its rhythm and shape.

WALLACE STEVENS (1879–1955)

Wallace Stevens was born in Reading, Pennsylvania, the son of a prosperous country lawyer. He was educated at the local high school and then went to Harvard, which he left without a degree to train to be a lawyer. In 1908 he secured a position with an insurance company in Hartford, Connecticut, and continued to work in insurance until his death. His life as a poet was equally undramatic. Nobody, apart from other poets, took much notice of the collections he frequently produced until his *Collected Poems* appeared in 1954. The Pulitzer prize and much wider recognition followed in 1955, but by then his life was ending.

He has been called 'the most complicated poet of modern times', and it is true that his work is difficult, often dealing with abstract ideas of appearance and reality and the way a poet creates new realities with each

American candour

Introducing the *Faber Book of Modern American Verse* in 1956, W.H. Auden stated that 'there is scarcely one American poet ... who can be mistaken for an Englishman'. Wallace Stevens pointed out that this was hardly surprising since, despite sharing a language, the British and Americans lived in 'two different physical worlds'. Critics have noted the particularly visual quality of American poetry and its distinctive seriousness, combined with a self-questioning, restless experimentation.

Robert Lowell with his second wife, the novelist Caroline Blackwood. A charismatic figure whose friends knew him as 'Cal' (after the emperor Caligula), Lowell suffered from lifelong manic depression.

ROBERT LOWELL (1917–77)

Robert Lowell has probably had more influence on the poetry of the past 50 years than any other poet. He invented what has come to be called 'confessional poetry', a term first used in a review of one of his early collections. As one critic has said: 'His poems tell us more of what it means to live, painfully and difficultly, in our century than any other writer has previously dared.' Lowell's central subject was his personal experience: his marriage, his madness, his drinking, his difficulty with what he called 'ordinary living', his 'fog-bound solitudes'.

Born in Boston into an old New England family, he was educated at Harvard and Kenyon College, jailed for six months as a conscientious objector, married the novelist Jean Stafford, converted to Roman Catholicism, divorced, remarried, went mad and recovered to write his first deeply personal book, *Life Studies*, in 1959. These poems are harrowing autobiographical sketches. Beginning with the admission that 'my mind's not right', Lowell uses bits of letters, conversations and memories to describe his most intimate experiences.

His early poems had been concerned simply to 'talk experience out' – to confess, in fact – but as he matured, he used his crazy states to release floods of images, associations and visionary material, which he transformed into powerful and moving poetry. Lowell's habitual style is, in his own phrase, 'gristly', incorporating rhyme, conventional metre, dialogue and mood changes to build tightly woven verse. Some critics felt that the confessional style Lowell pioneered made poetry prone not only to self-indulgence but also to slack writing – Sylvia Plath and Anne Sexton were his most successful followers, but there have been many more whose work is made tedious by a reliance on personal drama to produce poetry.

ELIZABETH BISHOP (1911–79)

Elizabeth Bishop was brought up by her grandparents in Nova Scotia after the death of her father and her mother's committal to a mental hospital. By the time she graduated from Vassar College in 1934, she was already writing seriously and in correspondence with Marianne Moore, who was in some senses a mother figure to her as well as a poetic mentor. Between 1935 and 1950 she lived in Brazil, where she wrote her first acclaimed collection, *North and South* (1946). Here she muses on the contrasts of cold and heat, reserve and passion, as well as on the restraint and extravagance in her own writing. *Cold Spring* followed in 1955, then *Questions of Travel* (1965) and *Geography III* (1976).

She is a quiet, elegant poet, concerned as much with 'all the untidy activity' of being alive as with creating miraculous imagined worlds, which themselves often begin with something as ordinary as breakfast. The *Complete Poems* (1969) reveals her as a supreme poet of description, whose gift is to suggest something large and general beyond the detail she sees.

JOHN ASHBERY (b.1927)

John Lawrence Ashbery started writing poems when he was 16 years old, and by the time he was 24 he was at the centre of a new school of poetry, the 'New York' school. The characteristic of the poets involved in the movement during the early 1950s – Frank O'Hara (1926–66), Kenneth Koch (b.1925) and James Schuyler (1923–91) – was a relaxed conversational, urban tone, collaged loosely with a 'surrealist shimmer'. In 1955 Ashbery left the United States and moved to France where he remained for ten years, reading the poetry of Arthur Rimbaud and Raymond Roussel, who, he felt, pointed to 'the republic of dreams'.

He experimented with making poems out of cut-up magazines, conversation, random meetings and reflections on what he calls the 'unknowable' aspects of being alive. He has been accused of 'playing games with language', and certainly he does, but the results are not superficial exercises but rather dreamy and ragged constructions, which roam around the cities he lives in, the thoughts he has, the absences he feels. A poem for Ashbery, he says, is 'a snapshot of whatever is going on in my head at the time'. There is never a consistent 'plot' or logical argument in an Ashbery poem. There is no strict metre nor rules about correct syntax in his work, but there is an energetic curiosity about the world, as well as a tenderness for the incoherent emptiness that he senses running through life's rich language and cheerful experience.

His first collection, *Some Trees* (1956), was chosen by W.H. Auden as a Yale Younger Poet selection, but his next, *The Tennis Court Oath* (1962), was too 'difficult' to be popular. *Rivers and Mountains* (1966) was more accessible, and his popularity increased steadily until the Pulitzer prize-winning *Self-Portrait in a Convex Mirror* in 1975, a work that made him the most celebrated poet in the United States. There have been ten more substantial collections since then. Ashbery now teaches at Bard College and lives part of the week in Hudson.

> ❛Father's death was abrupt and unprotesting.
> His vision was still twenty-twenty.
> After a morning of anxious, repetitive smiling,
> his last words to mother were:
> 'I feel awful'❜

ROBERT LOWELL, '*Terminal Days at Beverly Hills*'

The British Isles

After the modernist revolution engineered by Pound, Eliot and Yeats in the early 20th century, British poetry mostly turned its back on experimentation and settled into a less expansive mode than its US counterpart, both formally and thematically. Possibly constrained by a readership happier with recognizable, well-made, personal poetry, it moved away from 'movements' to concern itself with finding distinct individual voices.

DYLAN THOMAS (1914–53)

Dylan Marlais Thomas was born in Swansea, Wales. His father was a schoolmaster and poet, who recited Shakespeare to his infant son, and his mother was devoted to her asthmatic, pampered, naughty child. His manner through his schooldays was one of 'flamboyant idleness', and he left school when he was 17 years old to become a newspaper reporter in Swansea. The collection *18 Poems* appeared in 1934 – the year he moved to London – and his second collection, *25 Poems*, in 1936.

In London he led a life of journalism, broadcasting, film-making and drinking, quickly developing a reputation for exuberance and flamboyance – in both his life and his poetry. He married the long-suffering Caitlin Macnamara in 1937, and together they lived an impoverished, volatile life, not settling anywhere until 1947, when they moved to Laugharne in Wales with their collection of children. Thomas described himself as 'a freak user of words, not a poet', and critics have often agreed that his work depends more on sound than sense. His is a vibrant, tumbling world of repetition, echoes and bizarre juxtaposition, haunted everywhere by the 'moonless acre' of death. He wrote prose, autobiography and the radio play *Under Milk Wood* (1952) before his gruelling lifestyle of reading tours, alcohol abuse and emotional turmoil resulted in a heart attack in America when he was 39 years old.

PHILIP LARKIN (1922–85)

Regarded by some as the most significant English poet since the war, Philip Larkin was born in Coventry and spent his adult life working as a librarian. At Oxford University, where his friends included Kingsley Amis and John Wain, he read and loved the poetry of Dylan Thomas and Yeats but wrote later that for him 'the tradition of poetry' is 'emotion and honesty of emotion,

and it doesn't matter who it is written by or how, if this is conveyed'. His first book, *The North Ship* (1945), was followed by two novels, *Jill* (1946) and *A Girl in Winter* (1947), which are not generally highly valued.

The Less Deceived (1955) was the collection that first attracted widespread attention, and *The Whitsun Weddings* (1964) and *High Windows* (1974) consolidated his reputation. *The Collected Poems* appeared posthumously in 1988, along with his letters and a biography – both of which he had instructed should not appear. His task, he felt, was 'to preserve things I have seen/thought/felt', and poems were 'verbal devices' to enable that. His theme essentially is disappointment – time lost, opportunity wasted, the closing-in of death, the inescapable isolation of even a very social life. But he is rarely resentful or self-pitying, and his appeal is perhaps that he articulates a deep-felt, if wry, compassion for the quiet desperation of everyman.

TED HUGHES (1930–98)

Edward James Hughes was born in Mytholmroyd in Yorkshire. The harsh dialect and craggy landscape of his childhood informed the poetry he began writing in his teens and remained a consistent influence. His father was a veteran of the First World War, whose life and losses affected Hughes deeply, as did his brother's passion for hunting and fishing. After finishing his national service as a wireless mechanic in Yorkshire, he went to Cambridge University, where he switched from English to anthropology and archaeology and began his controversial relationship with the American poet, Sylvia Plath.

Hughes married Plath in 1956, and they went briefly to America, where she arranged for his collection *The Hawk in the Rain* to be published in 1957. Other works soon followed, continuing his preoccupation with the violence and beauty of the natural world. After *Lupercal* (1960) and *Wodwo* (1967), came the poem-sequence *Crow* (1970), which introduced the central symbol of the indestructible crow, 'screaming for blood' amid 'the horror of creation'. Later volumes include *Cave Birds* (1975), *Season Songs* (1976) and *Selected Poems* with Thom Gunn, whose work is frequently associated with Hughes's as marking a turning-point for English poetry. He became Poet Laureate in 1984. His final collection, *Birthday Letters* (1998), turned away from the violence of nature that had obsessed him to explore his relationship with Plath.

Right: Dylan Thomas's abundant feeling for language sometimes lead him to sacrifice sense for verbal music. Even so, his poetic achievement is substantial and would have been greater still if alcoholism had not led to his early death.

Below: Ted Hughes' upbringing in the harsh splendours of the English Pennines was a major influence on his poetry of the natural world.

SEAMUS HEANEY (b.1939)

Seamus Heaney is the undisputed leader of a group of Ulster poets – which includes Derek Mahon (b.1941), Michael Longley (b.1939), Paul Muldoon (b.1955), Tom Paulin (b.1949) and others – whose work constitutes a minor renaissance. His poetry, he has said, is 'an attempt to make the preserving, shifting marshes of Ireland ... a symbol of the preserving, shifting consciousness of the Irish people'. He carries with him the image of his father and grandfather, toiling with their spades. 'Between my finger and my thumb/The squat pen rests./I'll dig with it,' he explained in 'Digging'. He is concerned to understand the connections between the public 'troubles' and the most intimate of personal experiences, and he does so with patience and simplicity in poems that are technically accomplished and emotionally taut.

His early work was rooted in the Ireland of his youth: *Eleven Poems* (1965), *Death of a Naturalist* (1966) and *Door into the Dark* (1969). His later work is more densely written and poignant, brooding on the cultural supremacy of words, and it includes *The Haw Lantern* (1987), with its moving sequence of poems dedicated to his mother. In 1989 he was appointed professor of poetry at Oxford, and his contribution to international literature was rewarded by the Nobel prize in 1995.

> ❛Groping back to bed after a piss
> I part thick curtains, and am startled by
> The rapid clouds, the moon's cleanliness. ...
>
> ... and the plain
> Far-reachingness of that wide stare
>
> Is a reminder of the strength and pain
> Of being young; that it can't come again,
> But is for others undiminished somewhere.❜

PHILIP LARKIN, 'Sad Steps'

Modern masters

The United States and British Isles were fortunate in not experiencing any radical political destabilization after the end of the Second World War. Elsewhere, the world continued to be in turmoil, and the major poets of this generation inevitably wrote in reaction to this. If there is any common thread to these Nobel laureates, it is their passionate opposition to political tyranny and the sense of poetry as a necessary 'instrument of survival'.

CZESLAW MILOSZ (b.1911)

Czeslaw Milosz was born in Lithuania, in an environment that no longer exists – either culturally or physically. Before the Nazi terror and genocide and the Stalinist tyranny, Milosz's family was one in which primitive folk traditions continued side by side with a complex historical heritage. The contrast of this life with the oppressive regime in which he came of age – in the Polish town of Vilna (Wilno) – during the Cold War, which effectively exiled Milosz to Paris in 1951, is an integral part of his poetry. As his Nobel prize evaluation pointed out in 1980: 'The world that Milosz depicts in his poetry and prose and essays is the world in which man lives having been driven out of paradise.'

He is a difficult writer, in the best sense of the word: erudite and complex, provocative and dramatic, with swift changes of moods – furious or tender, abstract or extremely concrete. 'If I had to show what the world is for me,' he writes in the long poem 'Throughout Our Lands', 'I would take a hamster or a hedgehog or a mole/And place him on a theatre seat one evening/and ... listen to what he says about the spotlights.' This light-hearted tone is as typical as his inveighing against 'the human limitations which make us blind'. And despite critical focus on the 'intellectualism' of his writing, Milosz is a deeply sensual poet whose writing (in Polish), is renowned for its musical and rhythmic qualities and its linguistic richness. He has also written fiction and autobiography, the most significant non-poetry probably being *The Captive Mind* (1951), in which he discusses the experience of living in a totalitarian state.

EUGENIO MONTALE (1896–1981)

'I have felt completely out of harmony with the reality surrounding me ever since my birth,' Eugenio Montale wrote at one point. 'I have knocked desperately on the doors of the impossible, like one who awaits an answer.' He rejected any of the answers that dominated his native Italy – Roman Catholicism, communism and fascism – and spent his life expressing the disharmony of his particular poetic vision. He admired T.S. Eliot (whose work he translated), and his first collection, *Ossi di seppia* (*Cuttlefish Bones*, 1925), shares *The Waste Land*'s view of the world as a dry, barren and hostile place.

The growth of Italian fascism during the 1930s forced Montale to mask his real feelings and effect what he called an 'inner emigration', as did other European poets of this period. This led to some introverted and difficult volumes, which critics found obscure, although recently they have been seen as his most 'elemental', if dismaying, work. At this time he was concerned to transform his perceptions into symbolic metaphors. In 'The Eel', for example, a swimming fish becomes: 'A green soul seeking/life where only/dryness and desolation gnash.'

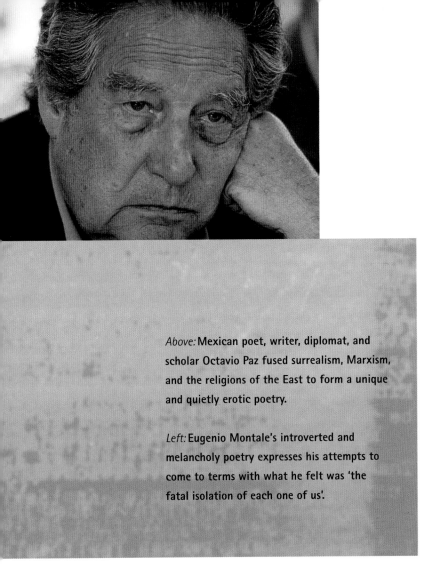

Above: Mexican poet, writer, diplomat, and scholar Octavio Paz fused surrealism, Marxism, and the religions of the East to form a unique and quietly erotic poetry.

Left: Eugenio Montale's introverted and melancholy poetry expresses his attempts to come to terms with what he felt was 'the fatal isolation of each one of us'.

After the death of his wife in 1964 Montale's work became more gentle, with a personal warmth that was absent from earlier collections. *Xenia* (1966) is a series of love poems, devoted to his wife's memory, expressing his pain and nostalgia in direct and simple language and evoking his desire through particular lost moments. He was awarded the Nobel prize in 1975.

OCTAVIO PAZ (1914–98)

Octavio Paz was born in Mexico City into a family that had been financially ruined by the Mexican Civil War. His first book, *Forest Moon*, was published when he was only 19 years old, but it was not until he had visited Spain and written his reflections on the Spanish Civil War, *Beneath Your Clear Shadow and Other Poems*, that he was internationally recognized as a writer of real promise. After Spain, he visited Paris where the surrealist movement was in full swing. That, together with Marxism, Buddhism and Hinduism, was to remain a prominent influence. His themes are difficult: man must overcome his existential solitude through erotic love and artistic creativity. 'The present is perpetual', 'I am where I was', 'We never arrive' and other abstract assertions are everywhere in his poetry. But there is also a frenzied eroticism – 'I drown myself and I do not touch myself' – and a tremendous lyricism to be enjoyed.

His supreme achievement is the extensive *Piedra del sol* (*Sun Stone*, 1957), which has been described as 'perhaps the outstanding long poem of this century'. Here the love of language and the language of love are inseparable as the poem moves towards an 'enormous instant' where 'everything is transfigured and sacred'. After this, Paz concerned himself increasingly with mystic questions of life and death and re-birth, most importantly in *East Slope* (1971), which was written in India. He was awarded the Nobel prize in 1990.

JOSEPH BRODSKY (1940–96)

Iosip Aleksandrovich Brodsky was born in Leningrad (now St Petersburg), where he left school when he was 15 years old and began to write poetry. His burgeoning reputation in the Leningrad literary scene was curtailed when he was charged with 'social parasitism' by the Soviet authorities and sentenced to five years' hard labour. This was ended after 18 months, when prominent literary figures there protested against the sentence. Nevertheless, Brodsky was subsequently 'invited' to leave Russia, and he settled in the United States, writing poetry of isolation, exile and, above all, survival. He remarked, 'It is difficult in Russia to know who is a human being,' but his poems are ultimately concerned with humans – particularly the women he loved – although not with personal history as much as with spiritual identity in the face of private grief.

'The poem is an instrument of survival,' he said, a 'linguistic event' that transcends the self. He admired poets with 'quiet voices' – Dostoesvky, Pasternak and Cavafy – and also Yeats, Auden, Dylan Thomas and Eliot, through whose work he learned English while he was in prison.

His own voice is meditative – never shrill, but powerful in its exploration of universal concerns of life, death and the meaning of existence. In 1987 he was awarded the Nobel prize.

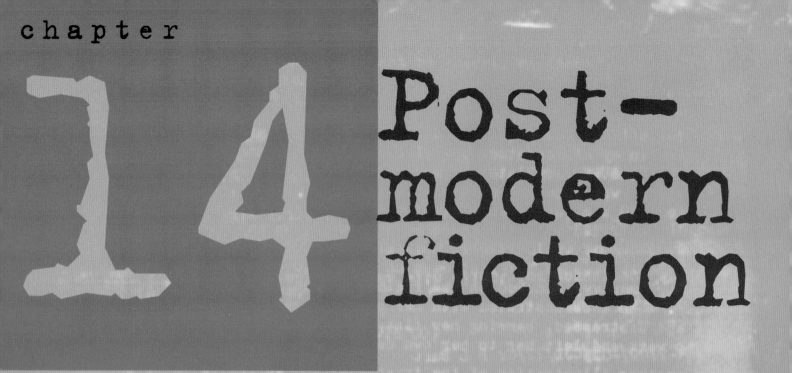

chapter 14 Post-modern fiction

Below: The film version of his novel *The Name of the Rose*, boosted the reputation of Italian academic Umberto Eco. His fictional treatment of post-modern ideas has earned a mixed reception from the critics.

Right: Jorge Luis Borges towards the end of his life when he was almost completely blind. Borges's fantastic short tales are unique in their imaginative depth and resonance.

The term 'post-modern' is notoriously vague. It supposedly refers to a state of mind common in Western culture: self-referential, allusive, 'playful' and ironic; given to parody; more interested in the surface of things than their depths; concerned with popular culture rather than universal truths. At worst, post-modernism is used as a cover for empty word-spinning. What is claimed to be a game between writer and reader can be both tedious and indulgent. The best post-modern writers – Borges, García Márquez, Pynchon and DeLillo – are very different from each other; but all regard writing as more than a mere game.

Literary latin

JORGE LUIS BORGES (1899–1986)

The Argentinian short-story writer, poet and essayist Jorge Luis Borges was almost unknown until he shared the prestigious Formentor prize with Samuel Beckett in 1961. He is now one of the most widely translated and highly regarded Latin American writers of the century. Born in a shabby suburb of Buenos Aires to a bourgeois family, in which both parents spoke English, he said he was not even aware that English and Spanish were separate languages until later in his childhood. 'I grew up in a garden,' he wrote, 'and in a library of unlimited English books.'

Borges's fame rests entirely on his short stories. His first collection, *Historia universal de la infamia* (*A Universal History of Infamy*, 1935), retells the lives of real and fictional criminals in such a way that there is no distinction between fact and fantasy. He was concerned to rid his writing of the florid, Romantic excess that he found in his poetry. The result was a concise, succinct style, a deceptively simple prose.

In 1938 he took a post in the library of Buenos Aires and, in an apparently minor accident, banged his head on a casement window - an injury leading to septicaemia, near death and temporary loss of speech. This led to a radical shift in his writing, from which he created the first of his 'fantastic' stories, 'Pierre Menard, Author of Don Quixote', in which he reviews a new version of Cervantes's *Don Quixote*, which has supposedly just been written, yet is exactly the same as the original but somehow different, because all the words in it have absorbed new meanings since they were first put together. From this time on Borges's themes were set: the relationship between reality and fiction, the double, the copy, the world as an illusion where 'all time has already transpired' – where all words have been used and we are doomed to repetition.

His best known and most influential collections are *Ficciónes* (*Fictions*, 1945) and *Labyrinths* (published in Paris in 1953), both of which were translated into English in the early 1960s. In short pieces, often no more than a few pages long, Borges articulates his ideas in a blend of fantastic fables, mysterious parables and dense invention. In 'The Other' the author meets himself (his double) on a park bench, then 14 years later finds himself again, this time much older, sprawled on a hotel bed. 'Funes the Memorious' is about a 19-year-old boy who is unable to forget anything. 'The Library of Babel' is an apparently scholarly account of the world as an endless library, in which generations of librarian caretakers try to make sense of the books.

Borges worked for some years himself in the municipal library in Buenos Aires, but under the Perón dictatorship in Argentina he was removed from his post, later to be reinstated as professor of English literature and director of the national library. By this time he was totally blind as a result of an hereditary condition and wrote by dictation to his mother or to friends and secretaries. He died on a visit to Switzerland, having produced several later collections of allegories, all blurring the distinction between prose and poetry.

Borges's writing is genuinely playful. His 'games with infinity' are informed by a staggeringly extensive knowledge of literature and philosophy. The ideas in his stories anticipate many of the concerns of later post-modernist writing, but, unlike some of his followers, Borges was primarily interested in the creative possibilities of his ideas rather than merely exploring a theoretical position.

'Through the years, a man peoples a space with images of provinces, kingdoms, mountains, bays, ships, islands, fishes, rooms, tools, stars, horses and people. Shortly before his death he discovers that the patient labyrinth of lines traces the image of his own face.'

BORGES *in conversation with the literary scholar, Richard Burgin*

Magic Realism

Unlike painting or music, fiction cannot easily be classified as belonging to particular movements, at least not in the short term. The term 'Magic Realism' refers to fiction that presents fantastic or magical events as if they were ordinary, but there is, in fact, no school of Magic Realist fiction. Strictly speaking, Magic Realism starts and finishes with the Colombian writer Gabriel García Márquez and applies mainly to his famous novel *One Hundred Years of Solitude*. Other writers have since adopted Magic Realist elements in their work – with varying degrees of success.

GABRIEL GARCÍA MÁRQUEZ (b.1928)

García Márquez is one of the outstanding writers of the century, and one of the few whose novels are immensely popular with the reading public while also being feted by critics as great literature. He was born in Colombia and grew up in a small town near the Caribbean coast. He studied law and journalism at university, then worked for some years as a journalist in Colombia, Venezuela, Mexico and Cuba.

Márquez's first published fiction, *La hojarasca* (*Leaf Storm and other Stories*, 1955), appeared while he was a foreign correspondent in Europe. In this collection of short stories he created the town of Macondo, an imaginary provincial town surrounded by swamps and mountains, and the town serves in Márquez's fiction as a microcosm for many of the features of Latin American history and society – just as Yoknapatawpha County represents the American South in the novels of William Faulkner ('my master', García Márquez called him). It is the setting for *No One Writes to the Colonel* (1961), a short novel about an eccentric war veteran and his efforts to secure his pension.

Recognition eluded García Márquez until the publication of *Cien años de soledad* (*One Hundred Years of Solitude*, 1967). The novel tells the story of seven generations of the Buendia family who founded Macondo. At the same time, it traces the history of the town through wars, drought, the arrival of the railway and cinema, to its eventual decay. It is a work of exceptional power; both grim and ironic, comic and gentle. Supernatural and fantastic phenomena – a priest levitating, conversations with the dead, people flying through the air – are described in the same tone as ordinary reality or horrific events, such as the massacre of 3000 political protestors. But what gives the novel its extraordinary charm and richness are not so much its magical aspects as García Márquez's superb gifts as a storyteller and a creator of characters. He sees Magic Realism as an appropriate and natural response to the 'outsized reality' of Latin America. When, at the age of 19, he read Kafka's *Metamorphosis* (in which a young man is transformed into a giant insect), he felt an immediate sense of recognition: 'That's how my grandmother used to tell stories, the wildest things with a completely natural tone of voice.' The idea of magic can be treated as a metaphor for the experience of wonder: what another Latin American writer has called the 'marvellous real'.

In García Márquez's subsequent novels, Magic Realism plays a much smaller part. The selection committee for the Nobel prize (which he was awarded in 1982) singled out *Le otoño del patriarca* (*The Autumn of the Patriarch*, 1977) as a work that compares

favourably with *One Hundred Years of Solitude*, although it differs considerably in its style and subject matter. It is a portrait of a half-mad but all-powerful dictator and his impact on the people he tyrannizes. García Márquez said the character was a composite of three Latin American dictators known for their cruelty and corruption. *Crónica de una muerte anunciada* (*Chronicle of a Death Foretold*, 1981) is a brilliant and strange reconstruction of a murder that occurred in the town where the author grew up. García Márquez himself figures as a character in the novel, interviewing people who remember the murder and studying court documents and other data such as dreams, gossip and weather reports.

With *El amor en los tiempos del coléra* (*Love in the Time of Cholera*, 1985) Márquez triumphantly brings together all his strengths as a writer. This story of a love that is requited only after 50 years has been highly praised for its mastery of technique, prose style, descrip-

tive power and, above all, its capacity to move the reader. In a review of the book, fellow novelist Thomas Pynchon finished by calling it 'this shining and heart-breaking novel'.

SALMAN RUSHDIE (b.1947)

Writers outside Latin America who have incorporated the effects and techniques of Magic Realism into their fiction include Angela Carter (see page 79), Toni Morrison (see page 178) and Günther Grass (see page 94), but only the Anglo-Indian novelist Salman Rushdie has made it the mainstay of his writing. At the start of *The Satanic Verses* (1988), the two chief characters fall from an exploded jumbo-jet, then land safely on a snow-covered English beach.

The novel that brought Rushdie to prominence, *Midnight's Children* (1981), is the story of Saleem Sinai, who is born at the stroke of midnight on the day India achieves independence. His life – related through a mixture of myth and fabulous tales, historical fact and realistic detail, political comment and satire – becomes emblematic of India's history in the years that follow. When *The Satanic Verses* was published, certain passages dealing with the life of Mohammed were seen as blasphemous. Ayatollah Khomeini, the leader of Iran's Shia Muslims, declared a *fatwa*, death sentence, on him, and Rushdie was driven into hiding for ten years until diplomatic pressure lifted the *fatwa*.

> Many years later, as he faced the firing squad, Colonel Aureliano Buendia was to remember that distant afternoon when his father took him to discover ice.

GABRIEL GARCÍA MÁRQUEZ, *One Hundred Years of Solitude* (1967)

Metafictions

Metafictions seek to make readers aware of the illusory nature of fiction and to disrupt their expectations. They are writings about writing, which play or experiment with the form of a novel or a short story. Authors such as Calvino and Barth are driven by philosophical ideas about language and writing. In the process, they may show considerable inventiveness, but their main impulse is intellectual – and, in Calvino's case, 'a massive weariness for literature'. It would not be entirely unfair to say that the archetypal metafiction is a novel about a novelist who is writing a novel about a novelist who is ...

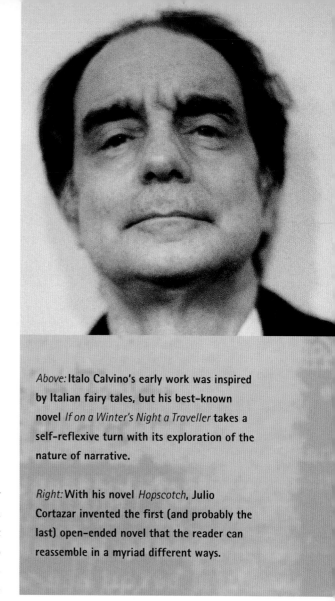

Above: Italo Calvino's early work was inspired by Italian fairy tales, but his best-known novel *If on a Winter's Night a Traveller* takes a self-reflexive turn with its exploration of the nature of narrative.

Right: With his novel *Hopscotch*, Julio Cortazar invented the first (and probably the last) open-ended novel that the reader can reassemble in a myriad different ways.

ITALO CALVINO (1923-85)

The Italian writer Italo Calvino worked as a publisher and critic, but his earliest short stories were based on his experiences of fighting in the resistance movement during the Second World War. From there, he turned to fantasy and allegory in novels such as *Il barone rampante* (*The Baron in the Trees*, 1957), *Cosmiconics* (1965) and *Il città invisibili* (*Invisible Cities*, 1972). The first is about a 19th-century aristocrat who decides to climb into the trees and never comes down again. These are delightful works of imaginative storytelling, in some cases inspired by Italian folk and fairy tales.

Calvino's change of direction towards a more explicitly avant-garde fiction, concerned with exploring theoretical ideas, came with *Il castello dei destini incrociati* (*The Castle of Crossed Destinies*, 1973). In this book mythical characters from classics of Italian literature stop at an overnight shelter and entertain each other by reciting their lives, using the sign-language of the Tarot pack. In Calvino's best known work, *Si una notte d'inverno un viaggiatore* (*If on a Winter's Night a Traveller*, 1979), has a writer who suffers from writer's block and who begins the same story over and over, each time in a different way.

Calvino was a member of the OULIPO (workshop of potential literature), a group of writers based in Paris, who were interested in various types of literary games. Another member, Georges Perec (1936-82), succeeded in writing an entire novel without using the letter 'e'.

The French title, *La Disparition* meaning 'The Disappearance', was changed to *A Void*, when the book was translated into English. Perec deliberately structured his fiction according to random patterns or principles drawn from logic or chess. His other novels, which include *La Vie: mode d'emploi* (*Life: A User's Manual*, 1978), have been described as 'the most crushingly boring works of fiction ever written'.

JULIO CORTAZAR (1914-84)

Another writer heavily preoccupied with metaphysical ideas, Julio Cortazar was born and educated in Argentina and moved in 1951 to Paris, becoming a French citizen and remaining there until his death.

As he himself conceded, he was 'over-intellectual'. His short stories and novels are like self-enclosed, abstract puzzles, frequently ingenious and full of dazzling word-play, but not easy to read. His short story 'The Devil's Drivel' was the basis for Michelangelo Antonioni's enigmatic film *Blow-up* (1966). Cortazar's most insistent theme was the possibility that a work of fiction could take different forking paths and that it could present alternative realities through different readings. In his best known book, *Hopscotch* (1966), he takes this idea to extreme lengths. It is an anti-novel or open-ended novel or, as he says in the table of instructions at the front, 'above all, it is two books'. The instructions invite the reader to discover an alternative story by reading the novel in a different sequence. The idea is that the reader will then be capable of imagining further ways of rearranging the chapters and sections.

JOHN BARTH (b.1930)

After studying music, the American John Simmons Barth pursued an academic career as a professor of English. With his third novel, *The Sot-Weed Factor* (1960), he made an absolute break with the conventional realism of his earlier work by writing it in a pastiche of 18th-century English prose. This lengthy picaresque tale about the adventures of a poet, Ebenezer Cooke, was followed by *Giles Goat-Boy: or, The Revised New Syllabus* (1966), an even more ambitious novel with a mythical hero, the 'horned human student' of the title, a religious prophet, and set in a world consisting wholly of computer-run universities. The book is fiendishly ingenious and clever, shot through with puns and other types of word-play and, at over 700 pages, somewhat difficult to finish for those who do not share the author's philosophical inclinations.

Barth is more interested in how a story is told than in the story itself. Like Calvino's *If on a Winter's Night a Traveller*, *Chimera* (1972) is in the vein of 'The Thousand and One Nights' ('Arabian Nights Entertainments') and retells variations on stories from Greek mythology, adopting many different narrative techniques.

UMBERTO ECO (b.1932)

The concept of post-modernism emanated from the universities, so it is appropriate that the writer who exemplifies the worst faults of the post-modern novel is an academic. Umberto Eco is professor of semiotics at the University of Bologna, Italy. His first novel, *Il nome della rosa* (*The Name of the Rose*, 1981), is a murder mystery set in a 14th-century Italian monastery. It brought him international fame, which was widened when a film version (1986) appeared, with Sean Connery cast as the medieval sleuth. Complete with a prologue, footnotes and invented scholastic research, the novel purports to be an exploration of the idea of 'truth' from the perspectives of theology, philosophy and history. Many readers were unable to finish the book. Eco's second novel, *Il pendolo di Foucault* (*Foucault's Pendulum*, 1989), is about three book editors who feed esoteric bits of knowledge into a computer as a game, and then find the game has serious consequences. But the story line is swamped by the interminable parade of erudition. His characters are paper-thin, and the narrative is incoherent. The text is dense with obscure references, scholarly allusions, lists and gestures towards profundity.

> ❛You are about to begin reading Italo Calvino's new novel ... Relax. Concentrate. Dispel every other thought. Let the world around you fade. Best to close the door.❜
> ITALO CALVINO, *If on a Winter's Night a Traveller* (1979)

Post-modern Americans

If there is one thing on which all definitions of post-modernity agree, it is that Western culture since 1945 has become uniquely fragmented and ephemeral. We now live in a world where fashions, design, lifestyles, our physical environment and even the words we use are in a constant state of flux. The American writers Pynchon, DeLillo and Vonnegut address this peculiarly modern phenomenon. Rather than individual lives, they take America itself as their subject.

THOMAS PYNCHON (b.1937)

In the era of the celebrity author, Thomas Pynchon is famous for his anonymity. He makes no public appearances and refuses to be interviewed, and the only photographs of him in existence date from his student days. Although he is sometimes regarded as the archetypal post-modern novelist, Pynchon the writer is as unclassifiable as the man is evasive. He is impossible to emulate; attempts by other authors to write like him have been miserable failures.

Pynchon's novels are long, elaborate and complex. All have a plot of a kind, although it is fantastically complicated by digressions and apparently irrelevant episodes. His first novel *V* (1963) follows the interweaving stories of ex-merchant seaman Benny Profane, 'the Whole Sick Crew' and a collection of albino alligators stalking the sewers of New York – to mention just some of its strands. Like most of his work, it cannot be read straight through, yet it is nonetheless entertaining and engrossing for its energy, exuberance and mastery of different fictional styles and techniques.

Pynchon studied physics at Princeton University before transferring to the English department. He is equally at home with the arts and the sciences, with popular and high culture. His novels display an amazing fund of knowledge, together with grotesque and bizarre tales, jokes, puns, songs, poems (some in the manner of 17th-century English poets) and startling pastiches of earlier 20th-century cultural idioms. Very disparate elements are held together by plots more or less centred on ideas of hidden codes, clandestine organizations and international conspiracies – on a paranoid vision of society and history as superficially chaotic but driven by a secret logic that can never be fully determined.

Much of *Gravity's Rainbow* (1973), his second major novel following the comparatively short *The Crying of Lot 49* (1966), is set in London during the Second World War. The story is loosely threaded around the fact that one of the characters has erections that coincide with the explosions of German V-2 rockets. But the reader is more likely to be struck by asides, such as the 20-page history of one light bulb, or by the accuracy with which Pynchon manages to register the feel of the period through radio programmes, catchphrases and popular songs.

This kind of fiction can run the risk of frustrating the reader's need for a coherent story line. *Vineland* (1990), Pynchon's next novel after a gap of 17 years, is a semi-political work, set in the Nixon-Reagan era. It has a fairly accessible story based on the lives of a group of people involved with the Californian counter-culture. *Mason & Dixon* (1997), about two British surveyors in 18th-century America and written in the literary style of the period, is less readable, despite the enormous critical attention it received.

DON DELILLO (b.1936)

Don DeLillo grew up in New York, in the South Bronx, the son of Italian immigrants, and he was raised as a Catholic, which has been responsible, he says, for 'the sense of last things' in his work. The novels that he produced during the 1980s are concerned with the decline of the American dream. They explore topics like the increase of violence, the potency of mass-communications, cult movements and terrorism. *Libra* (1988) deals with President John F. Kennedy's assassination; the hero of *White Noise* (1985) is a professor of Hitler studies who is sucked into the violent sub-culture of his campus town. In *Mao II* (1991) a famous writer who has withdrawn from the world becomes involved with terrorists.

Right: **Kurt Vonnegut's outlandish plots, gallows humour, and quirky imagination have secured him a large cult following in America and beyond.**

Below: **From the film of Kurt Vonnegut's satirical novel,** *Slaughterhouse-Five,* **where the central character Billy Pilgrim is kidnapped by aliens and taken to the planet Tralfamador.**

KURT VONNEGUT (b.1922)

Kurt Vonnegut, who was born in Indianapolis, studied biochemistry at Cornell University, before being drafted into the infantry in the Second World War. His first novels – *Player Piano* (1952), *The Sirens of Titan* (1959) and *Cat's Cradle* (1963) – take a science fiction form, although Vonnegut's highly individual style and ironic tone, which has been called 'wide-screen baroque', give them a much broader scope.

His most famous book is *Slaughterhouse-Five* (1969), which draws on his experience as a prisoner-of-war. It starts in a realistic vein with the central character, Billy Pilgrim, imprisoned in Dresden during the fire-bombing of the city, but it ends with him being kidnapped by aliens and taken to the planet Tralfamador, where he is mated in a public zoo with the actress Montana Wildhack. Vonnegut uses this outlandish plot as a framework for his meditations on war, human nature and the impossibility of telling the truth. 'So it goes', the refrain that appears here and throughout his fiction, expresses his characteristic mixture of pessimism, satire and black comedy ('gallows humour' in his own words). Among his later novels are *Breakfast of Champions* (1973), *Galapagos* (1985), *Bluebeard* (1987) and *Hocus Pocus* (1991).

DeLillo's characters are often obsessive, marginal figures in search of some system of belief in a world he depicts as corrupt, chaotic and bewildering. His novels – with their shambling plot lines, which move backwards and forwards in time and shift focus from one character to another – reflect the mood of contemporary America at the close of the century as few other works of modern fiction do. A terrific ear for dialogue and a jazzy, impressionistic style give DeLillo's writing a strong cinematic quality. The images he evokes are usually more resonant than events or personal experiences. In his most recent novel, *Underworld* (1997), he reverts to the 1950s, using a kind of documentary technique, with snapshots of dozens of characters mingled with real historical figures. This hugely ambitious book of more than 800 pages presents a brilliant collage of American life in an era shaped by the Cold War and the threat of nuclear annihilation.

15 The world in print

Below and right: **Japanese novelist Yukio Mishima was obsessed with violence, perversity and death. He was also an extreme nationalist who formed his own private army. After a sword-waving attack on an army HQ in Tokyo, Mishima harangued his soldiers from a balcony, then performed ceremonial suicide.**

The century has seen a tremendous cross-fertilization between literature of the past and the present and between national and global literature. Writers today are as likely to be influenced by Flaubert or Faulkner – whatever their cultural roots – as by the literary heritage of their own country. Travel, television, cinema, the wide availability of work in translation and the spread of English as a first and second language have all contributed to making world literature a genuinely international phenomenon.

The novel in Japan

PILLOW BOOK TO NOBEL PRIZE

Japan has its own distinguished and distinctive literary tradition, which extends as far back as the seventh century – the famous *The Pillow Book* (911–1000), for example, was written by a Japanese court lady, Sei Shonagon (966/7–1013). The 20th century, however, has been marked by the contradictory tendencies to both emulate and reject Western literature, which had been a potent influence on early novelists, who admired Zola enormously. Natsume Soseki (1867–1916), whom the Japanese regard as their greatest modern author, was an English teacher; even Kawabata and Mishima, who represent the conservative strain in later Japanese fiction, have been inevitably exposed to European influences.

The early work of Yasunari Kawabata (1899–1972) was influenced by Dadaism and surrealism. *The Izu Dancer* (1925) is an autobiographical account of his youthful infatuation with a dancer. In his Nobel prize acceptance speech (1968) he reflected that his overall concern was to beautify death and to seek harmony among men, nature and emptiness. To this end he concentrated mainly on lyrical tales of eroticism and fleeting beauty. *Snow Country* (1935, revised 1947), the tale of an elderly Tokyo womanizer and his relationship with a forlorn country geisha in a winter resort, is steeped with nostalgia for old Japan. *The Sound of the Mountain* (1954), which focuses on a sexually frustrated old man who is comforted by his daughter-in-law, is considered his best book. Kawabata committed suicide.

Kawabata's protégé, Yukio Mishima (1925–70), was an extreme nationalist, who even went to the extent of forming his own private army. He wrote about sex, violence and death, which he perceived as inextricably linked. His first novel, *Confessions of a Mask* (1947), is an autobiographical account of a young man's struggle to live with his homosexuality and sado-masochistic longings. His later work continued themes of self-inflicted torment and the impossibility of happiness. *The Temple of the Golden Pavilion* (1956) describes a typically troubled young man who burns down a temple because its beauty is unbearable to him. Mishima died having given a speech on a balcony at an army HQ, after which he committed *seppuku*, ritual self-disembowelment.

Kobo Abe (1924–93), novelist and playwright, is noted for his bizarre allegorical situations and black humour, which emphasize the isolation of the individual. While he was a student at the University of Tokyo, his wide reading included Dostoevsky, Heidegger, Kafka, Nietzsche and Poe. His own work, which has been called Kafkaesque, includes *The Woman in the Dunes* (1962) – made into an internationally successful film (1964) – *The Ruined Map* (1967) and *The Face of Another* (1964). His first collection of short stories to appear in English was *Beyond the Curve* (1990).

Kenzaburo Oë (b.1935) is both a novelist and an intellectual, whose work expresses the moral soul-searching of post-war Japan. When he was awarded the Nobel prize in 1994, he explained: 'I think I got it because I am still young and living.' By this he presumably meant that Japanese literature is so. His best known work, *The Silent Cry* (1967), is set in 1960 and is the story of two brothers who try to come to terms with their family's tumultuous history. A village is destroyed in the process. 'A sort of Japanese Joyce', Oë is steeped in many languages and literatures and – like Joyce – is more honoured than read in Japan: his style is difficult and complex. His son, severely disabled, about whom he wrote in *A Personal Matter* (1964), is a celebrated musician in Japan.

European novelists

It is noticeable that the strongest recent voices in European fiction have been more concerned with political and philosophical questions than their English-speaking counterparts. These writers are people who grew up during a war that was fought on their native soil and whose impact endured, in both personal and political terms, for the rest of their lives.

CAMILO JOSÉ CELA (b.1916)

Born in Galicia, of a Spanish father and Italian-English mother, Cela is a controversial but dominant figure in Spanish literature – disapproved of not only for his tireless obscenity and sexism but also for his personal history: he fought with the Nationalists in the Civil War and worked as a censor during Franco's early years. But he is indisputably talented, as his receipt of the Nobel prize in 1989 confirmed. Two of his earliest works are among his best known: *La familia de Pascual Duarte* (*The Family of Pascual Duarte*, 1942) and *La colmena* (*The Hive*, 1951). The first of these gave rise to the term the 'tremendista novel', so called because the shock of its brutality and horror are, literally, 'tremendous'. The novel – banned on publication – charts Pascual Duarte (a man who 'had no chance in life'), as he struggles with Oedipal guilt and existential terror and resolves his conflict by becoming a murderer. *The Hive* gives an alarmingly sordid account of life in Madrid after the Civil War through the activity that takes place at one café. After the book was published, Cela exiled himself to Majorca, where he still lives.

Other works include *Mrs Caldwell Speaks to her Son* (1953), which takes the form of letters written by a dead woman to her son and in which Cela's 'gallows humour' is at its peak, and *San Camilo, 1936* (1969), described as 'a disgusting book'. His most recent work is *The Murderer of the Loser* (1994).

JOSE SARAMAGO (b.1922)

The Portuguese writer Jose Saramago won the Nobel prize in 1998, 22 years after the publication of his first novel, which appeared when he was in his fifties. The prize committee celebrated him as a novelist 'who with parables sustained by imagination, compassion and irony ... enables us ... to apprehend an illusory reality'.

His books are projects on which he embarks as if they were journeys, to enlarge our collective imaginary map of the possible. *The Stone Raft* (1986) begins with a piece of the Iberian peninsula breaking off into the ocean. This unlikely incident sparks bureaucratic chaos and incredible personal experiences for the drifting inhabitants. *The History of the Siege of Lisbon* (1989) is a novel about a novel, which the proof-reader alters by inserting the word 'not'. This reverses the course of history (and allows Saramago enormous scope to delight in his own inventiveness). *The Gospel According to Jesus Christ* (1991) is a rewriting of the life of Jesus in which he has an affair with Mary Magdalene and argues with God – who is the villain of the piece.

Saramago's masterpiece, however, is *Baltasar and Blimunda* (1982) in which two young people – one handicapped and the other a visionary – transport

Above: A citizen of East Germany before the Berlin Wall came down, Christa Wolf trod a fine line between celebrating and criticizing the communist regime.

Left: A controversial but major figure in Spanish literature, Camilo José Cela won the Nobel prize in 1989, despite his sometimes obscene and sexist fiction.

themselves to heaven with a runaway priest. The flying machine they use is powered by Blimunda's psychic harnessing of swarms of human wills. 'It has the melancholy of magnificence,' one critic observed.

CHRISTA WOLF (b.1929)

Wolf is the most important female writer to have emerged from post-war East Germany, and it is a tribute to her subtlety and strength as a novelist that her work has been controversial both inside the German Democratic Republic (which saw it as critical) and in the world at large (which thought it collusive with the GDR).

Her first book, *Divided Heaven* (1963), was written with financial help from the GDR, which wanted life in East Germany to be recorded positively in fiction. Western critics were cynical of what they considered state propaganda, but the book is a lucid and moving love story about a woman whose lover leaves her for Europe.

The Quest for Christa T (1976) was denounced or ignored by East German critics but praised by those in the West. It is a richly imagined novel, narrated by a woman searching for her past through the life of a dead friend and working out along the way ideas about the conflict between individual fulfilment and social responsibility.

A Model Childhood (1976) is autobiographical. Wolf visits her birthplace and reflects on life under Hitler. Her vision of the strangeness of what seemed at the time an ordinary childhood in a normal Nazi family makes the story both convincing and resonant. *No Place on Earth* (1979), a historical romance of two writers who kill themselves, and *Accident: A Day's News* (1987), about the day of the Chernobyl disaster, are among her other considered and lyrical works.

THOMAS BERNHARD (1931–90)

'The most extraordinary of all modern Austrian writers', as Thomas Bernhard has been described, was actually born in the Netherlands, but he was raised in Austria where he lived alone in a farmhouse. His books are infused with a particular and vehement hatred – one critic has said he 'goes out of his way to be unpleasant and unfashionable'. Critically ill in 1949, he received the last rites, which may have influenced his nihilistic tendencies.

He established his reputation with *Gargoyles* (1967), which, like all his early fiction, is about Austrian peasants. The narrator accompanies his father, a doctor, on visits to increasingly deranged and nasty peasants. The final patient visited is a schizophrenic prince living in a decaying castle, an allegory of decaying Austria. *Corrections* (1979) is a fantastic portrait of the philosopher Ludwig Wittgenstein, which develops Bernhard's theory that madness is the only rational response to a meaningless existence.

The novels and autobiographies are written in mixtures of stream-of-consciousness monologues and Bernhard's long, complicated sentences, which make for difficult reading, but he is an intense and powerful writer whose charting of the disgusting is remarkably compulsive.

Latin American fiction

Latin American fiction is one of the strongest forces in world literature today. Since the 1960s, when the marvellous stories of Jorge Luis Borges and the Magic Realism of García Márquez became available in translation, there has been a surge of interest in their compatriots. Although it is mostly associated with Magic Realism, the literature of this region is as various as the three writers discussed here.

Above: Glenn Close in *The House of Spirits* (1993). Isabelle Allende's first and most overtly 'magical realist' novel is still regarded by many as her best.

Right: Novelist and playwright Mario Vargas Llosa. Chosen in 1989 as presidential candidate in his native country Peru, he narrowly lost the election after a large lead in the polls.

MIGUEL ANGEL ASTURIAS (1899–1974)

Born in Guatemala City, Miguel Angel Asturias was a poet, novelist and diplomat who was awarded the Nobel prize in 1967 and the Soviet Union's Lenin Peace Prize in 1966. His writing is dominated by his love of nature and the mythical world, and his first work was a collection of Guatemalan legends, the images and symbols of which were a source of inspiration throughout his writing career. This began in earnest in 1946, when his novel *El señor presidente* (*The President*) was published. A tragic satire of a dictator who makes life hell for his subjects, the book is written with Asturias's legendary passion.

Three years later *Hombres de maiz* (*Men of Maize*) appeared. Generally considered Asturias's masterpiece, this work depicts the seemingly irreversible misery of Indian peasants in a language described as 'bizarre and terrifying'. In 1950 Asturias began a trilogy of novels on the theme of the struggle against American trusts – epitomized by the fictional United Fruit Company – and their effects on the contemporary history of the 'banana republic'. Asturias's work, which was hailed as 'vast and bold' by the Nobel prize committee, contains language that 'assumed the bright splendour of the magical quetzal's feathers and the glimmering of phosphorescent insects'.

MAÑUEL PUIG (1932–90)

Born in General Villegas, Argentina, Puig learned English as a child by watching every American film he could. In 1957 he went to Rome to study film directing, then lived briefly in Stockholm and London. His film scripts were rejected when he returned to Buenos Aires, and he turned to writing fiction, his first novel, *La traición de Rita Hayworth* (*Betrayed by Rita Hayworth*, 1968), being a semi-autobiographical account of a boy who escapes from the boredom of South American life by fantasizing about Hollywood stars. Using shifting viewpoints, flashbacks and interior monologue, Puig described an existence driven by an escapist devouring of pulp fiction, comics and old movies.

Living through the consumption of another culture is described again in the detective novel, *The Buenos Aires Affair* (1973). What Puig's characters take from second-hand popular fiction is a store of possibilities, and his implication is that escapism may be one way (and perhaps the only way) of redeeming or actually altering a cripplingly diminished reality. *El beso de la mujer araña* (*Kiss of the Spider Woman*, 1976; film

1985) is a novel, told in dialogue between a middle-aged homosexual and a young revolutionary who find themselves in the same jail. In this work Puig moves into overt criticism of sexual and political repression, yet he still retains the poetry and particular tenderness that made his earlier works popular. Later works have

included *Angelic Pubis* (1979) and *Eternal Curse on the Reader of These Pages* (1980).

MARIO VARGAS LLOSA (b.1936)

Playwright, novelist and failed presidential candidate, Mario Vargas Llosa was born in Arequipa, Peru, and has since lived in Paris, London and Barcelona, where he settled in 1970. His first published work was a play, *The Escape of the Inca*. After this his stories appeared in Peruvian literary reviews while he worked as a journalist and broadcaster. In 1959 he moved to Paris, where he wrote his first novel, *La ciudad y los perros* (*The Time of the Hero*, 1963), which was translated into more than a dozen languages. Set in a military academy in Peru, the book describes a group of adolescents who are struggling to survive as individuals in a violent, hostile environment. *La casa verde* (*The Green House*, 1965) is

again about Peru, but it combines mythical, popular and heroic elements to capture the limited and seedily fragmented reality of its characters. In 1967 came *The Cubs, and Other Stories*, a disturbing psychoanalytical portrayal of a teenager who has been accidentally castrated. Other savagely critical works include *Conversación en la catedral* (*Conversations in the Cathedral*, 1969) and *Pantaléon y las visitadoras* (*Captain Pantoja and the Special Service*, 1973), a satire on Peruvian military and religious fanaticism.

Vargas Llosa has written critical works on García Márquez, Flaubert, Sartre and Camus. His plays, particularly *The Jest* (1986), have been performed in New York to great critical acclaim.

ISABEL ALLENDE (b.1942)

Isabel Allende is one of the few female Latin American writers whose work, translated into more than two dozen languages, can be found in bookshops worldwide. She spent her childhood in Chile, where her uncle, President Salvador Allende, was assassinated in a military coup in 1973. She fled to Venezuela with her husband and children and lived in exile until her grandfather, who had remained in Chile, was diagnosed as terminally ill. It was this, combined with her divorce, that spurred Allende's first novel, *Casa de los espiritus* (*The House of Spirits*, 1985). The book retold much of her own family history.

Allende considers herself part of a feminist literary awakening, which unites minority writers in a shared 'dimension of emotion, passion, obsession and dream'. It may have been these qualities that attracted her second husband, who said he fell in love with her through her novels. With him, Allende took up residence in San Francisco. Her fourth novel, *El plan infinito* (*The Infinite Plan*, 1991) is set there and was the work she said brought her closest both to her marriage and to America itself, a country that by now she deeply respected. Other works include *De amaor y de sombra* (*Of Love and Shadows*, 1984) and *Eva Luna* (*The Stories of Eva Luna*, 1989), which one critic described as 'getting your favourite storyteller to tell you a story and getting a hundred stories instead ... then hearing the storyteller's life as well'.

Post-colonial literature

Since the end of the Second World War Europe's former colonies have increasingly produced literature that has both celebrated and mourned the cultures upon which empire had intruded. In some cases, writers have self-consciously distanced themselves from the Western canon, but because they write almost exclusively in English, their work has, paradoxically, enriched the mainstream of Western culture, with many novelists and poets winning prestigious European literary prizes.

AFRICA

Since the 1950s Nigeria has witnessed a flourishing of new literature, which has drawn from both traditional oral sources and the rapid changes of present-day society to produce a vigorous body of fiction. Chinua Achebe (b.1930) is acclaimed for his unsentimental charting of the disorientation that has been an inevitable emotional consequence of Westernization.

Achebe rejects the European notion that art is un-accountable: it is 'and always was, at the service of man', his book of essays *Morning Yet on Creation Day: Essays* (1975) insists. 'Our ancestors told their stories for a human purpose.' His first, much translated, novel, *Things Fall Apart* (1958), tells of life in Igbo villages before the onset of modernity, and the tragic consequences that opposition to Christian and British interference has for its hero. *Anthills of the Savannah* (1987) and *Christmas in Biafra and Other Poems* (1973) are among the best of his works.

Wole Soyinka (b.1934) is Africa's most famous poet, dramatist, novelist and critic, who received the Nobel prize in 1986. His roots lie in the Yoruba culture, but his education was largely European. His work is vivid and harrowing, yet intensely poetic, with Yoruba mythology and ritual providing a lyrical undercurrent. Among his plays, *A Dance of the Forests* (1960) – a kind of African *A Midsummer Night's Dream* – and *Death and the King's Horseman* (1975) – a tragedy with cultic sacrificial death at its centre – are worth special mention.

His collection of poetry, *A Shuttle in the Crypt* (1972), was written while he was in prison for allegedly pro-Biafran activity during the Nigerian Civil War, and – like much of his work – is a reaction to that conflict, focusing on mental survival, human contact, anger and forgiveness.

Buchi Emechta (b.1944) is a novelist whose work portrays African womanhood, through characters that show what it means to be a mother in contemporary Nigeria. *In the Ditch* (1972) tells of a woman, living alone on a housing estate with her children, who is forced to accept charity. *The Joys of Motherhood* (1979), one of 15 other novels, continues her scrutiny of the difficulties facing women who struggle to be independent from the traditions of a male-dominated society.

THE WEST INDIES

Although many post-colonial writers chose to write in English – the language of their former colonizers – the Caribbean writers Derek Walcott and V.S. Naipaul have switched in and out of local Creoles and standard English to emphasize the multicultural and hybrid nature of the post-colonial world.

Derek Walcott (b.1930), who was born on St Lucia, was awarded the Nobel prize in 1992. He founded the Trinidad Theatre Workshop in 1959, where many of his own plays, among others, were first performed. His theatre mingles prose and verse, Creole vocabulary and

Left: Born in the West Indies of Indian descent, the highly regarded novelist V.S. Naipaul's melancholy and pessimistic vision has drawn comparisons with Conrad. Both writers chose to live in England.

Right: Indian writer Vikram Seth followed the runaway success of his verse novel *The Golden Gate* with *A Suitable Boy*, the second longest single volume work in English fiction.

calypso rhythms, and it is often preoccupied with national identity, with 'the choice of home or exile, self-realization or spiritual betrayal of one's country'. Among the better known of his plays are *Dream on Monkey Mountain* (1967), *O Babylon!* (1976) and *Viva Detroit* (1992). Walcott's poetry is also deeply concerned with the conflict between the heritage of European and West Indian culture. His rich, self-questioning, at times confessional collections include *In a Green Night: Poems 1948–60* (1962), *Omeros* (1981) and *The Fortunate Traveller* (1982).

V.S. (Vidiadhar Surajprasad) Naipaul (b.1932) was born in Trinidad but has lived in England since 1955. His recurrent themes of political violence, implicit homelessness and alienation have given rise to comparisons with Conrad, and certainly his intense and melancholy experience of contemporary human nature is somewhat similar. His first three books – *The Mystic Masseur* (1957), *The Suffrage of Elvira* (1958) and *Miguel Street* (1959) – were, however, comedies of manners set in Trinidad. *A House for Mr Biswas* (1961) was darker and was acclaimed for its study of colonial displacement and disorder. *The Middle Passage* (1962), in which he asserted that 'nothing was ever created in the West Indies', became infamous there. The Booker prize-winning *In a Free State* (1971), *A Bend in the River* (1979) and *The Enigma of Arrival* (1987) – his most introspective work yet – followed. Influential non-fiction works include *The Return of Eva Peron;*

with The Killings in Trinidad (1980) and a collection of personal and political essays, *The Overcrowded Barracoon* (1972). He was knighted in 1990. His brother, Shiva Naipaul (1945–85), was a distinguished novelist also.

INDIA

Much of the recent literature of India is, of course, well known to the world: Salman Rushdie, Arundahti Roy and Vikram Seth, for example – all bestselling authors – are discussed elsewhere in this book. Less well known is R.K. (Rasipuram Kirshnaswamy) Narayan (b.1906), who has produced a rich body of work, which was first published in Britain after Graham Greene's recommendation and which has been compared to Chekhov's for its tragi-comedy, its pathos and the tendency of its characters to have their hopes so frequently dashed.

Many of Narayan's novels, including his first, *Swami and Friends* (1935), are set in the imaginary town of Malgudi, the author's fictional microcosm of Indian society. Central to his vision is the iconoclastic anti-heroine and the forces of order, tradition and patriarchy she encounters in her creative self-willed lifestyle. *The Vendor of Sweets* (1967), *The Painter of Signs* (1976) and *The Tiger for Malgudi* (1983) – all set in Malgudi – are typical explorations of this idea. *The Financial Expert* (1952) drew more on his own life's experiences, particularly the tragic death of his wife. His autobiography, *My Days: A Memoir*, was published in 1974.

Literature in Australia and Canada

In the first part of the century both these former British dependencies tended to take their cultural lead from Britain (although in Canada, the influence of the United States was just as great), and many Australian and Canadian writers moved to Britain in order to develop their art. After the Second World War, however, a distinct national literature began to emerge in both countries, and these are now important strands in the body of English literature worldwide.

AUSTRALIA

After Patrick White's towering achievements (see page 119), Christina Stead (1902–83) has undoubtedly contributed more to Australian literature than anyone else.

A writer of great power and originality, she was consistently underrated during her lifetime. Her most renowned book, *The Man Who Loved Children* (1940), is a masterly study in selfishness, unconscious cruelty and savage domestic conflict, in which an idealistic but self-centred man drives his wife to suicide, although he 'never thought she meant it'. Stead's portraits of Sam Pollit, his strong-willed and intelligent wife and their seven children are immensely vivid; the story has a universality that led one distinguished critic to talk of 'an almost ecstatic pleasure of recognition'. Among the best of her other novels are *House of All Nations* (1938), an 800-page epic tracing the decline and collapse of a Swiss banking house, and *Cotters' England* (1967), about an unsuccessful left-wing journalist working in London. Stead is seen as a major feminist writer, although she would have rejected the label; as with her commitment to the political left, her feminism is characteristically personal and independent.

Thomas Keneally (b.1935), who was born in Sydney, trained for the Catholic priesthood but was never ordained – which may explain his fiction's later

fascination with spiritual and moral failure. His subject is almost always the individual in a hostile environment, who finds himself in opposition to religious, political or social systems. His first novel, *The Place at Whitton* (1964), is a murder mystery set in a seminary. *The Chant of Jimmie Blacksmith* (1972) describes the aboriginal Jimmie's effort to assimilate himself into white society, which in the end drives him to murder. His best known work, *Schindler's Ark* (1982), which was originally commissioned as a work of non-fiction but went on to win the Booker prize, tells of a German gentile, Oskar Schindler, who risks his life during the Second World War to save Polish Jews from the camps. It was filmed as *Schindler's List* (1993).

The novelist and short-story writer Peter Carey (b.1943) was born in Victoria and studied science before starting an advertising agency in Sydney. His first important book was a collection of short stories, *The Fat Man in History* (1974). A curious mix of the comic, the bizarre and the mundane, it is characteristically scathing in its critique of contemporary values but

Above: **Canadian novelist and playwright Robertson Davies, whose long and productive career included a spell as an actor at London's Old Vic theatre.**

Left: **Ralph Fiennes in** *The English Patient.* **Michael Ondaatje's novel about love and loss in wartime Egypt brought him to fame when it won the Booker prize in 1992.**

typical, too, in its compassion for the ungainly beings on whom Carey focuses. His first novel was *Bliss* (1981), but he is better known for *Illywhacker* (1985) and the Booker prize-winning *Oscar and Lucinda* (1988). The first is narrated by 139-year-old con-man, Illywhaker, whose function is partly to underline the general grasping and corrupt Australian society he supposedly dupes. *Oscar and Lucinda* is a dense and complex portrait of 19th-century Australia, featuring a young clergyman, who obsessively pursues his dream of building a glass church in the Australian outback.

CANADA

Alice Munro (b.1931) is second only to Margaret Atwood (see page 78) in her importance as a Canadian fiction writer of the 1970s and 1980s. Predominately a writer of short stories, her subjects are generally filtered through women's perceptions: their recognitions, betrayals and continuities. What is exciting in Munro is her vision of the strange world lying just beyond everyday reality. The novel *Lives of Girls and Women* (1971),

for example, ends with a metaphor of 'deep caves paved with kitchen linoleum' – the caves being the unknown depths of the psyche, as overlaid by the mundane details of ordinary life. Munro also excels at the documentation of psychological violence and the contradictory passions of relationships. Her short-story collection *Something I've Been Meaning to Tell You* (1974) explores questions of the relative power of men and women, in her characteristic 'naturalistic' style, which in fact connects bizarre unreal events to those of normal reality. Later works include *The Moons of Jupiter* (1982) and *Friend of My Youth* (1990), which reflect the rootlessness and unease of contemporary life.

Robertson Davies (1913–85) is one of Canada's most popular and prolific playwrights and novelists, whose work offers penetrating observations on the provincialism and prudery of the Canada he knew. His early reputation was based on the plays *Eros at Breakfast* (1949) and *At My Heart's Core* (1950), satires on Canadian values. Three trilogies of novels – the 'Salterton' trilogy, the 'Deptford' trilogy, which includes his best known work, *Fifth Business* (1970), and the 'Cornish' trilogy – secured his reputation as his country's foremost man of letters.

Davies was a traditional storyteller, but through his enduring interest in Jungian psychology – with its ideas about the collective unconscious and archetypes – he was concerned to explore the struggle of a coherent sense of identity.

Poet and novelist Michael Ondaatje (b.1943) was born in Sri Lanka but emigrated to Canada in 1962. His most ambitious and successful work is the Booker prize-winning novel *The English Patient* (1992), which was later made into a film (1996). It intertwines the lives of four characters during the Second World War, one of whom is a badly burned Englishman. Through the remembered love affair that the English Patient tells his nurse, the book becomes a lyrical meditation on history and war. Other novels include *Coming Through Slaughter* (1976), the story of jazz musician Buddy Bolden, and *In the Skin of the Lion* (1987), which is related through the consciousness of a child.

16 Modern writers

Literature today is commercialized as never before, with writers dependent on literary agents, who make deals with publishers on the strength of the potential sales figures of their work. Successful authors of serious fiction can expect enormous advances and substantial further earnings if the book sells well. Experimental, difficult or marginal work may not be published at all, however, which means that the fiction generally available is increasingly 'more of the same'. Whether this trend is temporary or will have a lasting effect on our culture is impossible to say. For the time being, we can be grateful that some writers of very good fiction remain popular and in print.

Below: A scene from the film *Kitchen*. It was based on the first novel by Banana Yoshimoto, which made her a literary spokesman for Japan's Generation X.

Right: Douglas Coupland, the novelist who first identified Generation X and mapped its contours most engagingly in his fiction, here exploring 'the depths of the shallow'.

Generation X

When the Canadian writer Douglas Coupland used the term 'Generation X' in the title of his first novel he was referring to his own 'socially disengaged' characters: middle-class, suburban North Americans who 'wanted to hop off the merry-go-round of status, money and social climbing'. Since then, the term has widened to the point where it means, more or less, the 'TV generation' – children of the information age, growing up in the 1960s and 1970s, for whom consumerism, media culture and youth culture are not features of a peculiarly post-modern experience but the norm.

DOUGLAS COUPLAND (b.1961)

Generation X: Tales for an Accelerated Culture (1991) is about three friends living in California, supporting themselves doing McJobs (Coupland's word for jobs with low pay, low prestige and little future). Nothing much happens to them, and the novel consists of the stories they tell about their lives. Their speech is dense with references to popular or junk culture. They typically use television programmes, brandnames and their own idioms (such as 'emotional ketchup burst') to make wry and sardonic comments on the world about them, and the tone is one of resignation and mild bitterness. For example, a bartender complains: 'My life had become a series of scary incidents that simply weren't stringing together to make for an interesting book.'

In *Microserfs* (1995) the heroes are young computer programmers working for Microsoft. Again, the plot is inconsequential. What gives the novel its fascination is the accuracy with which Coupland registers his characters' worldview and sub-culture, while also somehow making their undramatic, day-to-day lives interesting and engaging.

Girlfriend in a Coma (1998) returns to the social milieu of Generation X, taking six Vancouver friends from their teens in 1979, when one of them falls into a coma, through to 1997 when she wakes up. They have now found more engrossing jobs and are not so much dissatisfied with, as vaguely puzzled by, the course of their lives. Coupland has described his fiction as 'exploring the depths of the shallow'. But his characters are not in mourning for the passing of a less superficial existence, since they know no other; instead, they are, to a large extent, free from the passions and anxieties that occupy people in most fiction. This may be why some literary critics have refused to take his novels seriously. He is, however, a gifted writer whose stories are strangely endearing, in spite of their lack of dramatic incident or compelling plots.

BANANA YOSHIMOTO (b.1964)

Sometimes portrayed as an oriental Douglas Coupland, the Japanese writer Banana Yoshimoto has the same kind of readership. Her first collection of short stories, *Kitchen* (1994), was hugely popular with young Japanese adults, selling two million copies. An underlying concern in this and later works, such as *The Lizard* (1996) and *NP* (1994), is the contrast between traditional and modern Japanese culture.

Yoshimoto's protagonists are usually young women who have drifted away from their family. They work in bars and in coffee-shops, listen to Western pop music and pursue a somewhat dislocated existence. Their lives are marked by strange coincidences, off-beat experiences and conversations that seem to hold great significance but never actually lead anywhere. In a series of loosely connected episodes the narrator of *Amrita* (1998) comes to terms with her sister's death, aided by telepathic messages and a meeting with the guru-like Mr Mesmer.

Coupland's fiction assumes an intimate knowledge of American media (especially television) culture over the past two decades. For Western readers it is difficult to assess how far Yoshimoto succeeds in charting the consciousness of Japan's Generation X, because much of her language is, necessarily, untranslatable.

Recent American fiction

Novels are now packaged and branded like pop music, making it difficult to separate quality from mediocre fiction. Increasingly, literary merit is measured in sales figures, which explains why no one had heard of Cormac McCarthy until a few years ago – his first five books sold fewer than 2000 copies. Robert Stone and Paul Theroux are novelists of great accomplishment but are given less attention than newer, more transient talents.

ROBERT STONE (b.1937)

Robert Anthony Stone served in the US navy, went to Vietnam as a journalist and was later associated with Ken Kesey's Magic Bus. Informed by this background, his most celebrated novel, *Dog Soldiers* (1974), is a superb evocation of the Vietnam era and drug culture. It tells of an ex-marine who is persuaded by a journalist friend to smuggle heroin from Saigon to California, where he is pursued by corrupt narcotics agents to a hippie commune in Mexico.

Stone's novels frequently use the framework of the thriller to explore moral and political questions. *A Flag for Sunrise* (1982) has a complicated plot involving nuns, a priest, an anthropologist and a drifter caught up with revolutionaries in a poor Central American country. In *Damascus Gate* (1998) a journalist living in Jerusalem becomes entangled with religious zealots.

PAUL THEROUX (b.1941)

In a prolific writing career spanning nearly three decades, the American-born Paul Edward Theroux has spent much of his life outside America, including a long spell in London. His writing is unusual for its range of subjects and settings. Africa and Asia provide the background for early novels, such as *Girls at Play* (1969) and *Saint Jack* (1973). *The Family Arsenal* (1976) is about terrorism in London, while one of his finest works, *The Mosquito Coast* (1981; film 1986), has an American family trying to survive in a South American jungle.

Later novels include *O-Zone* (1993), a science fiction story set in a US that has been turned into a wasteland by a nuclear accident, and *Millroy the Magician* (1995), about a children's entertainer who becomes a TV entertainer.

Theroux's writing is unostentatiously skilful, witty in its unsparing observation of human vanity and pretence, and entertaining. 'I don't want to be a bore,' he said in an interview. 'I would rather open a beauty parlour – I swear.'

CORMAC MCCARTHY (b.1933)

Until the bestselling *All the Pretty Horses* (1992), the first novel in his 'Border' trilogy, McCarthy received little or no recognition, despite having published his first novel, *Orchard Keeper*, in 1965. He is now spoken of as a contemporary master, whose ornate, imagistic prose, coupled to a bleak (at times hellish and apocalyptic) view of existence, has drawn comparisons with

Above: As well as producing an extensive and varied body of fiction, Paul Theroux is celebrated for his entertaining and trenchant travel writing.

Left: Poster for the film of *The Right Stuff*. With this and other works like *The Electric Kool-Aid Acid Test*, Tom Wolfe established himself as the leading exponent of New Journalism before turning to the novel.

Faulkner and Herman Melville. McCarthy, who grew up in Tennessee, writes about an almost exclusively masculine world set in the American West. The characters in his early novels are maverick figures, living in outcast communities on the margins of society. The hero of *Suttree* (1979) has abandoned his wealthy family to live alone on a houseboat on the Tennessee river: 'Dear friend now in the dusty clockless hours of the town ... no soul shall walk save you.' *Blood Meridian* (1985), a brutal saga of bounty hunters in the 1850s, has been called the 'classic American novel of regeneration through violence'.

The '*Border*' trilogy is a dreamier, more romantic work, but still concerned mainly with men in their relationships with animals, each other and the wilderness.

BRETT EASTON ELLIS (b.1964)

Less than Zero (1985), the novel Ellis wrote while still a student, is about the decadent, sterile lifestyle of affluent Los Angeles youth. In a detached, laconic prose, it shows its 18-year-old hero and his circle engaging in a round of low-energy socializing, their sole interests being drugs, casual sex and rock music. Ellis's method of presenting a succession of brief episodes, which seemed to echo music video techniques, led critics to describe him as the voice of the new generation. None of his subsequent novels have enjoyed the same acclaim, although *American Psycho* (1991) caused some controversy for its grisly story of a Wall Street banker who also tortures and murders people.

JAY MCINERY (b.1955)

With his first novel, *Bright Lights, Big City* (1984), Jay McInery mapped similar territory to that explored by Brett Easton Ellis, telling the story of young New York professionals who are entirely given over to the pleasures of cocaine and night-clubbing. Like Ellis, he has continued to mine the same vein in much of his later fiction. He depicts American society as culturally and morally barren, but at the same time is absorbed in the antics of its most privileged members. His most ambitious novel, *Brightness Falls* (1992), which is also set in New York, follows a group of '30-somethings' in the publishing industry. They get involved in risky financial deals, consort with a famous author who has drug and sex problems, and worry whether having a family will hamper their careers.

TOM WOLFE (b.1930)

The work of Tom Wolfe illustrates the difficulty of making contemporary critical assessments. *The Bonfire of the Vanities* (1987) is about a New York stockbroker who is exploited by corrupt politicians after he kills a young black man in a car crash. A major bestseller, the book was praised extravagantly by many, dismissed by others as hype ('fit only for rapid reading on aeroplanes'). Wolfe began to be talked of (and to promote himself) as a social chronicler in the tradition of Dickens and Trollope. *A Man in Full* (1998) has the same surface glitter and panoramic sweep – and has again attracted extremes of derision and esteem.

Afro-American women writers

By the 1970s, with the rise of the women's movement, black literature came to be seen as staggeringly sexist, dealing with attitudes to race that were dictated by a male-dominated culture. Black women's literature was as critical of black men as of white ones, and it began a process of liberation, with imagined histories of individual suffering endured by people who were both female and black.

Above: America's pre-eminent black novelist Toni Morrison, whose gifts as a storyteller coupled with her blend of realism, myth and fantasy won her the Nobel prize for literature in 1993.

Right: The Color Purple, Alice Walker's poignant story of a young black girl's struggle to make sense of her life in the pre-war South was sensitively transferred to the big screen by Steven Spielberg.

MAYA ANGELOU (b.1928)

By the time she had reached her twenties Angelou had been a cook, a cocktail waitress, a dancer, a street-car conductor, a madam and a single parent. The following decades saw her emerge as a successful singer, actress and playwright, poet, civil rights activist, magazine editor in Egypt and author of five autobiographies. In 1993 she gave a reading of her poem 'On the Pulse of Morning' at President Clinton's inauguration: she had become one of the great voices of contemporary black literature.

Her first book of autobiographical stories was *I Know Why the Caged Bird Sings*, which was published in 1970 to critical and commercial applause. It established her as a writer with a rare idiomatic gift – an ability to recreate the texture of the past in a language that is both evocative, concise and tautly energetic. Her second volume continued her story, but moved on from the material of her unhappy childhood with her grandmother in Arkansas to describe her experience as a single parent in New York. *Gather Together in My Name* (1974) was not as successful as Angelou's first works, although one reviewer commented that she wrote 'like a song, and like the truth'. *Singin' and Swingin'* and *Gettin' Merry Like Christmas* (1977) dealt with her activities in the theatre, music and dance. *The Heart of a Woman* (1981) covered her engagement with the civil rights movement and brief marriage to exiled South African political activist, Vusumzi Make. The autobiographical series was completed with *All God's Children Need Travelling Shoes* (1986), which describes, with the particular mix of exuberance and thoughtfulness for which she was now famous, her four-year stay in Ghana.

Angelou is celebrated for her readings of her poetry, which stretches to five volumes, gathered together and published in 1994 as *The Complete Collected Poems of Maya Angelou*.

TONI MORRISON (b.1931)

Morrison has been called 'the most important black novelist in America since [Ralph] Ellison'. In 1993 she became the first African-American and the eighth woman ever to receive the Nobel prize, which followed many other awards for her fiction. Her work uses a blend of realism, history, myth, folktale and poetic fantasy to explore relationships between blacks and whites, men and women, the past and the present. Her language was described by the Nobel Committee as seeking 'to liberate from the fetters of race ... and [it] addresses us with the lustre of poetry'.

Her first novel was *The Bluest Eye*, which was published in 1970, after years of rejection. It traces the history of Pecola Breedlove – raped and driven mad by her father, and increasingly obsessed with Shirley Temple (whose eyes are truly blue). In the end, suffering an agonized schizophrenic withdrawal, she believes that she, too, has blue eyes.

Sula (1973) is an even bleaker book – 'a howl of love and rage,' according to one critic – which contrasts Sula, who ends as a witch, with her grandmother, who burns her own drug-addicted son. In 1977 came *Song of Solomon*, in which Morrison concerns herself with Milkman Dead, who finds he can fly, and his family in an epic

tale that surveys almost a century of American history as it impinges on one black family. *Tar Baby* (1981) remained on the bestseller list for four months, followed by the undisputed masterpiece and Pulitzer prize-winning, *Beloved* (1987). Through the lives of ex-slaves Sethe and her would-be lover, Paul D, the book is a dark and probing meditation on slavery. Margaret Atwood, reviewing the

book, wrote: 'Ms Morrison's versatility and technical and emotional range appear to know no bound.'

Jazz (1992) extended Morrison's range still further, using an unreliable, intrusive narrator to raise questions of her own responsibility in telling the tales of struggle she relentlessly embraces.

ALICE WALKER (b.1944)

Alice Malsenior Walker has co-founded a publishing company, been on the staff of the New York City Welfare Department and worked as both writer-in-residence and teacher of black studies at Jackson State College, Wellesley College and the University of Massachusetts, as well as writing a substantial body of poetry, fiction and essays.

Walker's most recent work is *Anything We Love Can Be Saved: A Writer's Activism* (1997), but she became a household name in 1985 when her Pulitzer prize-winning third novel, *The Color Purple* (1982), was filmed by Steven Spielberg. Celie, the heroine of the book, is in some senses an amalgam of all the women Walker had written about. She embodies their desperation and also their faith. Walker has said that 'the black woman is one of America's greatest heroes', and all her work centres on the oppressions, the loyalties and the triumphs of these people and their heritage.

In Love and Trouble: Stories of Black Women (1973), her first collection of short stories, was a searching examination of the experiences of 13 black women, whom she sees as mutilated mainly by 'the cruelty of the black man to his wife'. Men in *The Color Purple* are generally pathetic, weak and stupid, if they are not heartlessly cruel, yet Celie finally embodies a celebration of the human spirit over particular, harsh circumstances. *The Temple of My Familiar* (1989) featured several of the characters from her earlier novel, but was less well reviewed and seen by some as 'a manifesto' rather than a work of fiction.

Walker's collected poems, *Everything We Know: Earthling Poems 1965-90*, received high praise for her insistently 'strong, beautiful voice'.

' Dear God, I am fourteen years old. I am.(crossed out).
I have always been a good girl. maybe you can give me a
sign letting me know what is happening to me. '

ALICE WALKER, *The Color Purple* (1982)

Women writers in America

American fiction has been dominated by male writers to a far greater extent than elsewhere. The female voice has been a fairly recent one in the United States, notwithstanding the contribution of Edith Wharton, but it is now acknowledged as one of the most powerful and inventive there is. Writers such Grace Paley, Toni Morrison, Joyce Carol Oates and Amy Tan are as firmly at the forefront of international literature as any of their male contemporaries.

GRACE PALEY (b.1922)

Grace Paley's reputation as one of the most original and gifted of contemporary writers is based on just three collections of stories: *The Little Disturbances of Man* (1959), *Enormous Changes at the Last Minute* (1974) and *Later the Same Day* (1985).

Born in the Bronx to Russian-Jewish immigrant parents, Paley is a quintessentially New York writer. This is a city where 'dumbwaiters boom, doors slam, dishes crash; every window is a mother's mouth bidding the street shut-up, go skate somewhere else, come home'. Humour and poignancy are interwoven in largely plotless pieces to build a picture of paradigmatic ordinariness, where nothing and everything has its own importance. Her characters are mostly women, many of whom recur throughout her collections, bemoaning their children, their lovers, their feckless husbands, their parents, the litter in the parks or the war in Vietnam (against which Paley campaigned tirelessly). 'I could have done more for peace if I'd written about it,' she said, with the same honesty that illuminates her fiction. 'But I happen to like being in the streets.'

JOYCE CAROL OATES (b.1938)

Since her first collection of short stories was published when she was 25 years old, Oates has published about 120 titles. In essays, novels, plays, poetry, short stories and screenplays, her main theme has been violence, although not necessarily the physical kind. She is 'concerned with the violence that informs and distorts less apparently threatening acts,' one critic explained, 'the ones that look clean, easy, legitimate'. Her protagonists range from migrant workers to wealthy suburbanites, from slum-dwellers to distinguished poets, from religious zealots to feminist scholars. Much of her fiction is set in Detroit, where she lives, *A Garden of Earthly Delights* (1967), *Expensive People* (1968) and *Them* (1969) being three significant examples. Since completing these works, she has continued her exploration of American people and institutions in novels, which are often Gothic in nature, and short stories, which some judge to be her finest work. Of these, *Where Are You Going, Where Have You Been?* (1966),

an 'interlude of terror' in a teenager's life, is perfectly representative, using an unknown male intruder (who never completely intrudes, but could and might, after the story is told) to transform a reassuring domestic setting into a potential nightmare.

Above: **Amy Tam's** *The Joy Luck Club* gave a voice to Chinese-American women. It was received as enthusiastically by the critics as by the book-buying public.

Below, left: **Grace Paley** has achieved international fame on the basis of just three collections of short stories. 'Life is too short', she said, 'to spend it writing fiction'.

ANNE TYLER (b.1941)

Her early readings of Eudora Welty taught Anne Tyler that 'very small things are often really larger than the large things'. Her favourite theme is family life, as a microcosm of a world where people never quite connect. *Dinner at the Homesick Restaurant* (1982), her ninth and finest novel, is structured around Pearl Tull, a mother on her deathbed whose husband left years ago and whose children are 'closed off from her in some perverse way'.

The Accidental Tourist (1985), which was made into a successful film (1988), centres on an inhibited, disengaged protagonist, who writes travel guides for people who dislike travelling. Tyler's celebrated comic gift makes this portrait of a man 'moving slowly into life' both funny and touching.

The Pulitzer prize-winning *Breathing Lessons* (1988) follows Maggie Moran and her husband of 28 years as they travel to the funeral of an old friend and reflect on their lives together. Nothing definitive happens. Tyler is curious about how people are, rather than how they seem – or how they might be in the restrictions of a more formulaic fiction than hers.

MAXINE HONG KINGSTON (b.1940)

With its subtle shifts between the concrete and the mythical, the past and the present, the American and the Chinese perspective on life, Maxine Hong Kingston's work has been described as having 'a lucidity which verges on the eerie'. Blending autobiography with fiction, her first two books (which she considers 'one big book') chart the experience of first-generation Chinese immigrants to America, from both male and female points of view. *The Woman Warrior* (1976) is filled with Kingston's mother and her stories of Chinese women – the 'No Name' aunt, who is deliberately forgotten by her family when she has an illegitimate child, being perhaps the most memorable.

China Men (1980) tells of the wave of Chinese immigration to the New York of laundry and restaurant work. Contrasting Chinese with American heroism, the book is framed by a wedding and a funeral – with boys being born in plenty between. Kingston imagines versions of her father's life, inventing a dreamlike mix of identities for him to understand how he was '*the father from China*' and '*the American father*' at one and the same time.

AMY TAN (b.1952)

Like Kingston, Amy Tan is concerned with the balancing of Chinese and American identities. Her first novel, *The Joy Luck Club* (1989), which, she said, made her realize 'how very Chinese I was', describes three Chinese women who lived in San Francisco in the late 1940s, contrasting their lives with those of their daughters.

A young American woman, Pearl, who has a Chinese mother, Winnie, is at the centre of *The Kitchen God's Wife* (1991). Winnie's recounting of her arduous life before immigration brings Pearl closer to her and eventually leads to a revelation of her own. The book was admired for its bittersweet humour and 'enchanting' poignancy, qualities Tan mingled with the supernatural in her third novel *The Hundred Secret Senses* (1995), in which Olivia and Kwan are half-sisters, sharing the same Chinese father. A visit to China together involves the women in a life they shared in an earlier century.

Recent fiction in Britain

The Booker prize was started in 1969 and has been the benchmark of excellence in British fiction ever since, although it is interesting that Martin Amis has never won in spite of being internationally esteemed. This period, paradoxically, has coincided with a dearth of excellence by the standards of previous generations. No single novel stands out and no acknowledged major writer has emerged. Even so, there is a significant body of work that may be judged quite differently by the 21st century.

MARTIN AMIS (b.1949)

Amis has been compared to Vladmir Nabokov and Saul Bellow for his flamboyant language and exceptional stylistic skills. The son of the novelist Kingsley Amis (see page 110), his first novel, *The Rachel Papers* (1973), attracted attention for its comically squalid account of teenage sexual shenanigans, related by an intellectually precocious but callow 19-year-old boy. Amis's characters tend towards caricature – they are comic monsters who are always memorable but rarely likeable.

John Self, the hero of *Money* (1984), is a film producer trying to find financial backers. During a trip to New York his overwhelming drive to gratify his appetites for drink, pornography and sex leads to financial ruin – with the slightly unconvincing suggestion that he will be a better man for it. The book can be seen as a comment on materialist greed or, equally, as a study of identity (Self's sense of himself disintegrates when he is deprived of his worldly satisfactions).

Readers are likely to be more impressed by Amis's 'street-smart prose', his 'spot-on' metaphors, his faultless ear for idioms and phrases. These gifts come to the fore in *London Fields* (1989), which has two inspired creations: Nicola Six, a beautiful *femme fatale*, who foresees that she will be murdered and sets out to arrange her death on her own terms, and Keith Talent, the gross and amoral pub darts champion whom Six ensnares.

KAZUO ISHIGURO (b.1954)

Born in Nagasaki, Japan, Kazuo Ishiguro moved to Britain when he was five years old and later studied at the University of Kent. *A Pale View of Hills* (1982), the first of his novels, is about a middle-aged Japanese woman living in England who is haunted by her daughter's suicide. It was a book highly praised for its controlled prose and the 'delicate layering of its themes and images', virtues that some critics have seen as typically Japanese.

In *An Artist of the Floating World* (1986) the setting is Japan, where an ageing painter reflects on his life since the war. Similar themes concern Ishiguro's most successful novel, the Booker prize-winning *The Remains of the Day* (1989). An unmarried butler looks back on his days of service to an English aristocrat, and comes to see how he has sacrificed his chances of happiness to his sense of duty. Ishiguro tells the butler's story with a skill and restraint that makes it all the more poignant.

Unconsoled (1995) is a more experimental work about a pianist who finds himself in an East European city for a concert performance he does not remember arranging. A reviewer described it as 'one of the strangest novels in memory'.

A.S. BYATT (b.1936)

The English academic and novelist, Antonia Susan Byatt has said that her books 'try to be about the life of the mind, as well as of society and the relations between people'. The novel *Possession* (1990), which won the Booker prize, is the tale of two 1980s academics whose paths cross when they find that the two (fictitious) Victorian poets they are researching were linked in a passionate love affair. In a largely convincing pastiche of Victorian literary styles, Byatt imagines their letters, their diaries and even their poetry. The poets' love story casts an ironic light on the affair between the academics, who, for all their highly trained intellects, are singularly ill at ease with intimacy.

Above: Despite the presence of Anthony Hopkins, the film version of *The Remains of the Day* could not match the pathos of the novel's story of a retired butler, told with exceptional literary skill by Kazuo Ishiguro.

Left: Martin Amis, son of Kingsley Amis (see page 110), names Vladimir Nabokov and Saul Bellow as his literary mentors, but his own flamboyant prose has a quality all his own.

JAMES KELMAN (b.1946)

It was several years before the Scottish novelist and short-story writer James Kelman was recognized as the authentic voice of working-class Glasgow. His first stories were published in America, and *Not Not While the Giro* (1983) was produced by a student publishing company. By 1987, however, when his collection *Greyhound for Breakfast* was published, Kelman was accepted as an important literary force.

His early tales are of unemployed, ambitionless but generally stoic and heavy-drinking Glasgow men. A typical character would be the hero of the title story of *Greyhound for Breakfast*, who spends all his money on a dog, but then subsequenly realizes that he can't afford food for it. The humour of the piece is undercut by the man's misery, about which Kelman is unsentimental but nevertheless sympathetic. The novel *A Disaffection* (1989) developed Kelman's bleak social analysis with the uneventful story of a schoolteacher, taking a week off work.

How Late It Was, How Late (1994) won the Booker prize. As always in Kelman's writing, it is the language that drives the book – his unmatched ability to translate the speech and thoughts of his characters onto the page.

IAN McEWAN (b.1948)

Ian McEwan's gift is his ability to create a perfectly controlled, believable fictional world within which his characters are free to act out his disturbing and anarchic fantasies. Incest, rape, pornography and sexual power games figure largely.

First Love, Last Rites (1975) is a collection of stories about people who become caught up in sinister or bizarre scenarios. *The Comfort of Strangers* (1981) involves four people in an increasingly nightmarish train of events. In *Black Dogs* (1992) unpleasant things start to happen to a woman on holiday in France with her husband.

McEwan is not so much a stylist as a storyteller, whose notion of evil in the everyday makes chillingly compulsive reading.

International fiction now

With so much new fiction currently appearing – and being so quickly translated – it is hard to identify 'the best', but the following are writers of enduring merit, whose work continues to develop the tradition of literature worldwide, as they themselves develop and master their craft, 'to forge', perhaps, as James Joyce said 'the uncreated consciousness of the race'.

EUROPEANS

The Danish writer Peter Høeg (b.1957) turned to fiction after working as a sailor, dancer and actor. His first novel, *Miss Smilla's Feeling for Snow* (1993) – a murder mystery/thriller set in Greenland and Denmark, with metaphysical overtones – was an international best-seller. His later works have seen him leave the confines of the thriller to produce the intense but wholly uncategorizable *The Woman and the Ape* (1997) and *Tales of the Night* (1998). The latter includes eight short stories, set in different parts of the world, all dealing with 'love and conditions on the night of 29 March 1929'. Written in a graceful, meditative prose, it is noteworthy for its mix of ideas and baroque imagination. Other works include *Borderliners* (1994) and *The History of Danish Dreams* (1995).

Irish writer Roddy Doyle (b.1958) came to popular attention when *The Commitments* (1987) – the first in his 'Barrytown' trilogy – was filmed in 1991. Like *The Snapper* (1990) and *The Van* (1991; film 1996), the book describes certain characters in a family living on a housing estate in Dublin. The works are funny, gutsy, conversational and loud. *Paddy Clarke Ha Ha Ha* (1993) won the Booker prize for its sensitive view of the break-up of a marriage seen through the eyes of a ten-year-old boy.

German novelist Patrick Suskind (b.1949) had his first success with the work that remains his best known, *Perfume* (1985). A skilful pastiche of a whole range of literary styles, the book tells the story of an abandoned baby in 18th-century Paris whose only gift is an amazing sense of smell. He becomes a master perfume-maker, who stalks young women for their scent and then kills them. Suskind's subsequent work includes the less popular novellas *Pigeon* and *Mr Summer's Story*.

Orhan Pamuk (b.1952) is a Turkish writer who has been praised for the broad scope of his work and his Borgesian sentences. Two of his novels have been translated, *The White Castle*, an exquisitely lucid fable about an Italian slave and his Turkish master who exchange identities, and *The Black Book*, which attempts to chart the complexity of life in present-day Istanbul. This is a more experimental work, laced with games, paradoxes, stories about stories and about the nature of stories.

SOUTH OF THE EQUATOR

The Indian writer Vikram Seth (b.1952) came to fame with *The Golden Gate* (1986), a novel written entirely in verse. Using a metre modelled on Pushkin's *Eugene Onegin*, this long narrative poem is a witty and technically accomplished satire on middle-class life and manners in California (where Seth was studying). *The Golden Gate* was much admired for both its form and its content – and as an attempt to revitalize verse as a storytelling medium.

With *A Suitable Boy* (1993), Seth switched from poetry to prose, producing a novel that at 1349 pages has the distinction of being one of longest single-volume

works in English fiction. The book, which traces in exhaustive detail the linked histories of four Hindu families shortly after India gained its independence, enjoyed considerable popular and critical success, although some critics felt that it had sacrificed intensity for inclusiveness.

Another Indian writer Arundhati Roy (b.1961) won the Booker prize with her first novel, *The God of Small Things* (1997), which went on to become an international bestseller. Set in India in the 1960s, the book uses the story of a pair of young twins as a springboard for what has been likened to a jazz improvisation, spinning a myriad of interconnected yarns in highly charged poetic prose.

The South African J.M. Coetzee (b.1940) is the only novelist to have won the Booker prize twice, first in 1993 with *Life and Times of Michael K* and again six years later, in 1999, with *Disgrace. Life and Times of Michael K* is a Kafkaesque allegory about an ugly and slow-witted gardener in a Cape Town park who is trying to find a refuge for himself and his mother during a civil war. *Disgrace* is an equally dark meditation on the new South Africa from the perspective of a middle-aged white man, who is slowly reduced to the lowest of circumstances.

THE MIDDLE EAST

Israeli writer David Grossman (b.1954) has two novels currently in translation, *The Smile of the Lamb* (1983) and *See Under: Love* (1986), which Edmund White described as 'one of the most disturbing books I've ever read'. It tells the story of Momik, the only child of two holocaust survivors, who becomes 'infected with humanity' through listening to his great-uncle's stories. Its wider theme is that of Israel's refusal to acknowledge the damage done to its national psyche by the holocaust.

Amos Oz (b.1939) is one of Israel's true native voices, who charts its chaos and the soothing pattern of its daily life with equal care. His extensively translated work includes the powerful epistolary novel *Black Box* (1988), in which Illyana writes to her ex-husband Alex to ask for help with their illiterate son. Politics and personal destinies become increasingly intertwined in this tragi-comic tale of old scars being re-opened.

In 1988 Naguib Mahfouz or Mahfuz (b.1911) became the first Arab writer to win the Nobel prize. His best known fiction is the 'Cairo' trilogy, written between 1956 and 1957 but not published in translation until the 1990s. This massive work records the changes this century has wrought in Egypt through three generations of a middle-class family.

Nobel Prize for Literature Winners

1901	SULLY PRUDHOMME (*pen-name of* RENÉ FRANÇOIS ARMAND)
1902	CHRISTIAN MATTHIAS THEODOR MOMMSEN
1903	BJØRNSTJERNE MARTINUS BJØRNSON
1904	*The prize was divided equally between:*
	FRÉDÉRIC MISTRAL *and* JOSÉ ECHEGARAY Y EIZAGUIRRE
1905	HENRYK SIENKIEWICZ
1906	GIOSUÈ CARDUCCI
1907	RUDYARD KIPLING
1908	RUDOLF CHRISTOPH EUCKEN
1909	SELMA OTTILIA LOVISA LAGERLÖF
1910	PAUL JOHANN LUDWIG HEYSE
1911	COUNT MAURICE (MOORIS) POLIDORE MARIE
	BERNHARD MAETERLINCK
1912	GERHART JOHANN ROBERT HAUPTMANN
1913	RABINDRANATH TAGORE
1914	*The prize money for 1914 was allocated to the*
	Special Fund of this prize section.
1915	ROMAIN ROLLAND
1916	CARL GUSTAF VERNER VON HEI DENSTAM
1917	*The prize was divided equally between:*
	KARL ADOLPH GJELLERUP *and* HENRIK PONTOPPIDAN
1918	*The prize money for 1918 was allocated to the*
	Special Fund of this prize section.
1919	CARL FRIEDRICH GEORG SPITTELER
1920	KNUT PEDERSEN HAMSUN
1921	ANATOLE FRANCE (*pen-name of* JACQUES ANATOLE THIBAULT)
1922	JACINTO BENAVENTE
1923	WILLIAM BUTLER YEATS
1924	WLADYSLAW STANISLAW REYMONT (*pen-name of* REYMENT)
1925	GEORGE BERNARD SHAW
1926	GRAZIA DELEDDA (*pen-name of* GRAZIA MADESANI *née* DELEDDA)
1927	HENRI BERGSON
1928	SIGRID UNDSET
1929	THOMAS MANN
1930	SINCLAIR LEWIS
1931	ERIK AXEL KARLFELDT
1932	JOHN GALSWORTHY
1933	IVAN ALEKSEYEVICH BUNIN
1934	LUIGI PIRANDELLO
1935	*The prize money was allocated to the Main Fund (⅓) and to the*
	Special Fund (⅔) of this prize section.
1936	EUGENE GLADSTONE O'NEILL
1937	ROGER MARTIN DU GARD
1938	PEARL BUCK (*pen-name of* PEARL WALSH *née* SYDENSTRICKER)
1939	FRANS EEMIL SILLANPÄÄ
1940–43	*The prize money was allocated to the Main Fund (⅓) and to the*
	Special Fund (⅔) of this prize section.
1944	JOHANNES VILHELM JENSEN
1945	GABRIELA MISTRAL (*pen-name of* LUCILA GODOY Y ALCA-YAGA)
1946	HERMANN HESSE
1947	ANDRÉ PAUL GUILLAUME GIDE
1948	THOMAS STEARNS ELIOT
1949	WILLIAM FAULKNER
1950	EARL BERTRAND ARTHUR WILLIAM RUSSELL
1951	PÄR FABIAN LAGERKVIST
1952	FRANÇOIS MAURIAC
1953	SIR WINSTON LEONARD SPENCER CHURCHILL
1954	ERNEST MILLER HEMINGWAY
1955	HALLDÓR KILJAN LAXNESS.
1956	JUAN RAMÓN JIMÉNEZ
1957	ALBERT CAMUS
1958	BORIS LEONIDOVICH PASTERNAK (*Accepted first, later,*
	caused by the authorities of his country, to decline the prize.)
1959	SALVATORE QUASIMODO
1960	SAINT-JOHN PERSE (*pen-name of* ALEXIS LÉGER)
1961	IVO ANDRI´C
1962	JOHN STEINBECK
1963	GIORGOS SEFERIS (*pen-name of* GIORGOS SEFERIADIS)
1964	JEAN-PAUL SARTRE (*Declined the prize.*)
1965	MICHAIL ALEKSANDROVICH SHOLOKHOV
1966	*The prize was divided equally between:*
	SHMUEL YOSEF AGNON *and* NELLY SACHS
1967	MIGUEL ANGEL ASTURIAS
1968	YASUNARI KAWABATA
1969	SAMUEL BECKETT
1970	ALEKSANDR ISAEVICH SOLZHENITSYN
1971	PABLO NERUDA
1972	HEINRICH BÖLL
1973	PATRICK WHITE
1974	*The prize was divided equally between:*
	EYVIND JOHNSON *and* HARRY MARTINSON
1975	EUGENIO MONTALE
1976	SAUL BELLOW
1977	VICENTE ALEIXANDRE
1978	ISAAC BASHEVIS SINGER
1979	ODYSSEUS ELYTIS (*pen-name of* ODYSSEUS ALEPOUDHELIS)
1980	CZESLAW MILOSZ
1981	ELIAS CANETTI
1982	GABRIEL GARCÍA MÁRQUEZ
1983	SIR WILLIAM GOLDING
1984	JAROSLAV SEIFERT
1985	CLAUDE SIMON
1986	WOLE SOYINKA
1987	JOSEPH BRODSKY
1988	NAGUIB MAHFOUZ
1989	CAMILO JOSÉ CELA
1990	OCTAVIO PAZ
1991	NADINE GORDIMER
1992	DEREK WALCOTT
1993	TONI MORRISON
1994	KENZABURO OE
1995	SEAMUS HEANEY
1996	WISLAWA SZYMBORSKA
1997	DARIO FO
1998	JOSE SARAMAGO
1999	GÜNTER GRASS

1900 Sigmund Freud publishes
The Interpretation of Dreams

1901 Strindberg's *The Dance of Death*,
Rudyard Kipling's *Kim*,
Chekhov's *Three Sisters*

1903 First powered flight - Wright Brothers
The Way of All Flesh - Samuel Butler,
Henry James' *The Golden Bowl*.
Jack London's *Call of the Wild*

1905 Einstein's Special Theory of Relativity

1907 Joseph Conrad's *The Secret Agent*

1908 Arnold Bennett's *The Old Wives' Tale*

1908 Henry Ford's Model T, first production
line car

1913 Einstein's General Theory of Relativity
Guillaume Apollinaire's *Alcools*

1913-27 Publication of Marcel Proust's *A la
Recherche du Temps Perdu*
(*InRemembrance of Things Past*)

1914-18 The First World War

1915 Kafka's *The Metamorphosis*

1917 Russian revolution. Bolsheviks come to
power in Russia
First of Ezra Pound's *The Cantos*

1919 Sherwood Anderson's *Winesburg, Ohio*

1920 First radio broadcasts in US
Jaroslav Hasek's *The Good Soldier
Schweik*,
Edith Wharton's *The Age of Innocence*
D.H. Lawrence's *Women in Love*

1921 Luigi Pirandello's *Six Characters in
Search of an Author*

1922 T.S.Eliot's *The Waste Land* and
James Joyce's *Ulysses* published

1923 Rainer Maria Rilke's *Duino Elegies*,
Italo Svevo's *Confessions of Zeno*

1924 Thomas Mann's *The Magic Mountain*

1925 John Logie Baird invents TV
W.B. Yeats's *A Vision*
Franz Kafka's *The Trial* published
posthumously,
Scott Fitzgerald's *The Great Gatsby*,
Theodore Dreiser's *An American Tragedy*

1926 Franz Kafka's *The Castle* published
posthumously

1927 Alexander Fleming discovers penicillin,
the first anti-biotic
André Gide's *The Counterfeiters*
Hermann Hesse's *Der Steppenwolf*,
Virginia Woolf's *To the Lighthouse*,
Sinclair Lewis's *Elmer Gantry*

1929 Wall Street crash, start of the Depression
William Faulkner publishes *The Sound
and the Fury*.
Hemingway *A Farewell to Arms*

1930-32 Robert Musil's *The Man Without
Qualities*
Aldous Huxley's *Brave New World*

1933 Hitler comes to power
Federico Garcia Lorca's *Blood Wedding*

1934 Louis-Ferdinand Céline's *Journey to the
End of the Night*,
Evelyn Waugh's *A Handful of Dust*

1936-39 The Spanish Civil War

1937 Wallace Steven's *The Man with the Blue
Guitar*

1938 Jean-Paul Sartre's *Nausea*

1939 First TV broadcasts in US
Finnegans Wake's, James Joyce
John Steinbeck's *The Grapes of Wrath*

1939-45 The Second World War

1940 Ernest Hemingway's *For Whom the Bell
Tolls*,
Arthur Koestler's *Darkness at Noon*
Richard Wright's *Native Son*,
Christina Stead's *The Man Who Loved
Children*

1941 Bertolt Brecht's *Mother Courage*

1942 Camilo Jose Cela's *The Family of Pascual
Duarte*

1945 US drops atom bomb on Hiroshima

1946 First electronic computer built in USA
Eugene O'Neill's *The Iceman Cometh*

1947 Malcom Lowry - *Under the Volcano*,
Tennessee Williams - *A Streetcar named
Desire*
Jean Genet's *The Maids*,
Albert Camus *The Plague*

1948 Yasunari Kawabata's *Snow Country*

1949 George Orwell's *Nineteen Eighty-Four*
Arthur Miller's *Death of a Salesman*

1951 J.D. Salinger's *The Catcher in the Rye*

1952 Samuel Beckett's *Waiting for Godot*,
Ralph Ellison's *The Invisible Man*

1953 Crick and Watson decode DNA, the key
to human genetic code
Jorge Luis Borges's *Labyrinths*,
Arthur Miller's *The Crucible*

1954 William Golding's *Lord of the Flies*

1954-55 J.R.R. Tolkien's *The Lord of the Rings*

1955 Samuel Beckett's *Waiting for Godot*,
Nabokov's *Lolita*

1956 John Osborne's *Look Back in Anger*

1957 Jack Kerouac's *On the Road*

1958 Eugène Ionesco's *Rhinoceros*
Chinua Achebe's *Things Fall Apart*,
Boris Pasternak's *Doctor Zhivago*
José Maria Arguedas- *The Deep Rivers*

1959 William Burroughs's *The Naked Lunch*
Günter Grass' *The Tin Drum*

1960 Harold Pinter's *The Caretaker*

1961 Man in space, Russian Yuri Gagarin
Joseph Heller's *Catch-22*
V.S. Naipaul's *A House for Mr Biswas*

1962 Solzhenitsyn's *One Day in the Life of
Ivan Denisovich*

1963 John F. Kennedy, President of US,
assassinated

1964 Saul Bellow's *Herzog*

1967 *One Hundred Years of Solitude* - Gabriel
Garcia Marquez

1969 Moon landing
Kurt Vonnegut's *Slaughterhouse-Five*

1970 Patrick White's *The Vivisector*
Dario Fo's *Accidental Death of an
Anarchist*

1973 US forces withdraw from Vietnam
Thomas Pynchon's *Gravity's Rainbow*

1974 Robert Stone's *Dog Soldier*

1975 Wole Soyinka's *Death and the King's
Horseman*
John Ashberry's *Self-Portrait in a Convex
Mirror*

1977 Toni Morrison's *The Song of Solomon*

1979 Cormac McCarthy's *Suttree*

1981 Gabriel García Márquez's *Chronicle of a
Love Foretold*

1982 Alice Walker's *The Color Purple*

1984 David Mamet's *Glengarry Glen Ross*

1986 David Grossman's *See Under Love*

1987 Tom Wolfe's *Bonfire of the Vanities*

1989 Cold War ends, Berlin Wall comes down,
collapse of Communism in East Europe
Kazuo Ishiguro's *The Remains of the Day*,
Amy Tan's *The Joy Luck Club*
Iranian muslims impose a fatwa on
Salman Rushdie for *The Satanic Verses*

1992 Worldwide Web invented, Internet takes
off

1997 Thomas Pynchon's *Mason and Dixon*

1998 Don Delillo's *Underworld*

1999 Fatwa lifted on Salman Rushdie

Index

Page numbers in *italics* refer to illustrations.

18 Poems 152
25 Poems 152
291 33
2001: A Space Odyssey 133

A

Abe, Kobo 165
Absalom, Absalom! 63
Accident: A Day's News 167
Accidental Death of an Anarchist 128
Accidental Tourist 181
Achebe, Chinua 170
Adventures of Augie March, The 100
Advertisements for Myself 99
After the Fall 127
Afternoon Men 111
Age of Innocence, The 11
Age of Reason, The 89
Airport 145
Aitken, Conrad 81
Akhmatova, Anna 26
Albee, Edward 127
Album de vers anciens, L' 23
Alcools 49
Alexandria Quartet 54
All God's Children Need Travelling Shoes 178
All My Sons 126
All the Pretty Horses 176
All the Races 116
Allende, Isabel 169
Ambassadors, The 9
Ambler, Eric 136
Amen Corner, The 107
America 40
American Blues 126
American Buffalo 127
American Dream, An 99
American Dream, The 127
American Psycho 177
American Tragedy, An 16
Amis, Kingsley 110, *110*, 152
Amis, Martin 182, *183*
Amrita 175
An Angel at my Table 77
Anatomy Lesson, The 101
Ancient Evenings 99
And Where Were You, Adam? 95
Anderson, Sherwood 16, 50, 62
Andreas-Salome, Lou 23
Angelic Pubis 169
Angelou, Maya 178
Anglo-Saxon Attitudes 111
Animal Farm 82
Anna of the Five Towns 15
Another Country 107
Anthills of the Savannah 170
Antonioni, Michelangelo 160
Anything We Love Can Be Saved: A Writer's Activism 179
Apes of God, The 57
Apocalpyse Now 10
Apollinaire, Guillaume 48–9
Arguedas, Jose Maria 116–17
Arkin, Alan 103
Armies of the Night: the Novel as History, History as a Novel 99
Arms and the Man 13
Arp, Jean 32
Artist of the Floating World, An 182
As a Man Grows Older 69

As I Lay Dying 63
As If by Magic 111
Ashbery, John 55, 151
Asimov, Isaac 133
Aspects of the Novel 57
Assistant, The (Malamud) 101
Assistant, The (Walser) 67
Asturias, Miguel Angel 168
At My Heart's Core 173
Atwood, Margaret 78, 173, 179
Auden, W.H. 40, 55, 59, 81, 150, 151
Auto-da-Fe 67
Autobiography of Alice B. Toklas, The 48
Autumn Journal 81
Autumn of the Patriarch, The 158
Awake and Sing! 86

B

'Baa, Baa, Black Sheep' 11
Baal 70
Babbitt 60–61
Bacall, Lauren *141*
Balcony, The 123
Bald Prima Donna, The 122
Baldwin, James 94, 107, *107*
Ball, Hugo 32
Ballad of the Sad Cafe, The 103
Ballard, J.G. 135, *135*
Baltasar and Blimunda 166–7
Banks, Iain M. 135
Baron in the Trees, The 160
'Barrytown' trilogy 184
Barth, John 160, 161
Bates, Alan *101*
Beach, Sylvia 42
Bear, Greg 133
Beautiful and Damned, The 52
Beauty and the Beast 65
Beauvoir, Simone de 76, *76*, 89
Bech: A Book 102
Beckett, Samuel 43, 54, 70, 121, *121*, 157
Beerbohm, Sir Max 15, *15*
Being and Nothingness 89
Bell, The 113
Bell, Vanessa 37
Bell Jar, The 77
Bellow, Saul 100–101, *100*, 118
Beloved 179
Bend in the River, A 171
Beneath Your Clear Shadow and Other Poems 155
Benford, Gregory 133
Benjamin, Walter 39
Bennett, Alan 131, *131*
Bennett, Arnold 15
Bernhard, Thomas 167
Betrayed by Rita Hayworth 168
Betsy, The 144
Beyond the Curve 165
Beyond the Horizon 86
Big Sleep, The 140
Billiards at Half Past Nine 95
Binoche, Juliette *114*
Birthday Letters 152
Bishop, Elizabeth 105, 150
Black Book, The 184
Black Book: an Agon, The 54
Black Box 185
Black Boy 106
Black Dogs 183
Black Mischief 58
Black Power 106
Black Spring 54
Blackeyes 131
Blackwood, Caroline *151*
Blade Runner 134

Blair, Eric Arthur *see* Orwell, George
Blast: The Review of the Great English Vortex 32, 33
Blind Fireworks 81
Blish, James 134
Bliss 173
Blood Meridian 177
Blood Wedding 68
Blow-up 160
Blue Remembered Hills 131
Bluebeard 163
Bluest Eye, The 179
Bodily Harm 78
Bodysnatcher 116
Bogarde, Dirk 67, *101*
Bogart, Humphrey 140, *141*
Boll, Heinrich 94, 95
Bond, Edward 125
Bonfire of the Vanities, The 177
Book of Hours, The 23
Book of Laughter and Forgetting, The 114
Book of Poems (Lorca) 68
'Border' trilogy 177
Borderliners 184
Borges, Jorge Luis 156, 157, *157*, 168
Boy's Will, A 22
Bradford, Barbara Taylor 146, *147*
Braine, John 110
Braque 48
Brautigan, Richard 96
Brave New World 59, 133
Bread of our Early Years 95
Breakfast at Tiffany's 99
Breakfast of Champions 163
Breath 121
Breathing Lessons 181
Brecht, Bertolt 70–71, *71*
Breton, Andre 32, 33
Brideshead Revisited 59
Bridge of San Luis Rey, The 61
Bright Lights, Big City 177
Brightness Falls 177
Brimstone and Treacle 131
Brod, Max 40
Brodsky, Joseph 155
Buddenbrooks 66
Buenos Aires Affair, The 168
Bukowski, Charles 97
Bulgakov, Mikhail 83
Bunuel, Luis 68
Burgess, Anthony 108, 109, 133
Burning Perch 81
Burnt-Out Case, A 109
Burroughs, William 92, 93
Burton, Richard *148*
Butler, Samuel 14–15
Butor, Michel 90
Byatt, A.S. 182
Byrne, Gabriel *185*

C

Caeiro, Alberto *see* Pessoa, Fernando
'Cairo' trilogy 185
Caldwell, Erskine 85
Call for the Dead 137
'Call of Cthulhu, The' 142
Call of the Wild, The 17
Calvino, Italo 160, *160*
Campos, Alvaro de *see* Pessoa, Fernando
Camus, Albert *88*, 89, 122
Cancer Ward 94
Cannery Row 85
Can't Go Home Again 61

Can't Pay? Won't Pay! 128
Cantos, The 30, 31
Capote, Truman 93, 99, *99*
Captain Pantoja and the Special Service 169
Captive Mind, The 154
Caretaker, The 123
Carey, Peter 172–3
Carpentier, Alejo 116, 117, *117*
Carpetbaggers, The 144
Carrie 143
Carter, Angela 79, 159
Cartland, Barbara 147
Carver, Raymond 104, 105
Case of Peter the Lett, The 139
Casino Royale 137
Cassady, Neal 92, 93
Castle, The 40, 41
Castle of Crossed Destinies, The 160
Castle to Castle 64
Cat and Mouse 95
Cat on a Hot Tin Roof 126
Catch-22 102, 103
Catcher in the Rye, The 103
Cathedral 105
Cat's Cradle 163
Caucasian Chalk Circle, The 71
Cavafy, Constantine 24–5
Cave Birds 152
Ceasefire, The 114
Cela, Camilo Jose 166, *166*
Celine, Louis-Ferdinand 64
Chairs, The 122
Chambers, Jessie 44
Chandler, Raymond 140
Chart of Jimmie Blacksmith, The 172
Cheever, John 104
Chekhov, Anton 12, *13*
Cheri 73
Cherry Orchard, The 12
Chesterton, G.K. 75
Chicken Soup with Barley 125
Childermass 57
Childhood's End 133
Children of the Game 65
Chimera 161
China Men 181
Chips with Everything 125
Christie, Agathie 138–9, *138*
Christmas Garland, A 15
Christmas in Biafra and Other Poems 170
Chronicle of a Death Foretold 159
Chronicles of Clovis, The 15
'Chronicles of Thomas Covenant' 133
Cities of the Red Night 93
City and the Stars, The 133
Clancy, Tom 145
Clarke, Arthur C. 133
Clockwork Orange, A 109, 133
Close, Glenn *168*
Cocteau, Jean 39, 64, 65
Coetzee, J.M. *185*
Gold Spring 150
Colette, Sidonie Gabrielle 73, *73*
Collected Longer Poems (Auden) 81
Collected Poems (Frost) 23
Collected Poems (MacNeice) 81
Collected Poems (Stevens) 149
Collected Poems, The (Larkin) 152
Collected Shorter Poems (Auden) 81
Collected Stories (Lawrence) 45
Collins, Jackie 147

Color Curtain, The 106
Color Purple, The 179
Comfort of Strangers, The 183
Comforters, The 113
Coming Through Slaughter 173
Commitments, The 184
Complete Collected Poems of Maya Angelou 178
Complete Poems (Bishop) 150
Complete Poems (Lawrence) 45
Complicity 135
Compton-Burnett, Ivy 112–13
Concrete Island 135
Confederacy of Dunces, A 97
Confessions of a Mask 165
Confessions of Felix Krull, Confidence Man, The 66
Confessions of Zeno, The 69
Confidential Agent, The 136
Conformist, The 115
Connery, Sean 137
Connolly, Cyril 51
Conrad, Joseph 10, *10*, 44
Consider Phlebas 135
Conversations in the Cathedral 169
Cookson, Catherine 146
Copper, Gary *51*
'Cornish' trilogy 173
Cornwell, David *see* Le Carre, John
Corrections 167
Cortazar, Julio 160–61, *161*
Cotters' England 172
Count Zero 134
Counter-Attack 47
Counterfeiters, The 64
Coupland, Douglas 175, *175*
Couples 102
Cowley, Malcolm 92
Crane, Hart 34
Crane, Stephen 17
Crash 135
Creditors, The 13
Creeley, Robert 92
Crow 152
Crowds and Power 67
Crucible, The 127
Cry from Kensington 113
Cry, the Beloved Country 94
Crying of Lot 49, The 162
Cubs, and Other Stories, The 169
cummings, e.e. 34, *35*
Cuttlefish Bones 154

D

Daisy Miller 9
Dali, Salvador 68
Damascus Gate 176
Dance of Death, The 13
Dance of the Forests, A 170
Dance to the Music of Time, A 111
Darkness at Noon 83
Darkness Visible 108
Davies, Robertson 173, *173*
Day of the Jackal, The 145
Day of the Locust, The 61
Day Out, A 131
Day-Lewis, Daniel *114*
Days of Hope 65
Days Run Away Like Wild Horses Over the Hills 97
'Dayspring Mishandled' 11
Dean's December, The 101
Death and the King's Horseman 170
Death of a Naturalist 153
Death of a Salesman 126

Death on the Instalment Plan 64
Death on the Nile 138
Decline and Fall 58
Decline of the West, The 67
Deep Rivers 116
Delicate Balance, A 127
DeLillo, Don 156, 162–3
'Deptford' trilogy 173
Dharma Bums, The 93
Diaghilev 65
Dial, The 149
Diary (Nin) 74
Dick, Phillip K. 134
Dinner at the Homesick Restaurant 181
Disaffection, A 183
'Discworld' series 133
Disgrace 185
Divided Heaven 167
Do Androids Dream of Electric Sheep? 134
Doctor Zhivago 27
Dog Soldiers 176
Dog Years 95
Dolittle, Hilda 29
Dolores 112
Donaldson, Stephen 133
Donleavy, J.P. 96
Door into the Dark 153
Doors of Perception, The 59
Dos Passos, John 62, 63
Dourif, Brad *104*
Down and Out in Paris and London 82
Doyle, Sir Arthur Conan 138, *139*
Doyle, Roddy 184, *184*
Dr Faustus 66
Dracula 142
Dream on Monkey Mountain 171
Dream Play, A 13
Dreiser, Theodore 16, *17*
Driver's Seat, The 113
Drowned World, The 135
Dubliners 42
Duck Variations 127
Dufy, Raoul *28*
Duino Elegies 23
Duo 73
Duras, Marguerite 77, 90
Durrell, Lawrence 54
Duvall, Shelley *143*

E

Early Morning 125
Earthly Powers 109
East of Eden 85
East Slope 155
Eco, Umberto 161
Edible Woman, The 78
Edmond 127
Electric Kool-Aid Acid Test 96
Eleven Poems 153
Eliot, Henry 30
Eliot, T.S. 30, *30*, 31, 149, 152, 154
Ellis, Brett Easton 177
Ellison, Ralph 106
Elmer Gantry 61
Emechta, Buchi 170
Empire of the Sun 135
Enchantments 23
End of the Affair, The 109
Enderby Outside 109
Enemy of the Stars 32
English Patient, The 173
Englishman Abroad, An 131
Enigma of Arrival, The 171
'Enoch Soames' 15
Enormous Changes at the Last Minute 180
Enormous Room, The 34

Entertainer, The 124
Envoy from Mirror City, The 77
Erasers, The 90
Eros at Breakfast 173
Escape of the Inca, The 169
Espedair Street 135
Estate, The 118
Eternal Curse on the Reader of These Pages 169
Ethan Frome 11
'Evening' 26
Everything We Know: Earthling Poems 179
Excession 135
Executioner's Song: a Time Life Novel 99
Exile and the Kingdom 89
Expensive People 180

F

Face of Another, The 165
Family and a Fortune, A 113
Family Arsenal, The 176
Family Moskat, The 118
Family of Pascual Duarte, The 166
Farewell, My Lovely 140
Farewell to Arms, A 51
Farrell, James T. 85
Fat Man in History, The 172
Fat Woman's Joke, The 78
Father, The 13
Faulkner, William 62–3, *62*, 130
Fear and Loathing in Las Vegas 96
Fear of Flying 79
Ferlinghetti, Lawrence 92
Fictions 157
Fiennes, Ralph *173*
Fifth Business 173
Financial Expert, The 171
Finnegans Wake 43
Fire Next Time, The 107
Fires: Essays, Stories, Poems 105
First Circle, The 94
First Love, Last Rites 183
First Men in the Moon, The 133
Fitzgerald, F. Scott 52–3, *52*, 62, 130
Fitzgerald, Zelda 52
Fixer, The 101
Flag for Sunrise, A 176
Flaws in the Glass 119
Fleming, Ian 137
Fo, Dario 128
Fool, The 125
Ford, Ford Maddox 44, 49
Forest Moon 155
Forster, E.M. 44, 57, *57*
Forsyth, Frederick 145
Fortunate Traveller, The 171
Foucault's Pendulum 161
Four Wise Men, The 91
Fowles, John 97
Fox from Above and the Fox from Below, The 117
Frame, Janet 77
Franny and Zooey 103
French Lieutenant's Woman, The 97
French Lieutenant's Woman, The (screenplay) 123
Friday, or the Other Island 91
Friend of My Youth 173
Frost, Robert 22–3, *22*, 31

G

Gable, Clark 146, *147*
Galapagos 163
Gallagher, Tess 105
Garcia Lorca, Federico *see* Lorca, Federico Garcia

Garcia Marquez, Gabriel 156, 158–9, 168
Garden of Earthly Delights, A 180
Gargoyles 167
Gather Together in My Name 178
Gaudier-Brzeska, Henri 31
Gay, John 71
Generation X: Tales for an Accelerated Culture 175
Genet, Jean 70, 122–3
Geography III 150
Get Shorty 141
Getting Merry Like Christmas 178
Ghost Sonata 13
Ghost Writer, The 101
Gibson, William 134–5
Gide, Andre 23, 38, 64–5, *65*
Giles Goat-Boy: or, The Revised New Syllabus 161
Gilmore, Gary 99
Gimpel the Fool 118
Ginger Man, The 95
Ginsberg, Allen 92, 93
Giovanni's Room 107
Girl in Winter, A 152
Girlfriend in a Coma 175
Girls at Play 176
Girls of Slender Means, The 113
Glass Bead Game, The 19
Glass Menagerie, The 126
Glengarry Glen Ross 127
Go-Between, The 123
Go Tell It on the Mountain 107
Goalie's Anxiety at the Penalty Kick 129
God of Small Things, The 185
God's Little Acre 85
Golden Bowl, The 9
Golden Gate, The 184
Golden Notebook, The 77
Goldfinger 137
Golding, William 108
Gone with the Wind 146
Gonne, Maud 21
'Good Country People' 105
Good Morning, Midnight 75
Good Soldier, The 49
Good Soldier Schweik, The 68, 69
Good Woman of Setzuan, The 71
Goodbye Columbus 101
Goodbye to All That 55
Goodbye to Berlin 59
Gordimer, Nadine *118*, 119
Gorenko, Anna Andreevna *see* Akhmatova, Anna
Gospel According to Jesus Christ, The 166
Grapes of Wrath, The 84
Grass, Gunter 94–5, *95*, 159
Grass Harp, The 99
Grass is Singing, The 77
Graves, Robert 54–5, *55*
Gravity's Rainbow 162
Great Gatsby, The 53
Greco, Juliette 99
Green, Henry 59, 111
Green House, The 169
Greene, Graham 108–9, 136–7, *136*, 171
Greer, Germaine 77
Gregory, Lady Augusta 21, 87
Greyhound for Breakfast 183
Grisham, John 145
Grossman, David 185
Grosz, George 28
Growth of the Soil, The 18
Guest of Honour, A 119
Gulag Archipelago, The 94

Gumilev, Lev 26
Gumilyev, Nikolai 26
Gun for Sale, A 136
Gunn, Thomas 152
Guns of Navarone, The 144
Gypsy Ballads 68

H

Hailey, Arthur 145
Ham on Rye 97
Hammett, Dashiell 140
Hamsun, Knut 8, 18
Handful of Dust, A 58
Handke, Peter 129, 130
Handmaid's Tale, The 78
Hardy, Thomas 14, *14*
Hasek, Jaroslav 69
Havel, Vaclav 128
Haw Lantern, The 153
Hawk in the Rain, The 152
Heaney, Seamus 153
Heart is a Lonely Hunter, The 103
Heart of a Woman, The 178
'Heart of Darkness' 10
Heart of the Matter, The 109
Heartbreak House 13
Heaven and Hell 59
Heaven's My Destination 61
Heinlein, Robert 133
Heller, Joseph 100, 102, 103
Hemingway, Ernest 16, 48, 50–51, *50*, 62
Hemlock and After 111
Henry IV 70
Hepburn, Audrey 99
Herbert, Frank 133
Herzog 100
Hesse, Hermann 18–19, *19*, 97
High Windows 152
Hiroshima mon amour 77
History 115
History of Danish Dreams, The 184
History of the Siege of Lisbon, The 166
Hive, The 166
HMS Ulysses 144
Hobbit, The 133
Hoch, Hannah *28*
Hocus Pocus 163
Hoeg, Peter 184
Holdstock, Robert 133
Hollywood Wives 147
Hombre 141
Homage to Ctalonia 82
Honey for the Bears 109
Honors at Dawn 126
Honourable Schoolboy, The 137
Hope Abandoned 27
Hope against Hope 27
Hopscotch 161
Hotel 145
Hound of the Baskervilles, The 138
House and its Head, A 113
House for Mr Biswas, A 171
House of All Nations 172
House of Bernada Alba, The 68
House of Incest 74
House of Mirth, The 11
House of the Spirits, The 169
How Late It Was, How Late 183
How to Live on 24 Hours a Day 15
Howard's End 57
Howl and Other Poems 93
Hueffer, Ford Hermann *see* Ford, Ford Madox
Hughes, Langston 106
Hughes, Ted 55, 152, *153*

Hulme, T.E. 29
Humboldt's Gift 100
Hundred Secret Senses, The 181
Hunger 18
Hunt for Red October, The 145
Huxley, Aldous *58*, 59, 130, 133

I

I Know Why the Caged Bird Sings 178
Ibsen, Henrik 8, 12, 50
Ice Station Zebra 144
Iceman Cometh, The 86
If on a Winter's Night a Traveller 160
If This is a Man 114
Illywhacker 173
I'm Talking about Jerusalem 125
Immoralist, The 64
Impressions and Landscapes 68
In a Free State 171
In a Green Night: Poems 1948–60 171
In Cold Blood 99
In Love and Trouble: Stories of Black Women 179
In Our Time 51
In the Clearing 23
In the Ditch 170
In the Shadow of the Glen 13
In the Skin of the Lion 173
In Watermelon Sugar 96
Infinite Plan, The 169
Insurance Man, The 131
Interview with the Vampire 143
Investigation, The 129
Invisible Cities 160
Invisible Man 106
Ionesco, Eugene 70, 122, *122*
Iron in the Soul 89
Irving, Sir Henry 142
Isherwood, Christopher 59, 81, 130
Ishiguro, Kazuo 182
Island 59
It's a Battlefield 136
Izu Dancer, The 165

J

Jackie Brown 141
Jacob, Max 48
Jacob's Room 37
Jake's Thing 110
Jakob von Gunten 67
James, Emma 14
James, Henry 8, *8*, 9, 14
James, William 9
Jameson, Storm 74
Janco, Marcel 32
Jazz 179
Jealousy 91
Jest, The 169
'Jew Bird, The' 101
Jill 152
Jong, Erica 79, *79*
Journals (Gide) 65
Journey into Fear 136
Journey to the End of Night 64
Joy Luck Club, The 181
Joyce, James 31, 35, 36, 42–3, 42, 44, 69, 121
Joys of Motherhood, The 170
Jude the Obscure 14
Judgement Day 85
July's People 119
Jungle, The 85
Jungle Book, The 11
Junkie 93
Juno and the Paycock 86
Just So Stories 11

K

Kaddish and Other Poems 93
Kafka, Franz 36, 40–41, 67
Kallman, Chester 81
Kangaroo 45
Kaspar 129
Kavafis, Konstantinos Petrou
  see Cavafy, Constantine
Kawabata, Yasunari 165
Kelman, James 183
Keneally, Thomas 172
Kerouac, Jack 92–3, 92
Kesey, Ken 92, 96
Keynes, John Maynard 37
Kim 11
King, Stephen 142–3, 143
King Coal 85
Kingston, Maxine Hong 181
Kipling, Rudyard 11
Kiss of the Spider Woman 168–9
Kitchen (Yoshimoto) 175
Kitchen, The (Wesker) 125
Kitchen God's Wife, The 181
Koch, Kenneth 151
Koestler, Arthur 83
Korzeniowski, Jozef Teodor
  Konrad see Conrad, Joseph
Krapp's Last Tape 121
Kundera, Milan 114
Kuzmin, Mikhail 26

L

Labyrinths 157
Lady Chatterley's Lover 44
Lady from Dubuque, The 127
Lady Oracle 78
Lancaster, Burt 141
Larkin, Philip 106, 152
Lascaris, Manoly 119
Last Exit to Brooklyn 97
Last of Cheri, The 73
Last Year at Marienbad 91
Late Mattia Pascal 70
Later the Same Day 180
Laughable Loves 114
Lawrence, D.H. 31, 44–5, 45,
  57, 59, 75
Le Carre, John 137
Le Guin, Ursula 133
Leaf Storm and other Stories
  158
Lear 125
Leavetaking, The 128
Leavis, F.R. 44
Lees, Georgie Hyde 21
Leigh, Vivien 146, 147
Leonard, Elmore 140, 141
Less Deceived, The 152
Less than Zero 177
Lessing, Doris 76, 77
Letting Go 101
Levi, Primo 114–15
Lewis, Sinclair 52, 60–61, 60
Lewis, Wyndham 31, 31, 32, 57
Libra 162
Life, A 69
Life: A User's Manual 160
Life and Loves of a She-Devil,
  The 79
Life and Times of Michael K 185
Life is Elsewhere 114
Life of Galileo, The 71
Life Studies 150
Literary Taste: How to Form It
  15
Little Disturbances of Man, The
  180
Little Prince, The 65
Lives of Girls and Women 173
Living 59
Lizard, The 175
Llosa, Mario Vargas 169, 169

Lolita 102
London, Jack 16–17, 17
London Fields 182
Long Day's Journey into Night
  86
Longest Journey, The 57
Longley, Michael 153
Look Back in Anger 124, 125
Look Homeward, Angel 61
Look, Stranger! 81
Lorca, Federico Garcia 68, 68
Lord of the Flies 108
Lord of the Rings, The 133
Lost Steps, The 117
Love in the Time of Cholera 159
Lovecraft, H.P. 142
Loved One, The 59
Loving 59
Lowell, Amy 22, 29, 32
Lowell, Robert 99, 150, 151
Lowry, Malcom 108
Lucky Jim 110
Lupercal 152
Luther 124
Lying Days, The 119

M

Maclean, Alastair 144, 144, 145
Macnamara, Caitlin 152
MacNeice, Louis 81
'Magic Barrel, The' 101
Magic Mountain, The 66
Magic Toyshop, The 79
Magus 97
Mahfouz, Naguib 185
Mahon, Derek 153
Maids, The 122
Mailer, Norman 99, 100
Main Street 52, 60
Major Barbara 13
Make, Vusumzi 178
Malamud, Bernard 100, 101
Mallen Girl, The 146
Mallen Lot, The 146
Mallen Streak, The 146
Malone Dies 121
Malraux, Andre 64, 65
Maltese Falcon, The 140
Mamet, David 127, 130
Man and Superman 13
Man in Full, A 177
Man who had Three Arms, The
  127
Man Who Loved Children, The
  172
Man Without Qualities, A 66
Mandarins, Les 76
Mandelstam, Nadezhda 27
Mandelstam, Osip 26–7
Manhatten Transfer 63
Mann, Thomas 66, 66
Manor, The 118
Man's Estate 65
Manservant and Maidservant
  113
Mansfield, Katharine 72, 75, 75
Manuskripte 129
Mao II 162
Marat/Sade 128–9
Marinetti, Emilio 50
Marinetti, F.T. 32
Martin Eden 17
Mary 102
Mason & Dixon 162
Master and Margarita, The 83
Matisse 48
McCarthy, Cormac 176–7
McCullers, Carson 103
McDonald, Ross 140–41
McDowell, Malcolm 109
McEwan, Ian 130, 183
McInery, Jay 177
Member of the Wedding, The

  103
Memento Mori 113
Men of Maize 168
Men without Women 51
Mencken, H.L. 16
Metamorphosis 41
Microserfs 175
Middle Passage, The 171
Midnight's Children 159
Miguel Street 171
Miles, Barry 93
Miller, Arthur 126–7
Miller, Henry 54, 55, 74
Miller, June 74
Millroy the Magican 176
Milosz, Czeslaw 154
Mind Wars 93
Misfits, The 127
Mishima, Yukio 165, 165, 166
Miss Julie 13
Miss Lonelyhearts 61
Miss Smilla's Feeling for Snow
  184
Mister Buffo 128
Mitchell, Margaret 146
Model Childhood, A 167
Molloy 121
Money 182
Monroe, Marilyn 127
Montale, Eugenio 154–5, 154
Moons of Jupiter, The 173
Moore, Marianne 149, 150
Morante, Elsa 115
Moravia, Alberto 114, 115
More Die of Heartbreak 101
Morning Yet on Creation Day:
  Essays 170
Mornings in Mexico 45
Morrison, Toni 159, 178–9,
  178, 180
Mosquito Coast, The 176
Mosquitoes 62
Mother Courage 71
Mountain Interval 23
Mourning becomes Electra 86
Moveable Feast, A 48
Moving Target, The 140
Mr Norris Changes Trains 59
Mr Summer's Story 184
'Mrs Bathhurst' 11
Mrs Caldwell Speaks to her Son
  166
Mrs Dalloway 37
Muldoon, Paul 153
Munch, Edvard 19, 50
Muni, Paul 126
Munro, Alice 173
Munro, Hector Hugh see Saki
Murder of Roger Ackroyd, The
  139
Murder on the Orient Express
  138
Murderer of the Loser, The 166
Murdoch, Iris 113, 113
Murry, John Middleton 75
Musil, Robert 66–7
My Days: A Memoir 171
My Son's Story 119
Mysteries 18
Mysterious Affair at Styles, The
  138
Mystic Masseur, The 171
Myth of Sisyphus, The 89
'Mythago Wood' series 133

N

Nabokov, Vladmir 102, 102
Naipaul, Shiva 171
Naipaul, V.S. 170, 171, 171
Naked and the Dead, The 99
Naked Lunch 93
Naked Masks 70
Name of the Rose, The 161

Narayan, R.K. 171
Nash, Paul 46
Native Son 106
Natural, The 101
Nausea 89
Neruda, Pablo 25, 25
Neuromancer 134, 135
New Hampshire 23
New Poems (Lawrence) 45
Newman, Paul 127, 141
Night and Day 37
Night Flight 65
Night of the Iguana, The 126
Nin, Anais 74
Nineteen Eighty-four 59, 82,
  133
No Exit 89
No One Writes to the Colonel
  158
No Place on Earth 167
North 64
North and South 150
North of Boston 22
North Ship, The 152
Nostromo 10
Not I 121
Not Not While the Giro 183
Nothing Like the Sun 109
Nova Express 93
NP 175

O

O Babylon! 171
O-Zone 176
Oates, Joyce Carol 180
'Objects of Affection' 131
O'Casey, Sean 86, 87, 87
O'Cathasaigh, P. see O'Casey,
  Sean
Occasion for Loving 119
O'Connor, Flannery 104–5
Odets, Clifford 86–7
Oe, Kenzaburo 165
Of Love and Shadows 169
Of Mice and Men 84
Of Time and the River 61
Offending the Audience 129
Ogre, The 91
O'Hara, Frank 151
Oil! 85
Old Devils, The 110
Old Men at the Zoo, The 111
Old Wives' Tale 15
Olson, Charles 92
Omeros 171
On the Farm 102
On the Road 92
Ondaatje, Michael 173
One Day in the Life of Ivan
  Denisovich 94
One Flew Over the Cuckoo's
  Nest 96
One Hundred Years of Solitude
  158
O'Neill, Eugene 86, 86
Onetti, Juan Carlos 116
Orchard Keeper 176
Orphee 65
Orwell, George 82, 82, 83, 111,
  133
Osborne, John 110, 124, 124
Oscar and Lucinda 173
Our Game 137
Our Lady of the Flowers 122
Our Man in Havana 109
Our Town 61
Out of Sight 141
Outsider, The 89, 106
Overcrowded Barracoon, The
  171
Owen, Wilfred 47
Oxford Book of Light Verse,
  The 81

Oz, Amos 185

P

Paddy Clarke Ha Ha Ha 184
Painted Roofs 74
Painter of Signs, The 171
Pale View of Hills, A 182
Paley, Grace 180, 180
Pamuk, Orhan 184
Party Going 59
Passage to India, A 57
Passion of New Eve, The 79
Pasternak, Boris 27
Pastors and Masters 112
Paterson 35
Paton, Alan 94
Paulin, Tom 153
Paz, Octavio 155, 155
Pedersen, Knut see Hamsun,
  Knut
Pelican Brief, The 145
Pennies from Heaven 131
Perec, Georges 160
Perfume 184
Periodic Table, The 114
Personal Matter, A 165
Pessoa, Fernando 24
Peter Camenzind 19
Philosopher's Pupil 113
Picasso 48, 65
Pigeon 184
Pilgrimage 74
Pillow Book, The 165
Pincher Martin 108
Pincherle, Alberto see Moravia,
  Alberto
Pinter, Harold 70, 123, 123, 130
Pirandello, Luigi 50, 70, 71
Pirate, The 144
Place at Whitton, The 172
Plague, The 89
Plain Tales from the Hills 11
Plath, Sylvia 77, 150, 152
Playback 140
Playboy of the Western World,
  The 13
Player Piano 163
Plough and the Stars, The 86
Plumed Serpent, The 45
Poems (Eliot) 30
Point Counter Point 59
Portnoy's Complaint 101
Portrait of a Lady, The 9
Portrait of a Man Unknown 90
Portrait of the Artist as Young
  Man, A 42
Possession 182
Post Office 97
Potter, Dennis 131, 131
Pound, Ezra 21, 29, 30, 31, 31,
  35, 50, 152
Powell, Anthony 110–11
Powell, Dick 140
Pratchett, Terry 133
President, The 168
Prime of Miss Jean Brodie, The
  113
Proust, Marcel 36, 38–9, 39, 66
Puig, Manuel 168–9
Pygmalion 13
Pynchon, Thomas 156, 162

Q

Queer 93
Quest for Christa T, The 167
Questions of Travel 150
Quiet American, The 109

R

Rabbit at Rest 103
Rabbit is Rich 102
Rabbit Redux 102
Rabbit Run 102

Rachel Papers, The 182
Raise High the Roofbeam, Carpenter 103
Rame, Franca 128
Rank, Otto 74
Red Badge of Courage, The 17
Redford, Robert 53
Reginald in Russia 15
Reis, Ricardo *see* Pessoa, Fernando
Remains of the Day, The 182
Remembrance of Things Past 38–9
Reprieve, The 89
Resistible Rise of Arturo Ui 71
Restoration 125
Return of Eva Peron; with The Killings in Trinidad 171
Reyes, Ricard Eliecer Neftali *see* Neruda, Pablo
Rhinoceros 122
Rhys, Jean 74–5
Rice, Anne 143
Richardson, Dorothy 74
Rickword, Edgell 31
Riding, Laura 54
Right You Are (If You Think You Are) 70
Rigodon 64
Rilke, Rainer Maria 23, *23*
Rites of Passage 108
Rivers and Mountains 151
Road to Wigan Pier, The 82
Roads to Freedom, The 89
Robbe-Grillet, Alain 90–91
Robbins, Harold 144, *145*
Room, The 123
Room at the Top 110
Room of One's Own, A 37
Room with a View, A 57
Roots 125
'Rosary' 26
Rosenberg, Isaac 47
Rosshalde 19
Roth, Philip 100, 101
Roy, Arundahti 171, 185
Ruined Map, The 165
Rushdie, Salman 159, 171

S

Saint Jack 176
Saint-Exupery, Antoine de 64, 65
Saki 15
Salinger, J.D. 100, 103
'Salterton' trilogy 173
San Camilo 166
Saramago, Jose 166–7
Sarraute, Nathalie 90
Sartoris 62
Sartre, Jean-Paul 76, 89, 90, 130
Sassoon, Siegfried 47
Satan in Goray 118
Satanic Verses, The 159
Satori in Paris 93
Saturday Night and Sunday Morning 110
Saved 125
Scanner Darkly, A 134
Schindler's Ark 172
Schindler's List 172
Schmitz, Ettore *see* Svevo, Italo
Schuyler, James 151
Scoop 58
Scott, Ridley 134
Scott Moncrieff, C.K. 38, 39
Sea, the Sea, The 113
Seagull, The 12
Seascape 127
Season Songs 152
Second Sex, The 76
Secret Agent, The 10
See Under: Love 185

Selby Jr, Hugh 97
Selected Poems (Hughes) 152
Self-Portrait in a Convex Mirror 151
Servant 123
Seth, Vikram 171, *171*, 184–5
Sexton, Anne 150
Sexual Perversity of Chicago 127
Shadow of a Gunman 86
Shadow of the Coachman's Body, The 128
Shaw, George Bernard 13, *13*
She Came to Stay 76
Shining, The 143
Shipyard, The 116
Shonagon, Sei 165
Shuttle in the Crypt, A 170
Siddhartha 19
Silent Cry, The 165
Silent Honor 147
Sillitoe, Alan 110
Simenon, Georges 139, *139*
Simon, Claude 90
Sinclair, May 74
Sinclair, Upton 85
Singer, Isaac Bashevis 18, 118–19, *118*
Singin' and Swingin' 178
Singing Detective, The 131
Single and Single 137
Sirens of Titan, The 163
Sister Carrie 16
Six Characters in Search of an Author 70
Sixth One, The 116
Slaughterhouse-Five 163
Smile of the Lamb, The 185
Smiley's People 137
Smith, Maggie *112*
Smith, Wilbur 145
Snapper, The 184
Snow Country 165
Snyder, Gary 92
Soft Machine, The 93
Soft Voice of the Serpent, A 119
Soldier's Pay 62
Solzhenitsyn, Alexander 94
Some Trees 151
Something Happened 103
Something I've Been Meaning to Tell You 173
Song-Book 24
Song of Solomon 179
Songs (Lorca) 68
Sons and Lovers 44
Soseki, Natsume 165
Sot-Weed Factor, The 161
Sound and the Fury 62
Sound of the Mountain, The 165
Soyinka, Wole 170
Spark, Muriel 113
Speak, Memory 102
Speed-the-Plow 127
Spengler, Oswald 67
Spielberg, Steven 179
Spy Who Came in from the Cold, The 137
Stafford, Jean 150
Stamboul Train 136
Stanley and the Women 110
State of the Art, The 135
Stead, Christina 172
Steel, Danielle 146–7
Stein, Gertrude 48, 50, 51
Steinbeck, John 84–5, *84*
Stephen, Sir Leslie 37
Steppenwolf 19, 97
Stevens, Wallace 149, *149*, 150
Stick 141
Stoker, Bram 142
Stone 26
Stone, Robert 176

Stone Raft, The 166
Stoppard, Tom 130
Stories of Eva Luna, The 169
Straighthert's Delight 93
Stravinsky 65
Streetcar named Desire, A 126
Strindberg, August 13
Study in Scarlet, A 138
Subterraneans, The 93
Such Darling Dodos 111
Suddenly Last Summer 126
Suffrage of Elvira, The 171
Suitable Boy, A 184–5
Sula 179
Sun Also Rises, The 48, 51
Sun Stone 155
Suskind, Patrick 184
Suttree 177
Svevo, Italo 69
Swami and Friends 171
Sweet Bird of Youth 126
Synge, J.M. 13

T

Take Over, The 113
Tales of the Night 184
Talking Heads 131
Tan, Amy 180, 181, *181*
Tar Baby 179
Tarr 32
Taylor, Cora 17
Taylor, Elizabeth *127*
Tchekhov *see* Chekhov, Anton
Temple of My Familiar, The 179
Temple of the Golden Pavilion, The 165
Tender Buttons 48
Tender is the Night 53
Tennis Court Oath, The 151
Terminal Beach, The 135
Testament D'Orphee, La 65
Them 180
Theroux, Paul 176, *177*
Thief's Journal 122
Things Fall Apart 170
Third Man, The 109
This Side of Paradise 52
Thomas, Dylan 148, 149, 152, *153*
Thomas, Edward 22
Thompson, Hunter 96
Those Barren Leaves 59
Three Sisters, The 12
Three Soldiers 63
Three Stigmata of Palmer Eldritch, The 134
Three Tall Women 127
Threepenny Opera, The 71
Ticket that Exploded, The 93
Tiger for Malgudi, The 171
Time for a Tiger 109
Time Machine, The 133
Time of Indifference, The 115
Time of the Hero, The 169
Tin Drum, The 94–5
Tinker, Tailor, Soldier, Spy 137
To Him Who Wants It! 35
To The Island 77
To the Lighthouse 37
Tobacco Road 85
Toklas, Alice B. 48
Tolkein, J.R.R. 133, *133*
Tolstoy, Leo *13*
Toole, John Kennedy 97
Torrents of Spring, The 16
Tortilla Flat 84
Tough Guys Don't Dance 99
Tournier, Michel 91
Tower, The 21
Town and the City, The 92
Train was on Time, The 95
Tree of Man, The 119
Trial, The 40, 41

Tristia 27
Tropic of Cancer 54
Tropisms 90
Trotsky in Exile 129
Trout Fishing in America 96
Tulips and Chimneys 34
Twenty Love Poems and a Song of Despair 25
Twin In The Clouds, A 27
Twyborn Affair, The 119
Tyler, Anne 181
Tzara, Tristan 32

U

Ulysses 42–3
Unbearable Lightness of Being, The 114
Uncle Tom's Children 106
Uncle Vanya 12
Unconsoled 182
Under Milk Wood 152
Under the Net 113
Under the Volcano 108
Under Western Eyes 10
Underground Man, The 141
Underworld 163
Universal History of Infamy, A 157
Unnamable, The 121
Updike, John 59, 102–3
USA 63

V

V 162
Vagabond 73
Valery, Paul 23
Vampire Lestat, The 143
Van, The 184
Vanishing Point, The 128
Vendor of Sweets, The 171
Vermilion Sands 135
'Verona Notes, The' 27
Victory 10
View from the Bridge, A 127
Vile Bodies 58
Vineland 162
Vision, A 21
'Vision of the World, A' 104
Visions and Beliefs in the West of Ireland 21
Viva Detroit 171
Vivisector, The 119
Vogt, A.E. van 133
Void, A 160
Vollmer, Joan 93
Vonnegut, Kurt 163, *163*
Vote, Vote, Vote for Nigel Barton 131
Voyage Out, The 37
Voyeur, The 91
Vries, Peter de 15

W

Wain, John 152
Waiting for Godot 121
Waiting for Lefty 86
Walcott, Derek 170–71
Walker, Alice 179
Walser, Robert 67
War of the Worlds, The 133
Waste Land, The 30, 31
Watch It Come Down 124
Waugh, Evelyn 58–9, *58*
Waves, The 37
Way of All Flesh, The 14
We 83
Web and the Rock, The 61
Weekley, Frieda 44, 45, *45*, 75
Weill, Kurt 71
Weird Tales 142
Weiss, Peter 128–9

Weldon, Fay 78–9, *78*
Wells, H.G. 133
Wenders, Wim 129
Wesker, Arnold 125, *125*
West, Nathanael 60, 61, 130
West, Rebecca 74
Wharton, Edith 9, 11, 180
What Maisie Knew 9
What We Talk About When We Talk About Love 105
Wheels 145
When She Was Good 101
Where Angels Fear to Tread 57
Where Are You Going, Where Have You Been? 180
Where Eagles Dare 144
White, Edmund 185
White, Patrick 119, 172
White Buildings 34
White Castle, The 184
'White Flock' 26
White Ma, Listen! 106
White Noise 162
White Peacock, The 44
Whitsun Weddings, The 152
Who's Afraid of Virginia Woolf? 127
Wilder, Thornton 60, 61
Will You Please be Quiet, Please? 105
Williams, Tennessee 126
Williams, Ella Gwendolen Rees *see* Rhys, Jean
Williams, William Carlos 31, 34–5, *35*
Wilson, Angus 111, *111*
Wilson, Edmund 51
Winding Stair, The 21
Wings of Desire 129
Wings of the Dove, The 9
Winsburg, Ohio 16
Winterson, Jeanette 78
Wisdom of the Sands, The 65
Wise Blood 104
Wodwo 152
Wolf, Christa 167, *167*
Wolfe, Thomas 60, 61
Wolfe, Tom 96, 177
Woman and the Ape, The 184
Woman in the Dunes, The 165
Woman of Rome, The 115
Woman of Substance, A 146
Woman Warrior, The 181
Woman's Hand, A 119
Woolf, Virginia 36, *36*, 37, 74, 75
Word Child, A 113
Words 89
World's End 85
Wrench, The 115
Wright, Richard 106
Wrong Set, The 111

X

Xenia 155

Y

Yeats, W.B. 13, *20*, 21, 31, 152
Yerma 68
Yoshimoto, Banana 175
Young Lonigan: A Boyhood in Chicago Streets 85
Young Manhood of Studs Lonigan, The 85
Young Torless 66

Z

Zamyatin, Yevgeny 83
Zoo Story, The 127
Zuckerman Unbound 101
Zuleika Dobson 15

Acknowledgements

In source order

Corbis UK Ltd /Bettmann Front Cover top left, Front Cover bottom right, /Colita Front Cover centre left, /Hulton Getty Front Cover top right, Front Cover bottom left, **Hulton Getty Picture Collection** Front Cover centre right,

AKG, London 7, 23, 25 left, 25 right, 27 left, 28, 40-41, 48, 50-51, 63, 67, 68, 73, 91, 167 /Associated Press 95, /Marion Kalter 76 left, 107 left, 117, 160, 161, /Gret Widmann 19 left; **Arena**/Eric Richmond 175;

Bridgeman Art Library, London/New York/The Illustrated London News Library 138-139 Centre, /Imperial War Museum 46, /Library of Congress, Washington DC 60/ (c) Munch Museum/Munch-Ellingsen Group, BONO, Oslo, DACS, London 2000 19 right, /National Museum and Gallery of Wales, Cardiff (c) Courtesy of the artist's estate 153 right, /Private Collection 13 right, 45 left, 83, (c) Estate of Max Beerbohm 16, (c) Estate of Mrs G.A. Wyndham Lewis, By Permission 31, /Stapleton Collection, (c) Estate of Mrs G.A. Wyndham Lewis, By Permission 33, (c) ADAGP, Paris and DACS, London 2000 29, /Whitney Museum of American Art, New York 75 right;

Camera Press/Miriam Berkley 118 left /Jane Bown 181 /Basso Cannarsa 163 right, 180-181 /B. Charlon 157 /Lionel Cherruault 76 right /Ralph Crane 144 /Debbie Humphrey 78 /J. J. Menee 166 /Richard Open 184-185 /P-A Decrane L'Express 118-119 /R/T 111 /Beryl Sokoloff 79 /David Steen 145 /Mark Stewart 147 left;

Corbis UK Ltd 66 /Archivo Iconografico, S.A. 71 left /Bettmann 10, 17 right, 22, 35 right, 42, 45 right, 49, 51, 52, 58, 62, 71, 82, 84 Bottom, 86-87, 87, 92 right, 92, 107 right, 125, 149, 164, 165, 178 /Colida 169 /Jerry Cooke 99 /The Everett Collection 143, 163 left, 185 /Hulton Getty 11, 14-15, 55 left, 57, 58 left, 84 Top, 88, 102, 121, 122, 123, 124 /Jacques M. Chenet 173 /Barry Lewis 41 /Robert Maass 120 /Frederico Patellani 154 /Underwood & Underwood 17 left /Oscar White 35 left; **Mary Evans Picture Library** 13 left, 27 right, 30, 65, 138-139 Top, /Explorer Archives 39 /Jeffrey Morgan 136; **Hulton Getty Picture Collection** 6, 8, 20, 36, 43, 75 left, 80, 89, 90-91, 110, 113, 126, 139, 151 /Chris Ball 130-131 /Daniel Farson 55 right /John Minihan 170-171; **Kobal Collection**/Warner Bros. 141 /Castelofilm/Neue Constantin 168-169 /20th Century Fox 112 /Columbia 56 /Columbia/Merchant-Ivory 183 right /France 3/Halmedia/Ariane/Soprofilm 158-159 /MGM/Avon 127 /Paramount 53 /Paramount/Filmways 103; **Rex Features** 131, 133, 134-135, 135, 179 /Richard Gardner 182 left /Nils Jorgensen 171 /Julian Makey 143 left /N.J. 153 left, /RGA 140 /Rosenlund 100-101 /Kerry Thais 177 /Tschaen 155; **The Ronald Grant Archive** 69, 72, 94-95, 97, 98, 101, 104-105, 105, 108-109, 109, 114, 115, 129, 137, 148, 156, 174, 176 /MGM 132, 147 /Miramax 172-173